5 STEPS TO A >5

500
AP English Literature Questions
to Know by Test Day

Also in the 5 Steps Series:

Also in the 500 AP Questions to Know by Test Day series:

5 STEPS TO A >5

500

AP English Literature Questions
to Know by Test Day

Second Edition

Shveta Verma Miller

Mc
Graw
Hill
Education

New York   Chicago   San Francisco   Athens   London   Madrid
Mexico City   Milan   New Delhi   Singapore   Sydney   Toronto

SHVETA VERMA MILLER has taught English literature and English as a foreign language at the high school and college level in the United States, England, India, Japan, and China. She currently works as an instructional coach for middle and high school literacy specialists and English Language Arts teachers. She has a bachelor's degree in English literature from the University of California, Berkeley, and a master's degree in modern literature from the University of London, England. She most recently taught AP English Literature in New York City public schools.

1 2 3 4 5 6 7 8 9   QFR   22 21 20 19 18 17

ISBN   978-1-259-83663-3
MHID   1-259-83663-0

e-ISBN   978-1-259-83664-0
e-MHID   1-259-83664-9

McGraw-Hill Education products are available at special quantity discounts to use as premiums and sales promotions or for use in corporate training programs. To contact a representative, please visit the Contact Us pages at www.mhprofessional.com.

CONTENTS

PREFACE

Even though students have been enrolling in AP English literature classes and taking the AP exam for decades, there is a noticeable shortage of multiple-choice practice and guides in the test prep world. This book is intended to *complement* a test-prep curriculum guidebook like McGraw-Hill Education *5 Steps to a 5: AP English Literature*, which provides extensive instruction on the content covered in the exam, including terms, concepts, writing skills, and some multiple-choice practice. *5 Steps to a 5: 500 AP English Literature Questions to Know by Test Day*, however, is unique and essential in that it provides extensive practice for the multiple-choice section alone, which comprises 45 percent of the total AP exam score. The book provides 500 practice questions and detailed answer explanations. The questions are comparable to those found on the AP exam, covering similar content and genres.

This book is intended for students to use to prepare for the AP exam independently, in addition to the preparation they may be doing in an actual AP English literature classroom. The book is also useful for teachers to use in their AP and non-AP classrooms for extra practice and assessment. Students who do not intend to take the AP exam can still benefit from using this book because the passages, questions, and answer explanations will train any student of literature how to develop a subtle and insightful appreciation for and understanding of the technique, form, style, and purpose of complex literary texts, all skills necessary for the reading comprehension section of the SAT and other standardized exams in reading comprehension.

How to Use This Book

The book is divided into eight chapters that are categorized by geographic region and genre. The multiple-choice questions for the AP exam in English literature consist mostly of fiction and poetry. Of the fiction passages, most passages are taken from novels and short stories, while occasionally a passage from a play or even expository prose (excerpts from essays, prefaces, etc.) might be used.

Terms written in bold are terms and concepts that will reappear in multiple questions and should be reviewed for the AP exam. Many of these terms can be studied in McGraw-Hill Education *5 Steps to a 5: AP English Literature*. In certain situations, words or letters that are *italicized* indicate this author's emphasis to make the answer explanations clearer.

The questions all ask you to *choose the best answer* from the available choices, so even though multiple answer choices may be "correct," the right answer is always the *best* answer because it may be more specific, detailed, or all-encompassing than the other choices.

Studying with the Passages

Identify a genre (American poetry, drama, expository prose, etc.) with which you are the least familiar and start with that chapter's passages. Which genre have you had the least experience with or the most difficulty studying? Or, have you already read and studied some of the texts or authors in the book? Try starting with those passages to test your ability on texts you already have some confidence with; then move on to unfamiliar texts, authors, and genres.

After completing a passage and questions, write your own explanations for your answers and then compare your explanations to the ones in the book. This exercise will force you to think carefully about why you are picking certain answers. It may help you avoid picking certain answers on a whim if you know you will have to justify those choices later.

As you practice the questions, read the answer explanations of the questions you get wrong and the explanations of the questions you get right so you know why you got a question right and learn the logic of how right answers are reached on the exam.

Highlight the terms and concepts you are unfamiliar with that are written in bold in the answer explanations, even in the explanations of questions you answer correctly. Once you have completed several passages, you will be able to notice which terms you consistently misunderstand in the questions. Review these terms by reading the answer explanations and looking up their definitions in *5 Steps to a 5: AP English Literature* or ask your teacher for a list of resources.

Highlight and study any unfamiliar vocabulary, especially from the answer choices. This book has followed the AP Exam's example in the level of vocabulary used in the answer choices. The words are reflective of a college-level vocabulary. If you take the time to learn new words as they appear, you will notice that over time you will begin to recognize more of the words in the answer choices. You will develop a nuanced vocabulary to express what is happening in a complex text, one that will also enhance your clarity of thinking, along with your written and oral expression.

There are only 10–15 questions per passage, but there are countless additional questions that could be asked for each passage in this book. Try creating additional questions for passages that ask about nuances, effects, stylistic choices, and meaning that have not already been covered. Use the book's questions as a model. Thinking like the test-writers will train you to read closely and critically, and it will help you recognize why certain wrong answers appear, why they are distracting or tempting, and ultimately not as cogent as the correct answer.

Strategies for Answering the Questions

Use the Questions to Guide Your Re-reading of the Passage

It is common for readers to feel confused after their preliminary read through the passage. The questions focus on the most subtle, complex, and relevant portions of a passage, so they will guide you to the areas where a second read, a closer look, will help you gain a deeper understanding of the passage. Approach the passages with the mindset that your understanding will develop over multiple reads of key lines that the questions direct you to. Remain flexible as you move through questions, open to the possibility that your first impression may not have been the most astute.

Notice Key Words in the Questions

- **"paraphrase," "summarizes," "stated as," "means"**

  These key words tell you not to infer, interpret, or analyze the given lines. You are being asked about your comprehension of what is directly stated or indicated in the passage. Avoid answer choices that require you to draw conclusions, assume, or analyze.

- **"suggest," "implies," "it can be inferred," "is best interpreted as"**

  These key words give you license to analyze the lines or passage. As you analyze, you must rely on textual evidence from the passage. Avoid choosing answers that re-state or indicate what is directly or explicitly stated in the passage and focus only on answers that would reflect analysis of the lines.

- **"primarily," "most," "best"**

  These can be the most challenging questions since you will likely encounter multiple answer choices that are correct, but you are being asked to consider the larger themes, purpose, tone, style, and function of the passage to identify the most fitting answer choice. For example, if you are asked how a character is primarily characterized, avoid choosing an answer that describes a less significant feature of the character that is only mentioned once or that actually falls under the purview of another answer choice. Look in all the paragraphs to identify a recurring pattern or consistency to the portrayal of the character.

- **"in context"**

  When asked about a phrase or word "in context," you are being reminded to consider how the phrase is being used in this specific situation. Beware of answer choices that provide common usages of the word or phrase, as the writer is likely using the word/phrase in a less common way. You may try crossing out the given word/phrase in the passage, reading the surrounding lines, and then predicting your own word/phrase to replace the current one. In so doing, you will force yourself only to consider the context when deciding what idea should be expressed in that spot. Choose the answer that most closely matches the tone and meaning of your own predicted word.

- **"all of the following *except*"**

  Four of the choices do answer the question and one does not. Keep your eyes out for the lone wolf in the group—which word/phrase does not belong with the other four? This type of question can be more time-consuming than others. Consider whether you should skip it and return if time allows.

Process of Elimination

When challenging vocabulary or terms appear in answer choices, do not eliminate them as possible choices because these answers could be correct. Look closely at the answer choices you do understand and consider whether those answers articulate the "best" response to the question. If you suspect there is something better out there, then eliminate these choices and choose one of the answers you did not fully comprehend.

Remember that there can only be one correct answer. If you identify a common theme to three or four of the answer choices, consider that the correct answer is often the one that is different from the others.

Creating Practice Tests from This Book

At the start of the year, create a full-length diagnostic exam from the passages in the book. Choose five to six passages totaling 50–60 questions. Select a balance of prose and poetry. The diagnostic exam will help you determine what types of passages (American poetry, drama, British fiction, etc.) and questions (main idea, in context, narrative point of view, etc.) you struggle with most, which can help you identify where you should focus your study.

At the beginning of your practice, complete passages untimed to gain familiarity and confidence with the format and content. When you are ready for timed practice, start with doing one passage at a time, allowing yourself 10–15 minutes.

When you are ready for full-length practice exams, choose five to six passages with a variety of prose (choose from novels, short stories, expository prose, and drama) and poetry. Many of the passages in this book contain more questions than the exam generally includes for a passage so that you may select certain questions and discard others while still having enough to constitute a full-length practice test.

Students' comfort level, confidence, and efficiency generally improve the more practice tests they take. Set a reasonable goal and schedule for yourself when planning how many practice tests you will take before the official exam.

After each test, carefully review the answer explanations in the book and look up unfamiliar terms and vocabulary before attempting another practice test.

Testing Instructions

One hour for 55 multiple-choice questions. This section is 45 percent of the total score.

Your multiple-choice score is determined only by the number of questions you answer correctly. Points are not deducted for incorrect answers. It is not expected that students will be able to answer every question correctly. For that reason, do not spend too much time on any given question. Return to the harder questions if you have time remaining at the end.

For Teachers

- When your students are beginning their practice, let them complete passages without a time limit so they can first adjust to the style, content, and expectations of the exam.

  While they are getting familiar with the test, you may also want to have them work in groups on one passage. They should discuss their rationale for choosing an answer and debate each other when there are disagreements. They will have to justify their own answers and explain their reasoning using references to the passages, which will train them to become more sensitive readers and to think carefully about *why* they are choosing an answer. While they are trying to convince their peers of their answer choice, they may realize they have misinterpreted something in the passage and they will come to appreciate the level of close reading and analysis the exam requires.

- You may also ask students to create additional questions for a passage. What are other significant images, devices, effects, and subtle ideas that have not been addressed by the 10–15 provided questions? When students mimic the test-maker, they will need to consider what is significant about a passage or poem, they will need to identify possible misinterpretations in order to create attractive but incorrect answer choices, and they will need to carefully articulate a correct response that holds up to any good reader's valid interpretation.

- When students are ready to practice on their own in a timed setting, have them practice a passage and check their answers but *not* read the answer explanations. Have them go back to the passage and write their own answer explanations for their chosen answers. Then they should test their explanations against the ones in the book to see exactly where and how their misinterpretation occurred.

AP Teachers: Assessments

- At the start of the year, create a full-length diagnostic exam from the passages in the book. Choose five to six passages totaling 50–60 questions. Select a balance of prose and poetry. The diagnostic exam will help you determine what types of passages (American poetry, drama, British fiction, etc.) and questions (vocabulary in context, main idea, inference, etc.) the students struggle with most, which can inform your teaching throughout the year.

All English Teachers

- If you plan to teach one or more of the texts used in the book, you may want to use that text's passage and questions as a prereading assessment when beginning the unit on that text to see how well students are already reading that particular text on their own, before receiving instruction on it.

- If you plan to teach one or more of the texts used in the book, you may want to use that text's passage and questions as a formative assessment to determine students' progress with rigorous close reading.

- For practice and assessment throughout the year, create full-length practice exams that consist of five to six passages with a variety of prose (choose from novels, short stories, expository prose, and drama) and poetry. Many of the passages contain more questions than the exam generally includes for a passage so that you may select certain questions and discard others while still having enough to constitute a full-length practice test.

- Any teacher of English literature can make extensive use of the passages and questions provided in this book. Like AP teachers, non-AP teachers can use the passages as diagnostics and assessments if they are teaching units on any of the texts included in the book.

- Non-AP teachers can also use the book to prepare students who are on the AP track or to challenge the higher-performing students in their classes.

ACKNOWLEDGMENTS

I would first like to thank my AP English students for their insightful contributions to our class discussions and written assignments on many of the texts used in this book.

Thank you to Dr. Sean Miller for his expert literary analysis of certain passages, Dr. Vikas Bhushan for his guidance on the art of the multiple-choice question, and the editorial team at McGraw-Hill Professional for their editorial comments. A special thank you to Yael McShane Wulfhart for helping to vet the questions in this book with her shrewd close-reading skills.

INTRODUCTION

Congratulations! You've taken a big step toward AP success by purchasing *5 Steps to a 5: 500 AP English Literature Questions to Know by Test Day*. We are here to help you take the next step and score high on your AP exam so you can earn college credits and get into the college or university of your choice!

This book gives you 500 AP-style multiple-choice questions that cover all the most essential course material. Each question has a detailed answer explanation. These questions will give you valuable independent practice to supplement your regular textbook and the groundwork you are already doing in your AP classroom.

This and the other books in this series were written by expert AP teachers who know your exam inside out and can identify the crucial exam information as well as questions that are most likely to appear on the exam.

You might be the kind of student who takes several AP courses and needs to study extra questions a few weeks before the exam for a final review. Or you might be the kind of student who puts off preparing until the last weeks before the exam. No matter what your preparation style, you will surely benefit from reviewing these 500 questions, which closely parallel the content, format, and degree of difficulty of the questions on the actual AP exam. These questions and their answer explanations are the ideal last-minute study tool for those final few weeks before the test.

Remember the old saying "Practice makes perfect." If you practice with all the questions and answers in this book, we are certain you will build the skills and confidence needed to do great on the exam. Good luck!

Editors of McGraw-Hill Education

5 STEPS TO A >5™

500
AP English Literature Questions to Know by Test Day

CHAPTER 1

British Poetry

Passage 1. Elizabeth Barrett Browning, "Sonnet 32"

THE FIRST time that the sun rose on thine oath
To love me, I looked forward to the moon
To slacken all those bonds which seemed too soon
And quickly tied to make a lasting troth.
Quick-loving hearts, I thought, may quickly loathe;   5
And, looking on myself, I seemed not one
For such man's love;—more like an out-of-tune
Worn viol, a good singer would be wroth
To spoil his song with, and which, snatched in haste,
Is laid down at the first ill-sounding note.   10
I did not wrong myself so, but I placed
A wrong on *thee*. For perfect strains may float
'Neath master-hands, from instruments defaced,—
And great souls, at one stroke, may do and dote.

1. In contrast to the sun, the moon is portrayed as
    (A) hindered
    (B) gloomy
    (C) menacing
    (D) anticipated
    (E) calculating

2. What is "too soon/ And quickly tied" (3–4)?
      I. "thine oath"
     II. "those bonds"
    III. "a lasting troth"
    (A) I only
    (B) II only
    (C) I and II only
    (D) II and III only
    (E) I, II, and III

3. The words "Quick" and "quickly" in line 5 serve to emphasize
    (A) the fickle nature of attraction
    (B) the partner's manic behavior
    (C) the degree of the speaker's regret
    (D) the musicality of the poem
    (E) the speaker's chastisement of her partner

4. A contrast to the speaker's initial assumption is found in which of the following line(s)?
    (A) line 4
    (B) lines 6–7
    (C) lines 7–10
    (D) line 10
    (E) lines 11–12

5. The speaker uses a simile to emphasize her
    (A) view of her inadequacies
    (B) mistake in loving an unworthy mate
    (C) prudence in entering a romantic relationship
    (D) hope that her mate will deem her worthy of his love
    (E) regret over her hasty betrothal

6. In line 9, "the song" is likely a symbol for
    (A) wasted passion
    (B) estimable love
    (C) the temporality of love
    (D) the mate's musical talent
    (E) the speaker's love

7. The connotation of "ill-sounding note" in line 10 is most in line with the idea expressed in which other phrase in the poem?
    (A) "I seemed not one/ For such man's love!"
    (B) "I looked forward to the moon"
    (C) "Quick-loving hearts"
    (D) "For perfect strains may float"
    (E) "snatched in haste"

8. The speaker implies that her initial concerns would have been abated if
   - (A) her vows were heartfelt
   - (B) her mate had been genuine
   - (C) she exercised more patience
   - (D) she and her mate procrastinated
   - (E) their commitment had been made over time

9. In the final four lines of the poem, the speaker reveals
   - (A) her error in judging herself too harshly
   - (B) her regret at overestimating her mate's love
   - (C) her paranoia about her mate's potential infidelity
   - (D) her underestimation of her mate's potential
   - (E) her concern that she married too quickly

10. The poem's central idea is developed mainly through
    - (A) onomatopoeia
    - (B) extended metaphor
    - (C) repetition
    - (D) parallelism
    - (E) an oxymoron

11. Throughout the poem, the speaker experiences
    - (A) reflection
    - (B) guilt
    - (C) fear
    - (D) foresight
    - (E) infatuation

Passage 2. Gerard Manley Hopkins, "God's Grandeur"

The world is charged with the grandeur of God.
It will flame out, like shining from shook foil;
It gathers to a greatness, like the ooze of oil
Crushed. Why do men then now not reck his rod?
Generations have trod, have trod, have trod;   5
And all is seared with trade; bleared, smeared with toil;
And wears man's smudge and shares man's smell: the soil
Is bare now, nor can foot feel, being shod.
And for all this, nature is never spent;
There lives the dearest freshness deep down things;   10
And though the last lights off the black West went
Oh, morning, at the brown brink eastward, springs—
Because the Holy Ghost over the bent
World broods with warm breast and with ah! bright wings.

12. "It" in lines 2 and 3 refers to

    (A) God's greatness
    (B) foil
    (C) the world
    (D) humanity
    (E) oil

13. The change in sound from the first three lines to line 4 is

    (A) a change from a mellifluous sound to a harsh sound
    (B) a change from a tranquil sound to a placid sound
    (C) a change from a confusing sound to a clear sound
    (D) a change from an inconsistent sound to a steady sound
    (E) a change from an indistinct sound to a distinct sound

14. The sound devices in line 4 serve to emphasize

    (A) the superiority of men to God
    (B) the unity between men and God
    (C) the noteworthy independence of men
    (D) man's obliviousness to God's grandeur
    (E) man's dislike of God's wrath

15. In context, the repetition in line 5 highlights

    (A) man's preference for the natural world
    (B) the inexorable nature of man's mistakes
    (C) the monotonous demands of an earthly life
    (D) man's temporary preference for industry and materiality over God
    (E) man's dissatisfaction with the material world

16. Lines 6 and 7 share which of the following characteristics?

    I. internal rhyme
    II. parallel structure
    III. negative imagery

    (A) I only
    (B) II only
    (C) I and II only
    (D) I and III only
    (E) I, II, and III

17. The change in tone from lines 1–3 to lines 4–8 is

    (A) a change from reverential to ambivalent
    (B) a change from perplexed to dismayed
    (C) a change from awe-inspired to dirgelike
    (D) a change from optimistic to skeptical
    (E) a change from confident to pitiful

18. The structure and form of the poem indicates that it is

    (A) a pastoral
    (B) an elegy
    (C) a Petrarchan sonnet
    (D) an ode
    (E) a Shakespearean sonnet

19. The alliteration in the final six lines reinforces

    I. God's eminence
    II. the speaker's confidence
    III. God's harmony with the world

    (A) I only
    (B) I and II only
    (C) III only
    (D) II and III only
    (E) I, II, and III

20. The last six lines differ from the first eight in that
    (A) the sound changes but the tone stays the same
    (B) God is portrayed as less powerful
    (C) the focus is more on man than on God
    (D) they reassure rather than question
    (E) they contain skepticism instead of curiosity

21. In the context of the poem, the tone of the word "broods" (14) is best described as
    (A) foreboding
    (B) intimidating
    (C) paternal
    (D) avuncular
    (E) cheerful

22. The theme of the poem is best expressed by which one of its phrases?
    (A) "It gathers to a greatness, like the ooze of oil" (3)
    (B) "all is seared with trade; bleared, smeared with toil" (6)
    (C) "Why do men then now not reck his rod" (4)
    (D) "nature is never spent" (9)
    (E) "Generations have trod, have trod, have trod" (5)

23. The poem ends on a note of
    (A) bemusement
    (B) unrestrained awe
    (C) didacticism
    (D) qualified hope
    (E) constructive criticism

Passage 3. Andrew Marvell, "To His Coy Mistress"

Had we but world enough, and time,
This coyness, lady, were no crime.
We would sit down and think which way
To walk, and pass our long love's day;
Thou by the Indian Ganges' side   5
Shouldst rubies find; I by the tide
Of Humber would complain. I would
Love you ten years before the Flood;
And you should, if you please, refuse
Till the conversion of the Jews.   10
My vegetable love should grow

Vaster than empires, and more slow.
An hundred years should go to praise
Thine eyes, and on thy forehead gaze;
Two hundred to adore each breast,   15
But thirty thousand to the rest;
An age at least to every part,
And the last age should show your heart.
For, lady, you deserve this state,
Nor would I love at lower rate.   20

But at my back I always hear
Time's winged chariot hurrying near;
And yonder all before us lie
Deserts of vast eternity.
Thy beauty shall no more be found,   25
Nor, in thy marble vault, shall sound
My echoing song; then worms shall try
That long preserv'd virginity,
And your quaint honour turn to dust,
And into ashes all my lust.   30
The grave's a fine and private place,
But none I think do there embrace.

Now therefore, while the youthful hue
Sits on thy skin like morning dew,
And while thy willing soul transpires   35
At every pore with instant fires,
Now let us sport us while we may;
And now, like am'rous birds of prey,
Rather at once our time devour,
Than languish in his slow-chapp'd power.   40
Let us roll all our strength, and all
Our sweetness, up into one ball;
And tear our pleasures with rough strife
Thorough the iron gates of life.
Thus, though we cannot make our sun   45
Stand still, yet we will make him run.

24. The actions described by the speaker throughout the first stanza
    (lines 1–20) are

    (A) regrettable
    (B) currently happening
    (C) in the future
    (D) hypothetical
    (E) inevitable

25. In context, the word "coyness" in line 2 most likely means

(A) sedentary lifestyle

(B) hurried state

(C) procrastination

(D) seduction

(E) modesty

26. The references to the "Indian Ganges" (5), the "Humber" (7), the "Flood" (8), and the "Jews" (10) serve to

(A) flatter and impress

(B) confound and shock

(C) startle and mystify

(D) persuade and elude

(E) degrade and vilify

27. The phrase "vegetable love" (11) is

(A) indicative of the speaker's duplicity

(B) meant to undermine the speaker's integrity

(C) intended to emphasize the speaker's immediate desire

(D) a symbol of the seductive powers of the natural environment

(E) a metaphor for the speaker's long-lasting love

28. It can be inferred that the phrases "the rest" (16) and "every part" (17) are references to

(A) the speaker's other emotions

(B) the addressee's desirable qualities

(C) other attractive women

(D) romantic acts

(E) the speaker's lust

29. The second stanza differs from the first in that

   I. the imagery changes from libidinous to morbid

  II. the tone changes from arrogant to desperate

III. the flattery is abandoned

(A) I and II only

(B) I and III only

(C) II only

(D) II and III only

(E) I, II, and III

30. The effect of the device used in the phrase "Time's winged chariot hurrying near" (22) is

  (A) the power of time is undermined
  (B) time is portrayed as a savior
  (C) the speed of time's passage is dramatized
  (D) time is portrayed as negligent
  (E) the speaker's argument is called into question

31. The word "quaint" in line 29 hints at the speaker's

  (A) respect for his addressee's prudence
  (B) disdain for chastity
  (C) admiration for his addressee's steadfastness
  (D) immodest proposition
  (E) true view of his addressee's virginity

32. The simile in line 34 serves to

  (A) impress the addressee
  (B) underscore the addressee's ephemeral youth
  (C) distract the addressee
  (D) point out the addressee's natural beauty
  (E) question the addressee's beauty

33. In line 40, "his" refers to

  (A) the speaker
  (B) the addressee
  (C) "birds of prey"
  (D) "instant fires"
  (E) time

34. Which of the following devices enhances the speaker's declaration in the last two lines of the passage?

  I. end rhyme
  II. alliteration
  III. personification
  IV. oxymoron

  (A) I and II only
  (B) II and IV only
  (C) I, II, and III only
  (D) I, III, and IV only
  (E) II, III, and IV only

35. The speaker's strategy in the passage as a whole consists of

    (A) an introduction to a problem, deductive reasoning, criticism, and solution

    (B) soothing sounds, cogent examples, and personal anecdotes

    (C) seduction, accurate data, and historical examples

    (D) a major premise, minor premise, and conclusion

    (E) agreement and contradiction

Passage 4. Christina Rossetti, "Winter: My Secret"

I tell my secret? No indeed, not I;
Perhaps some day, who knows?
But not today; it froze, and blows and snows,
And you're too curious: fie!
You want to hear it? well: 5
Only, my secret's mine, and I won't tell.

Or, after all, perhaps there's none:
Suppose there is no secret after all,
But only just my fun.
Today's a nipping day, a biting day;   10
In which one wants a shawl,
A veil, a cloak, and other wraps:
I cannot ope to everyone who taps,
And let the draughts come whistling thro' my hall;
Come bounding and surrounding me,   15
Come buffeting, astounding me,
Nipping and clipping thro' my wraps and all.
I wear my mask for warmth: who ever shows
His nose to Russian snows
To be pecked at by every wind that blows?   20
You would not peck? I thank you for good will,
Believe, but leave the truth untested still.

Spring's an expansive time: yet I don't trust
March with its peck of dust,
Nor April with its rainbow-crowned brief showers,   25
Nor even May, whose flowers
One frost may wither thro' the sunless hours.

Perhaps some languid summer day,
When drowsy birds sing less and less,
And golden fruit is ripening to excess,
If there's not too much sun nor too much cloud,
And the warm wind is neither still nor loud,
Perhaps my secret I may say,
Or you may guess.

30

36. The questions in lines 1 and 21 indicate the speaker

    (A) is inquisitive
    (B) is confused
    (C) is responding
    (D) is dubious
    (E) is hopeful

37. The tone of line 6 is best understood as

    (A) juvenile
    (B) hostile
    (C) aggressive
    (D) vexing
    (E) irritable

38. The main purpose of the first stanza is to

    (A) introduce a quandary
    (B) establish the rhyme scheme
    (C) describe the setting
    (D) characterize the speaker as power-hungry
    (E) develop the relationship between the speaker and addressee

39. The "wraps" mentioned in line 12 serve, for the speaker, mainly as

    (A) a way to rhyme line 12 with line 13
    (B) a physical embodiment of her secret
    (C) a metaphorical savior
    (D) a figurative refuge
    (E) a means for staying chaste

40. In lines 14–17, the speaker is doing which of the following?

    (A) using a rhythmical and jovial tone to match her perspective on winter
    (B) using iambic pentameter and alliteration to match the consistency of the poem's rhythm
    (C) using end rhyme, internal rhyme, anaphora, and metaphor to dramatize a threat
    (D) using alliteration, metaphor, and irony to question an idea
    (E) using repetition and figurative language to intimidate and tease her addressee

41. According to the speaker, spring differs from winter and summer in its

    (A) steadfastness
    (B) monotony
    (C) interminability
    (D) capriciousness
    (E) uniformity

42. Winter, spring, and summer are treated in the poem

    (A) objectively, to indicate the best temperature for revealing a secret
    (B) absurdly, to further exasperate the addressee with random digressions
    (C) rhythmically, to establish a musical tone
    (D) figuratively, to illustrate pestering meddlers
    (E) symbolically, to portray people's inquisitiveness as a result of nature

43. It can be interpreted that the speaker withholds her secret for all of the following reasons *except*

    (A) her addressee is overzealous
    (B) she does not actually have one
    (C) she is concerned about the potential reaction
    (D) it will spread uncontrollably
    (E) withholding something coveted is playfully powerful

44. It can be inferred that the speaker's attitude toward her addressee is mainly one of

    (A) mild amusement
    (B) censorious disapproval
    (C) fond appreciation
    (D) willingness to engage
    (E) sincere avoidance

45. The speaker gives symbolic significance to

    I. the weather
   II. a house
  III. clothing
  IV. a nose

  (A) I only
  (B) I and III only
  (C) II, III, and IV only
  (D) I, II, and III only
  (E) I, II, III, and IV

46. In response to the final line of the poem, the addressee most probably feels

  (A) attacked
  (B) passionate
  (C) resentful
  (D) satisfied
  (E) hopeful

47. Which of the following best describes the effect of the final stanza's syntactical structure?

  (A) The end rhymes and steady beat correspond to the eventual revelation that will conclude the poem.
  (B) The repetition of the word "Perhaps" highlights the speaker's antipathy.
  (C) The uncommon adjectives modify ordinary nouns, which presents the secret as exclusive.
  (D) The stanza is made up of a periodic sentence, which heightens the sense of anticipation.
  (E) The final stanza is written in passive voice, which shows the speaker is in control of her secret.

Passage 5. William Wordsworth, "The world is too much with us"

The world is too much with us; late and soon,
Getting and spending, we lay waste our powers:
Little we see in nature that is ours;
We have given our hearts away, a sordid boon!
This Sea that bares her bosom to the moon;   5
The Winds that will be howling at all hours

And are up-gathered now like sleeping flowers;
For this, for every thing, we are out of tune;
It moves us not—Great God! I'd rather be
A Pagan suckled in a creed outworn;   10
So might I, standing on this pleasant lea,
Have glimpses that would make me less forlorn;
Have sight of Proteus coming from the sea;
Or hear old Triton blow his wreathed horn.

48. The poem is formally divided into

  (A) couplets
  (B) quatrains
  (C) a sestet and an octave
  (D) tercets
  (E) asides

49. The subject of "Getting and spending" in line 2 is

  (A) the world
  (B) we
  (C) God
  (D) nature
  (E) our powers

50. The phrase "sordid boon" (4) is

  (A) a call for an end to industry
  (B) a sarcastic expletive that mocks our "hearts"
  (C) a paradox that deplores human nature
  (D) an oxymoron that points out the irony of society's advancement
  (E) a celebration of nature's benefits

51. The function of the figurative language in lines 5 and 6 is
   (A) to dramatize the potential danger of the world
   (B) to alleviate the speaker's regret
   (C) to underscore the majestic qualities of nature
   (D) to question the relationship between man and the sea
   (E) to create an intimidating tone

52. The image created in lines 5 and 6 coincides with the image from which of the poem's other line(s)?
   (A) line 2
   (B) line 4
   (C) lines 7–8
   (D) line 10
   (E) lines 13–14

53. The word "this" in line 8 refers to
   I. "sleeping flowers"
   II. "The Winds"
   III. "all hours"

   (A) I only
   (B) II only
   (C) I and III only
   (D) I and II only
   (E) I, II, and III

54. In context of the poem as a whole, we can infer that the word "world" means
   (A) humanity
   (B) London
   (C) the man-made world
   (D) nature
   (E) people

55. The metaphor in line 10 compares
   (A) a religion to a mother's breast
   (B) Paganism to an outdated belief system
   (C) beliefs to mothers
   (D) religion to breast milk
   (E) Pagans to mothers

56. The allusions in lines 13–14 illustrate

(A) the speaker's sanguinity
(B) the speaker's predicament
(C) the speaker's desire
(D) the speaker's knowledge
(E) the speaker's solution

57. The theme of the poem as a whole can best be stated as

(A) nature is better than technology
(B) the natural world has more to offer than people
(C) the natural world is a panacea for our troubles
(D) it is regrettable that we have immersed ourselves in industry and lost touch with the natural world
(E) we can forget our sins by personifying nature as godlike

Passage 6. William Butler Yeats, "That the Night Come"

She lived in storm and strife.
Her soul had such desire
For what proud death may bring
That it could not endure
The common good of life,   5
But lived as 'twere a king
That packed his marriage day
With banneret and pennon,
Trumpet and kettledrum,
And the outrageous cannon,   10
To bundle Time away
That the night come.

58. It can be inferred from the poem as a whole that "She" views "the common good of life" as all of the following *except*

(A) unappreciated
(B) undesirable
(C) unappealing
(D) unendurable
(E) not enjoyable

59. The subject(s) of the poem is/are
    (A) "a king"
    (B) "She"
    (C) "the common good of life"
    (D) "Time"
    (E) "She" and "a king"

60. Line 1 is distinct from each of the other lines in the poem in that it
    (A) contains alliteration
    (B) describes the subject of the poem
    (C) contains figurative language
    (D) is comprised of an independent clause
    (E) is objective

61. The word "it" in line 4 refers to
    (A) "death"
    (B) "Her"
    (C) "soul"
    (D) "desire"
    (E) "She"

62. The main difference emphasized in the poem between "She" and the "king" is
    (A) their gender
    (B) their way of living
    (C) the object of their desire
    (D) their attitude
    (E) their class status

63. The speaker's point of view is most like that of
    (A) a harsh critic
    (B) an indifferent observer
    (C) an indulgent friend
    (D) a mentor
    (E) an omniscient narrator

64. The simile in line 6 reveals

(A) the king's superiority to the woman
(B) the king's love for his wife
(C) the woman's anticipation of her wedding night
(D) the woman's regret that she did not marry
(E) the woman's excitement about death

65. Which of the following devices creates a sense of frenetic energy in lines 8–10?

(A) unconventional verbs
(B) alliteration
(C) polysyndeton
(D) enjambment
(E) internal rhyme

66. The poem characterizes night as

I. remote
II. unavoidable
III. interminable

(A) I only
(B) II only
(C) I and III only
(D) II and III only
(E) I, II, and III

67. The phrase "To bundle Time away" (11) means

(A) to pass time
(B) to protect time
(C) to waste time
(D) to save time
(E) to ignore time

CHAPTER 2

American Poetry

Passage 1. Anne Bradstreet, "The Author to Her Book"

Thou ill-form'd offspring of my feeble brain,
Who after birth did'st by my side remain,
Till snatcht from thence by friends, less wise than true,
Who thee abroad exposed to public view,
Made thee in rags, halting to th' press to trudge,   5
Where errors were not lessened (all may judge).
At thy return my blushing was not small,
My rambling brat (in print) should mother call.
I cast thee by as one unfit for light,
The visage was so irksome in my sight,   10
Yet being mine own, at length affection would
Thy blemishes amend, if so I could.
I washed thy face, but more defects I saw,
And rubbing off a spot, still made a flaw.
I stretcht thy joints to make thee even feet,   15
Yet still thou run'st more hobbling than is meet.
In better dress to trim thee was my mind,
But nought save home-spun cloth, i' th' house I find.
In this array, 'mongst vulgars may'st thou roam.
In critics' hands, beware thou dost not come,   20
And take thy way where yet thou are not known.
If for thy father askt, say, thou hadst none;
And for thy mother, she alas is poor,
Which caused her thus to send thee out of door.

68. The word "Thou" in line 1 indicates

(A) the poem is a letter
(B) the poem is an invocation
(C) the speaker is employing apostrophe
(D) the speaker uses arcane vocabulary to make a point
(E) the poem is outdated

69. Who is the subject of the verb "Made" (5)?
    (A) the press
    (B) friends
    (C) the speaker
    (D) the book
    (E) the offspring

70. What is ironic about the effort the speaker puts forth to improve her book?
    (A) it is futile
    (B) she is a worse writer than she thought
    (C) it exacerbates the situation
    (D) the "blemishes" are actually amended
    (E) she only partially improves it

71. In which line does the speaker suggest she is without the skills and tools to improve her book?
    (A) "less wise than true" (3)
    (B) "I washed thy face, but more defects I saw" (13)
    (C) "Yet still thou run'st more hobbling than is meet" (16)
    (D) "But nought save home-spun cloth, i' the' house I find" (18)
    (E) "thou hadst none" (22)

72. The speaker implies her book is all of the following *except*
    (A) unfinished
    (B) disseminated prematurely
    (C) fallible
    (D) irreparable
    (E) polemical

73. The tone of the poem is
    (A) mournful
    (B) nurturing
    (C) self-deprecating
    (D) vengeful
    (E) acerbic

74. Based on the poem as a whole, the speaker's relationship to her critics can best be described as

    (A) friendly
    (B) productive
    (C) wrought
    (D) unconventional
    (E) acrimonious

75. The poem's rhythm is composed of

    I. parenthetical phrases
    II. first person point of view
    III. heroic couplets

    (A) I only
    (B) I and II only
    (C) II and III only
    (D) III only
    (E) I, II, and III

76. The relationship between the speaker and her addressee is most similar to the relationship between

    (A) a teacher and a student
    (B) a nurturing father and a child
    (C) a boss and an employee
    (D) a fastidious artist and her painting
    (E) a director and an actor

77. The main topic of the poem is

    (A) an artist's relationship with her work
    (B) an artist's dislike for her work
    (C) the need for editing before publication
    (D) unreasonable critics
    (E) the hardships of motherhood

78. The poem is developed mainly through

    (A) rhyme
    (B) iambic pentameter
    (C) simile
    (D) metaphor
    (E) conceit

Passage 2. Countee Cullen, "I Have a Rendezvous with Life"

I have a rendezvous with Life,
In days I hope will come,
Ere youth has sped, and strength of mind,
Ere voices sweet grow dumb.
I have a rendezvous with Life,   5
When Spring's first heralds hum.
Sure some would cry it's better far
To crown their days with sleep
Than face the road, the wind and rain,
To heed the calling deep.   10
Though wet nor blow nor space I fear,
Yet fear I deeply, too,
Lest Death should meet and claim me ere
I keep Life's rendezvous.

79. The word "Ere" most nearly means

    (A) until
    (B) before
    (C) when
    (D) after
    (E) because

80. The first sentence (1–4) and the second sentence (5–6) are similar in that

    I. each makes a reference to time
    II. each creates a mood of anticipation
    III. they share a rhyme

    (A) I only
    (B) II only
    (C) III only
    (D) I and III only
    (E) I, II, and III

81. The "hum" in line 6 is likely a reference to

    (A) the speaker's conscience
    (B) God's ominous voice
    (C) vexing insects buzzing in spring
    (D) the sounds of life that signal spring's arrival
    (E) the speaker's imagined heaven

82. The poem indicates that "some" (7) are inhibited by their

    (A) obliviousness to what "Life" has to offer
    (B) tendency to take risks
    (C) inclination to avoid challenges
    (D) self-consciousness
    (E) proclivity for introversion

83. In comparison to "some" (7), the speaker indicates he, too, is

    (A) fearsome
    (B) frightened
    (C) reluctant
    (D) brave
    (E) audacious

84. In line 12, the speaker is literally doing which of the following?

    (A) pitying himself
    (B) humanizing himself
    (C) distinguishing himself
    (D) drawing a parallel between himself and others
    (E) inciting empathy

85. The speaker's use of the word "space" (11) is in response to

    (A) stormy obstacles he may encounter
    (B) his eagerness for "Spring's herald hum"
    (C) his fear of death
    (D) his anticipation for his rendezvous with life
    (E) the "road" feared by "some"

86. Based on the poem as a whole, the word "Life" is best interpreted to mean

    (A) romantic love
    (B) the speaker's desired mate
    (C) breathing
    (D) all that the world has to offer
    (E) strictly the pleasures of youth

87. The word "rendezvous" can be replaced with all of the following *except*

    (A) encounter
    (B) meeting
    (C) engagement
    (D) date
    (E) interview

88. The words "Life" and "Death" are capitalized in order to

    (A) portray them as intimidating the speaker
    (B) capture the speaker's view that life and death hold sway over him
    (C) personify them as menacingly influential
    (D) allude to them as Greek gods
    (E) humanize them to decrease their fearsome qualities

89. The speaker's main concern is

    (A) the inevitability of dying young
    (B) the drawbacks of aging
    (C) the temporality of the seasons
    (D) the crippling fear that prohibits people from experiencing life
    (E) the need to make the most of life

Passage 3. Emily Dickinson, "Success is counted sweetest …"

Success is counted sweetest
By those who ne'er succeed.
To comprehend a nectar
Requires sorest need.

Not one of all the purple host   5
Who took the flag to-day
Can tell the definition,
So clear, of victory,

As he, defeated, dying,
On whose forbidden ear   10
The distant strains of triumph
Break, agonized and clear!

90. In context, the word "comprehend" in line 3 most likely means

    (A) to eat
    (B) to figure out
    (C) to determine
    (D) to analyze
    (E) to truly know

91. The alliteration in the first stanza serves to

    (A) soothe the reader
    (B) highlight the envious tone
    (C) complement the assonance in the first stanza
    (D) contrast the consonance in the second stanza
    (E) emphasize the appeal of success by creating an appealing sound

92. According to the speaker, who can best understand the definition of "victory" (8)?

    I. "the purple host" (5)
    II. "those who ne'er succeed" (2)
    III. "he, defeated, dying" (9)

    (A) I and II only
    (B) I and III only
    (C) II and III only
    (D) III only
    (E) I, II, and III

93. The words "day" (6) and "victory" (8) provide an example of

    (A) exact rhyme
    (B) slant rhyme
    (C) double entendre
    (D) oxymoron
    (E) antithesis

94. Based on the poem, it can be inferred that the color purple is symbolic of

    (A) jealousy
    (B) royalty
    (C) comeraderie
    (D) victory
    (E) compensation

95. The words "agonized" and "strained" are used in reference to "triumph" because

    (A) those who do not win long for a second chance
    (B) the joy of victory is tainted by the jealousy of others
    (C) the sounds of victory are emotionally hard to hear for those who have lost
    (D) the triumph was not rightfully earned
    (E) competition inevitably creates antipathy

96. The poem as a whole presents a contrast between
    (A) those with and without success
    (B) a well-earned and undeserved victory
    (C) competition and collaboration
    (D) soreness and sweetness
    (E) clear and distant

97. The structure of the poem consists of
    (A) a hypothesis, reasoning, and a solution
    (B) a proposition and evidence
    (C) a maxim and illustrations of that maxim
    (D) a theory and examples
    (E) a question answered by hypothetical situations

98. The overall tone of the poem is
    (A) sorrowful
    (B) sanctimonious
    (C) moralistic
    (D) adagelike
    (E) envious

99. The poem can be summarized by which of the following sentences?
    (A) Only those who have achieved success understand its sweetness.
    (B) Success comes only to those who risk and persevere.
    (C) Success is best won through hard work.
    (D) Only those who have not achieved success understand its sweetness.
    (E) The victor is always better off.

Passage 4. T. S. Eliot, "Morning at the Window"

They are rattling breakfast plates in basement kitchens,
And along the trampled edges of the street
I am aware of the damp souls of housemaids
Sprouting despondently at area gates.
The brown waves of fog toss up to me   5
Twisted faces from the bottom of the street,
And tear from a passer-by with muddy skirts
An aimless smile that hovers in the air
And vanishes along the level of the roofs.

100. In line 5, the "waves" are

(A) evidence of a recent flood that has ravaged the town
(B) a metaphor for the fog that carries images from down below up to the speaker at his window
(C) part of the poem's bigger conceit that compares the scene below to an ocean
(D) part of a hypothetical situation thought up by the speaker
(E) a hallucination that characterizes the speaker as depressed and delusional

101. The subject to which the word "tear" (7) refers is

(A) a passer-by
(B) the speaker
(C) the brown waves
(D) an aimless smile
(E) damp souls

102. The words "fog ... faces from" (5–6) are an example of

(A) consonance
(B) repetition
(C) anaphora
(D) assonance
(E) alliteration

103. The poem's assonance

(A) is found in the words "muddy skirts" (7) and emphasizes the ugliness of the scene being described
(B) is found in the words "faces from" (6) and creates a soothing sound to ease the speaker's discomfort
(C) is found in the words "fog toss" (5) and creates a feeling of upward movement to complement the movement of the waves
(D) is found in the words "brown waves" (5) and emphasizes the disparity between ugliness and beauty
(E) is found in the word "rattling" (1) and allows the reader to hear what the speaker hears

104. Regarding the scene he is describing, the speaker is
    (A) removed and observant
    (B) obsessed and upset
    (C) optimistic
    (D) fatalistic
    (E) apathetic

105. The people described in the poem are characterized mostly as
    (A) ghostlike
    (B) penurious
    (C) starving
    (D) pathetic
    (E) grotesque

106. The speaker is differentiated from the people he describes by
    I. his wealth
    II. his location
    III. his actions

    (A) I only
    (B) I and II only
    (C) II only
    (D) II and III only
    (E) III only

107. The tone of the poem is developed through
    (A) eerie diction, sensory images, and metaphor
    (B) rhyme, metaphor, and consistent rhythm
    (C) similes, personification, and grotesque imagery
    (D) unconventional verbs, allusions, and speculation
    (E) haunting images, couplets, and double meanings

Passage 5. Phyllis Wheatley, "An Hymn to the Evening"

Soon as the sun forsook the eastern main
The pealing thunder shook the heav'nly plain;
Majestic grandeur! From the zephyr's wing,
Exhales the incense of the blooming spring.
Soft purl the streams, the birds renew their notes,   5
And through the air their mingled music floats.

Through all the heav'ns what beauteous dies are spread!
But the west glories in the deepest red:
So may our breasts with ev'ry virtue glow,
The living temples of our God below!   10

Fill'd with the praise of him who gives the light,
And draws the sable curtains of the night,
Let placid slumbers sooth each weary mind,
At morn to wake more heav'nly, more refin'd;
So shall the labours of the day begin   15
More pure, more guarded from the snares of sin.

Night's leaden sceptre seals my drowsy eyes,
Then cease, my song, till fair Aurora rise.

108. The verbs in lines 1–6 are notable because they are

    (A) passive
    (B) mundane
    (C) repetitive
    (D) literal
    (E) sensory

109. The antecedent to the pronoun "their" in line 6 is

    (A) "mingled music"
    (B) "the birds"
    (C) "the streams"
    (D) "notes"
    (E) "blooming spring"

110. The speaker consistently responds to her observed environment with

    (A) restrained awe
    (B) unabashed reverence
    (C) fearful respect
    (D) whimsical enthusiasm
    (E) sincere shock

111. Line 9 marks a transition in the poem from

    (A) objectivity to subjectivity
    (B) a focus on nature to a focus on people
    (C) exclamation to consternation
    (D) daybreak to nightfall
    (E) an appreciation of nature to an appreciation of God

112. What do the "living temples of our God below" (10) symbolically represent?

    (A) devout souls
    (B) churches erected in honor of God
    (C) "beauteous dies"
    (D) secularism
    (E) "all the heav'ns"

113. Considering the poem as a whole, the speaker implies that slumbers are placid as a result of

    (A) quietude
    (B) drawn curtains
    (C) "labours of the day"
    (D) "Night's leaden scepter"
    (E) our piety

114. The speaker indicates that sleep can have all of the following effects *except*

    (A) to restore
    (B) to mollify
    (C) to stimulate
    (D) to ready
    (E) to purify

115. The speaker most probably views the "leaden sceptre" (18) with

    (A) anxiety
    (B) some skepticism
    (C) nervousness
    (D) ambivalence
    (E) veneration

116. The speaker attributes which of the following behaviors to God?

    I. regulates
    II. inspires
    III. intimidates

    (A) I only
    (B) I and II only
    (C) II and III only
    (D) III only
    (E) I, II, and III

117. The alliteration in the poem's final couplet primarily functions to

    (A) contrast the poem's earlier lines
    (B) create a sense of foreboding
    (C) evoke the sound of slumber
    (D) disrupt the rhyme scheme
    (E) present God as harmonious

118. The context of the poem suggests that "Aurora" is symbolic of

    (A) a companion
    (B) the speaker's muse
    (C) music
    (D) light
    (E) the morning

119. In the final two lines, the speaker seeks to convey a feeling of

    (A) intimidation
    (B) threat
    (C) imminence
    (D) eminence
    (E) repose

120. In order to convey its central message, the poem relies repeatedly on all of the following *except*

    (A) understatement
    (B) exclamation
    (C) couplets
    (D) metaphor
    (E) sensory images

Passage 6. Walt Whitman, "O Captain! My Captain!"

O Captain! my Captain! our fearful trip is done!
The ship has weathered every wrack, the prize we sought is won.
The port is near, the bells I hear, the people all exulting,
While follow eyes the steady keel, the vessel grim and daring.

But, O heart! heart! heart!
Leave you not the little spot
Where on the deck my Captain lies,
Fallen cold and dead.

5

O Captain! my Captain! rise up and hear the bells!
Rise up! for you the flag is flung, for you the bugle trills: 10
For you bouquets and ribboned wreaths; for you the shores a-crowding:
For you they call, the swaying mass, their eager faces turning.

O Captain! dear father!
This arm I push beneath you.
It is some dream that on the deck   15
You've fallen cold and dead!

My Captain does not answer, his lips are pale and still:
My father does not feel my arm, he has no pulse nor will.
But the ship, the ship is anchored safe, its voyage closed and done:
From fearful trip the victor ship comes in with object won!   20
Exult, O shores! and ring, O bells!
But I, with silent tread,
Walk the spot my Captain lies,
Fallen cold and dead.

121. The best paraphrase of line 4 is

   (A) all eyes are watching the formidable vessel
   (B) witnesses are focused on the vessel's departure
   (C) bystanders are concerned about the vessel's arrival
   (D) we follow the eyes of all these people as we pull into the port
   (E) people are in awe of the damage done to our vessel

122. Lines 5–8 can best be summarized as

   (A) I should never forget the moment of my captain's death.
   (B) I love my captain.
   (C) My heart is breaking upon seeing my captain die.
   (D) I will never leave this spot where my captain has died.
   (E) I will never forget this moment.

123. It can be inferred that the "bells," "flag," "bugle," "wreaths," and crowds
    (lines 9–12)

   (A) are meant to be ironic
   (B) are part of the speaker's hallucination
   (C) describe both a victory celebration and a funeral
   (D) are metaphors for the captain
   (E) are similes for the captain

124. In lines 19–20, the ship is like the captain in all of the following ways
except

   (A) they have both ended their heroic journeys
   (B) they have achieved their goals
   (C) they are both metaphorical
   (D) they have both arrived home safely
   (E) they are both celebrated

125. The references to the captain change

   (A) from exclamations in the first and third stanzas to calm statements in the fifth stanza
   (B) to direct addresses in the fifth stanza
   (C) to internal thoughts in the fifth stanza
   (D) to dialogue in the third stanza
   (E) to exclamations in the fifth stanza

126. The three segments (stanzas 1, 3, and 5) of the poem are divided according to

   (A) the speaker's shock, anger, and disbelief
   (B) the speaker's discovery, denial, and acceptance
   (C) death, funeral, and denial
   (D) theory, research, and conclusion
   (E) argument, counterargument, and solution

127. The repetition of the phrase "O Captain! my Captain" contributes to

   (A) the uplifting tone of the poem
   (B) the elegiac tone of the poem
   (C) the idea that mourning is musical
   (D) the poem's rhyme scheme
   (E) a sense of the speaker's exultation

128. In the final stanza, there is a contrast between

   (A) the speaker and the ship
   (B) land and sea
   (C) noisy rejoicing and quiet mourning
   (D) splendid victory and regrettable surrender
   (E) life and death

129. Based on the poem as a whole, which of the following could the captain most likely symbolize?

    (A) a nation's beloved leader
    (B) an excellent seafarer who has suddenly died
    (C) a controversial leader
    (D) the mighty naval industry
    (E) the speaker himself

130. The poem's style and content are most similar to those of

    (A) a limerick
    (B) a satire
    (C) a screed
    (D) an ode
    (E) an elegy

131. The poem ends with the speaker in a state of

    (A) optimism
    (B) disappointment
    (C) celebration
    (D) denial
    (E) mourning

World Poetry

Passage 1. Kahlil Gibran, "Defeat"

Defeat, my Defeat, my solitude and my aloofness;
You are dearer to me than a thousand triumphs,
And sweeter to my heart than all world-glory.

Defeat, my Defeat, my self-knowledge and my defiance,
Through you I know that I am yet young and swift of foot   5
And not to be trapped by withering laurels.
And in you I have found aloneness
And the joy of being shunned and scorned.

Defeat, my Defeat, my shining sword and shield,
In your eyes I have read   10
That to be enthroned is to be enslaved,
and to be understood is to be leveled down,
And to be grasped is but to reach one's fullness
and like a ripe fruit to fall and be consumed.

Defeat, my Defeat, my bold companion,   15
You shall hear my songs and my cries and my silences,
And none but you shall speak to me of the beating of wings,
And urging of seas,
And of mountains that burn in the night,
And you alone shall climb my steep and rocky soul.   20

Defeat, my Defeat, my deathless courage,
You and I shall laugh together with the storm,
And together we shall dig graves for all that die in us,
And we shall stand in the sun with a will,
And we shall be dangerous.   25

132. The poem as a whole is written as a(n)

(A) allegory
(B) anecdote
(C) letter
(D) speech
(E) apostrophe

133. In the second stanza, the speaker reveals that

(A) "Defeat" is a characteristic of the young
(B) "Defeat" is an actual person
(C) he sees value in "Defeat" because it makes him incorrigible
(D) he sees value in "Defeat" because it makes him self-aware
(E) he has a sarcastic attitude toward "Defeat"

134. The parallel structures in the third stanza serve to

(A) portray "Defeat" as unrelenting
(B) present "Defeat's" messages as overwhelming
(C) communicate the cohesion of "Defeat's" messages
(D) create rhythm with a discordant sound
(E) create a regular beat with a predictable sound

135. The metaphor of the "sword and shield" (9) is meant to

(A) emphasize "Defeat's" emboldening powers
(B) characterize the speaker as invincible
(C) contradict the previous stanza's imagery
(D) change the poem's tone from sarcastic to laudatory
(E) emphasize "Defeat's" valiant nature

136. The third stanza reveals that the speaker thinks success is

(A) hypocritical
(B) unimaginable
(C) overrated
(D) easily obtained
(E) better than "Defeat"

137. The simile in lines 13–14 compares

(A) "ripe fruit" to consumption
(B) "Defeat" to fruit
(C) ripeness to satisfaction
(D) "ripe fruit" to "one"
(E) comprehensibility to fullness

138. The speaker characterizes "Defeat" as all of the following *except*
    (A) second best to success
    (B) distinct
    (C) useful
    (D) brave
    (E) bold

139. The poem's refrain
    (A) is found in lines 1, 4, 9, 15, and 21 and characterizes "Defeat" as alone
    (B) is found in all lines beginning with "And" and highlights the theme
    (C) is found in all lines beginning with "And" and emphasizes the speaker's point
    (D) is found in lines 1, 4, 9, 15, and 21 and enhances the poem's ode-like quality
    (E) is the entire last stanza and contains the theme

140. The speaker's address to "Defeat" as his "deathless courage" (21) shows
    (A) the poem's ironic tone
    (B) the speaker's appreciation of death
    (C) that courage and death are opposites
    (D) that with "Defeat" comes immortality
    (E) that with "Defeat" comes temerity

141. The speaker sees "Defeat" primarily as his
    (A) friend
    (B) mentor
    (C) adversary
    (D) obstacle
    (E) parent

142. The mood that is established by the end of the poem is one of
    (A) confidence
    (B) cynicism
    (C) desire
    (D) destruction
    (E) wistfulness

Passage 2. Jayadeva, Excerpt from *Gita Govinda*

Beautiful Radha, jasmine-bosomed Radha,
All in the Spring-time waited by the wood
For Krishna fair, Krishna the all-forgetful,—
Krishna with earthly love's false fire consuming—
And some one of her maidens sang this song:—   5

I know where Krishna tarries in these early days of Spring,
When every wind from warm Malay brings fragrance on its wing;
Brings fragrance stolen far away from thickets of the clove,
In jungles where the bees hum and the Koil flutes her love;
He dances with the dancers of a merry morrice one,   10
All in the budding Spring-time, for 'tis sad to be alone.

I know how Krishna passes these hours of blue and gold
When parted lovers sigh to meet and greet and closely hold
Hand fast in hand; and every branch upon the Vakul-tree
Droops downward with a hundred blooms, in every bloom a bee;   15
He is dancing with the dancers to a laughter-moving tone,
In the soft awakening Spring-time, when 'tis hard to live alone.

Where Kroona-flowers, that open at a lover's lightest tread,
Break, and, for shame at what they hear, from white blush modest red;
And all the spears on all the boughs of all the Ketuk-glades   20
Seem ready darts to pierce the hearts of wandering youths and maids;
Tis there thy Krishna dances till the merry drum is done,
All in the sunny Spring-time, when who can live alone?

Where the breaking forth of blossom on the yellow Keshra-sprays
Dazzles like Kama's sceptre, whom all the world obeys;   25
And Pâtal-buds fill drowsy bees from pink delicious bowls,
As Kama's nectared goblet steeps in languor human souls;
There he dances with the dancers, and of Radha thinketh none,
All in the warm new Spring-tide, when none will live alone.

Where the breath of waving Mâdhvi pours incense through the grove,   30
And silken Mogras lull the sense with essences of love,—
The silken-soft pale Mogra, whose perfume fine and faint
Can melt the coldness of a maid, the sternness of a saint—
There dances with those dancers thine other self, thine Own,
All in the languorous Spring-time, when none will live alone.   35

Where—as if warm lips touched sealed eyes and waked them—all the bloom
Opens upon the mangoes to feel the sunshine come;
And Atimuktas wind their arms of softest green about,
Clasping the stems, while calm and clear great Jumna spreadeth out;
There dances and there laughs thy Love, with damsels many a one,
In the rosy days of Spring-time, for he will not live alone.

40

143. The first verse serves as the poem's

    (A) overture
    (B) invocation
    (C) climax
    (D) denouement
    (E) coda

144. The appositives in lines 1–5 provide

    (A) epithets for Radha and Krishna
    (B) examples
    (C) additional details about the setting
    (D) stereotypical descriptions
    (E) the problem that will be discussed in the poem

145. The simile in line 25 serves to

    (A) imply that nature can be destructive
    (B) emphasize Krishna's infidelity
    (C) compare the season to a war
    (D) compare flowers to people
    (E) highlight the commanding powers of spring

146. The phrase "pink delicious bowls" (26) is intended as

    (A) an example of personification
    (B) a metaphor for the nourishing flower petals
    (C) a description of a rare species of flower
    (D) an oxymoron
    (E) a symbol of the bees' hunger

147. In line 27, "Kama's nectared goblet steeps in languor human souls" most likely refers to

    (A) the drunken feeling of love
    (B) the smallness of human ambition
    (C) the awakening of desire
    (D) the wetness of springtime
    (E) the intoxicating effects of alcohol

148. The consistent repetition of the word "alone" emphasizes the contrast between

 (A) celibacy and marriage
 (B) loneliness and mating
 (C) independence and submission
 (D) monogamy and polygamy
 (E) the speaker and Radha

149. The poem's refrain serves to

 (A) describe spring
 (B) reinforce the speaker's empathy for Krishna
 (C) make Radha feel lonelier
 (D) introduce new characters
 (E) question Krishna's intentions

150. Krishna's attitude toward Radha can best be described as

 (A) scornful
 (B) indifferent
 (C) ambivalent
 (D) coy
 (E) calculating

151. In line 34, "thine other self, thine own" refers to

 (A) Krishna
 (B) Radha
 (C) Mâdhvi
 (D) Mogra
 (E) Kama

152. The maidens' attitude toward Krishna can best be described as

 (A) mercurial
 (B) ambivalent
 (C) sanctimonious
 (D) incriminating
 (E) apologetic

153. In context, the word "Love" (40) is a reference to

 (A) Radha's possession
 (B) Radha's desire
 (C) spring
 (D) Radha
 (E) Krishna

154. We can infer from the poem's context that words like "Kroona," "Ketuk," "Keshra," "Pâtal," and "Mogras" are all

(A) allusions
(B) names of characters
(C) names of gods
(D) names of types of foliage
(E) names for spring

155. The implication from the maidens' song is that Krishna is all of the following *except*

(A) faithful
(B) promiscuous
(C) dexterous
(D) charming
(E) indulgent

156. The overall mood of the poem can best be described as

(A) jealous
(B) exultant
(C) reticent
(D) admonishing
(E) conciliatory

Passage 3. Rabindranath Tagore, "The Home"

I paced alone on the road across the field while the sunset was
hiding its last gold like a miser.

The daylight sank deeper and deeper into the darkness, and the
widowed land, whose harvest had been reaped, lay silent.

Suddenly a boy's shrill voice rose into the sky. He traversed   5
the dark unseen, leaving the track of his song across the hush of
the evening.

His village home lay there at the end of the waste land, beyond
the sugar-cane field, hidden among the shadows of the banana and
the slender areca palm, the cocoa-nut and the dark green   10
jack-fruit trees.

I stopped for a moment in my lonely way under the starlight, and
saw spread before me the darkened earth surrounding with her arms
countless homes furnished with cradles and beds, mothers' hearts
and evening lamps, and young lives glad with a gladness that   15
knows nothing of its value for the world.

157. The simile in line 2

    (A) compares gold to a cheapskate to emphasize the town's poverty

    (B) compares the sun to a scrupulous saver to convey the disappearance
        of sunlight

    (C) contrasts the gold to a miser to show the town's poverty

    (D) contrasts the sun to a miser to show how dark it has become

    (E) symbolizes darkness

158. Line 3 contains an abundance of

    (A) anaphora

    (B) personification

    (C) hyperbole

    (D) assonance

    (E) alliteration

159. The phrases "widowed land" (4) and "her arms" (13) are best understood
as

    (A) commentary on harsh agricultural practices

    (B) conflicting references to the speaker's society

    (C) metaphors for the tribulations of women

    (D) personifications of a depleted and nurturing earth

    (E) symbols of the speaker's longing

160. The sentence that comprises the second stanza of the poem differs from that
of the first in that

    (A) it evokes a mood of stillness instead of movement

    (B) it contains a simile

    (C) it emphasizes light instead of darkness

    (D) it describes the setting

    (E) it is focused on the speaker's actions

161. The third stanza contains a contrast between

    (A) night and day
    (B) boy and sky
    (C) boy and man
    (D) sound and silence
    (E) light and dark

162. The phrase "waste land" (8) implies that

    (A) the setting is hellish
    (B) the "home" is in the middle of nowhere
    (C) a war has just taken place
    (D) the people of this town are devastated
    (E) the boy's home is isolated

163. What is the primary function of the fourth stanza?

    (A) to provide the precise location of the speaker
    (B) to develop the personification of the land
    (C) to provide a glimpse into the culture and background of the people
    (D) to illustrate the home as distinctly different from its surroundings
    (E) to emphasize the remoteness of the home

164. The poem's final sentence can best be paraphrased as

    (A) Happy families are unaware of how valuable their bliss is to the world.
    (B) The dark, lonely earth is lit up by the people who inhabit it.
    (C) I wish I were part of one of these families.
    (D) Home is where the heart is.
    (E) The natural world protects families and makes them glad.

165. The list in lines 14–15 is intended to convey a feeling of

    (A) exclusivity
    (B) envy
    (C) mild satisfaction
    (D) indulgence
    (E) reassurance

166. The poem's form and style are characteristic of a(n)

    (A) ballad
    (B) ode
    (C) elegy
    (D) sonnet
    (E) free-verse poem

CHAPTER 4

British Fiction

Passage 1. Frances Burney, *Evelina*

We are to go this evening to a private ball, given by Mrs. Stanley, a very fashionable lady of Mrs. Mirvan's acquaintance.

We have been a-shopping as Mrs. Mirvan calls it, all this morning, to buy silks, caps, gauzes, and so forth.

The shops are really very entertaining, especially the mercers; there seem to be 5 six or seven men belonging to each shop; and every one took care by bowing and smirking, to be noticed. We were conducted from one to another, and carried from room to room with so much ceremony, that I was almost afraid to go on.

I thought I should never have chosen a silk: for they produced so many, I knew not which to fix upon; and they recommended them all so strongly, that I 10 fancy they thought I only wanted persuasion to buy every thing they showed me. And, indeed, they took so much trouble, that I was almost ashamed I could not.

At the milliners, the ladies we met were so much dressed, that I should rather have imagined they were making visits than purchases. But what most diverted me was, that we were more frequently served by men than by women; and such 15 men! so finical, so affected! they seemed to understand every part of a woman's dress better than we do ourselves; and they recommended caps and ribbands with an air of so much importance, that I wished to ask them how long they had left off wearing them.

The dispatch with which they work in these great shops is amazing, for they 20 have promised me a complete suit of linen against the evening.

I have just had my hair dressed. You can't think how oddly my head feels; full of powder and black pins, and a great cushion on the top of it. I believe you would hardly know me, for my face looks quite different to what it did before my hair was dressed. When I shall be able to make use of a comb for myself I cannot tell; for my 25 hair is so much entangled, frizzled they call it, that I fear it will be very difficult.

I am half afraid of this ball to-night; for, you know, I have never danced but at school: however, Miss Mirvan says there is nothing in it. Yet, I wish it was over.

Adieu, my dear Sir, pray excuse the wretched stuff I write; perhaps I may improve by being in this town, and then my letters will be less unworthy your 30 reading. Meantime, I am, Your dutiful and affectionate, though unpolished, EVELINA

167. The mercers are primarily characterized as

(A) solicitous
(B) excessive
(C) redundant
(D) generous
(E) conscientious

168. The speaker's tone in the phrase "and such men!" (15–16) can best be described as

(A) perturbed
(B) frightened
(C) bewildered
(D) disappointed
(E) disturbed

169. In context, the word "affected" in line 16 most likely means

(A) unnatural
(B) influential
(C) concerned
(D) moved
(E) stirred

170. Lines 20–21 reveal that the speaker is impressed by the shops'

(A) dresses
(B) communication
(C) efficiency
(D) respect
(E) accommodation

171. Regarding her "dressed" (22) hair, the speaker feels

(A) disillusioned
(B) relieved
(C) dissatisfied
(D) proud
(E) disoriented

172. Based on the passage as a whole, it can be interpreted that the speaker is "half afraid" (27) mostly due to her

(A) fear of the unpredictable
(B) new hairstyle and clothing
(C) the newness of everything she has experienced
(D) insecurity and apprehension
(E) poor dance skills

173. The reader can infer that the speaker is here primarily

(A) to ingratiate herself
(B) to become refined
(C) to please her "dear Sir"
(D) to meet a husband
(E) to study

174. The closing lines (32–33) indicate that the passage is

(A) an interior monologue
(B) stream of consciousness
(C) nonfiction
(D) excerpted from a journal
(E) part of a missive

175. The qualification in the final line of the passage serves to

(A) characterize Evelina as obtuse
(B) underscore Evelina's self-awareness
(C) berate Evelina
(D) contrast Evelina with her addressee
(E) undermine Evelina's authority

176. The purpose of the passage as a whole is

(A) to criticize the values of a particular society
(B) to characterize the speaker as guileless and uncouth
(C) to detail the oddities of a culture from a stranger's perspective
(D) to reveal the speaker's perception of her experiences
(E) to characterize the speaker as tenacious and wise

Passage 2. Joseph Conrad, *Heart of Darkness*

The Nellie, a cruising yawl, swung to her anchor without a flutter of the sails, and was at rest. The flood had made, the wind was nearly calm, and being bound down the river, the only thing for it was to come to and wait for the turn of the tide.

The sea-reach of the Thames stretched before us like the beginning of an   5
interminable waterway. In the offing the sea and the sky were welded together without a joint, and in the luminous space the tanned sails of the barges drifting up with the tide seemed to stand still in red clusters of canvas sharply peaked, with gleams of varnished sprits. A haze rested on the low shores that ran out to sea in vanishing flatness. The air was dark above Gravesend, and farther back still   10
seemed condensed into a mournful gloom, brooding motionless over the biggest, and the greatest, town on earth.

The Director of Companies was our captain and our host. We four affectionately watched his back as he stood in the bows looking to seaward. On the whole river there was nothing that looked half so nautical. He resembled a pilot, which to   15
a seaman is trustworthiness personified. It was difficult to realize his work was not out there in the luminous estuary, but behind him, within the brooding gloom.

Between us there was, as I have already said somewhere, the bond of the sea. Besides holding our hearts together through long periods of separation, it had the effect of making us tolerant of each other's yarns—and even convictions. The   20
Lawyer—the best of old fellows—had, because of his many years and many virtues, the only cushion on deck, and was lying on the only rug. The Accountant had brought out already a box of dominoes, and was toying architecturally with the bones. Marlow sat cross-legged right aft, leaning against the mizzen-mast. He had sunken cheeks, a yellow complexion, a straight back, an ascetic aspect,   25
and, with his arms dropped, the palms of hands outwards, resembled an idol. The director, satisfied the anchor had good hold, made his way aft and sat down amongst us. We exchanged a few words lazily. Afterwards there was silence on board the yacht. For some reason or other we did not begin that game of dominoes. We felt meditative, and fit for nothing but placid staring. The day was end-   30
ing in a serenity of still and exquisite brilliance. The water shone pacifically; the sky, without a speck, was a benign immensity of unstained light; the very mist on the Essex marsh was like a gauzy and radiant fabric, hung from the wooded rises inland, and draping the low shores in diaphanous folds. Only the gloom to the west, brooding over the upper reaches, became more sombre every minute, as if   35
angered by the approach of the sun.

And at last, in its curved and imperceptible fall, the sun sank low, and from glowing white changed to a dull red without rays and without heat, as if about to go out suddenly, stricken to death by the touch of that gloom brooding over a crowd of men.   40

177. The word "it" in line 3 refers to

(A) a vessel
(B) the water
(C) the flood
(D) the sun
(E) the wind

178. Lines 5–6 ("It was difficult...brooding gloom") suggest which of the following about the Director's "work"?

(A) It is nautical.
(B) It takes place in foreign lands.
(C) It is adventurous.
(D) It is meaningful.
(E) It is municipal.

179. The sentence in lines 9–11 ("The air was dark ... earth") expresses what type of mood?

(A) wicked
(B) lugubrious
(C) irreverent
(D) diabolical
(E) placid

180. In the first and second paragraphs, the setting is described using all of the following devices *except*

(A) sensory imagery
(B) simile
(C) metaphor
(D) personification
(E) oxymoron

181. The Director of Companies is

(A) affectionate and authoritative
(B) demonstrative and trustworthy
(C) naval and venerable
(D) principled and brooding
(E) gregarious and esteemed

182. How many people are with the narrator?

 (A) three
 (B) four
 (C) five
 (D) fewer than three
 (E) more than five

183. The context of the passage suggests that a potential reason the crew "did not begin that game of dominoes" (29–30) is that

 (A) the setting induces stillness
 (B) they are growing slightly intolerant of each other's yarns and convictions
 (C) they have just come out of a period of long separation
 (D) each crew member is occupied with another task
 (E) "The Accountant" does not intend to share his dominoes

184. The word "diaphanous" (34) describes

 (A) the mist
 (B) the landscape
 (C) the water
 (D) the light
 (E) the shore

185. In context, the reference to "a crowd of men" (39–40) is most likely used to

 (A) refer reverentially to the city's denizens
 (B) subtly mock the city's bureaucrats
 (C) evoke a sense of a restive majority
 (D) suggest imminent doom for the hapless citizens
 (E) objectively describe the setting

186. Lines 30–36, "The day was ending … approach of the sun," contrast

 (A) the opening paragraph
 (B) day and night
 (C) the crew and their environs
 (D) light and dark
 (E) the west and the south

187. The passage's final sentence creates what type of mood?

(A) morbid

(B) ominous

(C) sanguine

(D) sorrowful

(E) regretful

188. The passage as a whole serves primarily to

    I. foreshadow later events

    II. establish a symbolic setting

    III. characterize the main character

(A) I only

(B) II only

(C) I and II only

(D) I and III only

(E) I, II, and III

Passage 3. Joseph Conrad, *Heart of Darkness*

"I left in a French steamer, and she called in every blamed port they have
out there, for, as far as I could see, the sole purpose of landing soldiers and
custom-house officers. I watched the coast. Watching a coast as it slips by the
ship is like thinking about an enigma. There it is before you—smiling, frown-
ing, inviting, grand, mean, insipid, or savage, and always mute with an air of   5
whispering, 'Come and find out.' This one was almost featureless, as if still in the
making, with an aspect of monotonous grimness. The edge of a colossal jungle,
so dark-green as to be almost black, fringed with white surf, ran straight, like
a ruled line, far, far away along a blue sea whose glitter was blurred by a creeping mist. The sun was fierce, the land seemed to glisten and drip with steam.   10
Here and there greyish-whitish specks showed up clustered inside the white surf,
with a flag flying above them perhaps. Settlements some centuries old, and still
no bigger than pinheads on the untouched expanse of their background. We
pounded along, stopped, landed soldiers; went on, landed custom-house clerks
to levy toll in what looked like a God-forsaken wilderness, with a tin shed and   15
a flag-pole lost in it; landed more soldiers—to take care of the custom-house
clerks, presumably. Some, I heard, got drowned in the surf; but whether they
did or not, nobody seemed particularly to care. They were just flung out there,
and on we went. Every day the coast looked the same, as though we had not
moved; but we passed various places—trading places—with names like Gran'   20
Bassam, Little Popo; names that seemed to belong to some sordid farce acted in
front of a sinister back-cloth. The idleness of a passenger, my isolation amongst
all these men with whom I had no point of contact, the oily and languid sea,
the uniform sombreness of the coast, seemed to keep me away from the truth

of things, within the toil of a mournful and senseless delusion. The voice of the   25
surf heard now and then was a positive pleasure, like the speech of a brother. It
was something natural, that had its reason, that had a meaning. Now and then a
boat from the shore gave one a momentary contact with reality. It was paddled
by black fellows. You could see from afar the white of their eyeballs glistening.
They shouted, sang; their bodies streamed with perspiration; they had faces like   30
grotesque masks—these chaps; but they had bone, muscle, a wild vitality, an
intense energy of movement, that was as natural and true as the surf along their
coast. They wanted no excuse for being there. They were a great comfort to look
at. For a time I would feel I belonged still to a world of straightforward facts;
but the feeling would not last long. Something would turn up to scare it away.   35
Once, I remember, we came upon a man-of-war anchored off the coast. There
wasn't even a shed there, and she was shelling the bush. It appears the French had
one of their wars going on thereabouts. Her ensign dropped limp like a rag; the
muzzles of the long six-inch guns stuck out all over the low hull; the greasy, slimy
swell swung her up lazily and let her down, swaying her thin masts. In the empty   40
immensity of earth, sky, and water, there she was, incomprehensible, firing into a
continent. Pop, would go one of the six-inch guns; a small flame would dart and
vanish, a little white smoke would disappear, a tiny projectile would give a feeble
screech—and nothing happened. Nothing could happen. There was a touch of
insanity in the proceeding, a sense of lugubrious drollery in the sight; and it was   45
not dissipated by somebody on board assuring me earnestly there was a camp of
natives—he called them enemies!—hidden out of sight somewhere."

189. Lines 1–10, "'I left in a French steamer . . . a creeping mist,'" describe the
     sea as

    I. cryptic
   II. laconic
  III. obfuscated

  (A) I only
  (B) II only
  (C) I and III only
  (D) II and III only
  (E) I, II, and III

190. In context of the passage as a whole, lines 13–19, "'We pounded along, ...
     on we went,'" suggest that the speaker sees his job on the French steamer as

  (A) perfunctory
  (B) cumbersome
  (C) onerous
  (D) critical
  (E) vexing

191. The tone of the sentence in lines 13–17 ("'We pounded along . . . presumably'") is enhanced by

(A) tactile imagery
(B) anaphora
(C) personification
(D) simile
(E) hyperbole

192. All of the following keeps the speaker in a delusional state *except*

(A) idleness
(B) alienation
(C) the sea
(D) the uniformity of the coast
(E) the voice of the surf

193. The speaker is relieved to see the "'black fellows'" (29) because

(A) they provide him with comic relief
(B) their grotesque faces are intriguing
(C) they provide a sense of verity
(D) they make the Europeans look better
(E) they are an entertaining diversion

194. Line 35 ("'but the feeling ... away'") contains

(A) regret
(B) foreshadowing
(C) antithesis
(D) vacillation
(E) paradox

195. The sentence in lines 38–40 ("'Her ensign . . . masts'") provides a fully drawn image due, in part, to the use of

(A) onomatopoeia, which makes the sounds of the guns audible
(B) simple syntactical structures, which emphasizes the calmness of the scene
(C) hyperbole and understatement, which show the hypocrisy of the situation
(D) alliteration and simile, which underscore the futility and absurdity of the scene
(E) allegory and allusion, which compare the strangeness of the scene to something more familiar

196. The word "'she'" in line 41 refers to

(A) the hull
(B) the sea
(C) France
(D) the man-of-war
(E) the masts

197. In the two sentences in lines 42–44 ("'Pop . . . could happen'"), the narrator is doing which of the following?

   I. describing an object by using onomatopoeia
  II. creating a sense of futility by using parallel structure and repetition
 III. emphasizing the tone by creating sentence variety

(A) I only
(B) II only
(C) I and II only
(D) II and III only
(E) I, II, and III

198. In line 45, "'drollery'" most likely means

(A) boredom
(B) contention
(C) sadness
(D) dark absurdity
(E) insanity

199. The speaker's tone in the phrase "'he called them enemies!'" (47) communicates

(A) relief
(B) incredulity
(C) distress
(D) remorse
(E) disappointment

200. The passage as a whole

(A) expresses yearning for an unforgettable journey
(B) questions assumptions about racial inequality
(C) questions the value of imperial outposts
(D) describes past events objectively
(E) describes experiences myopically

Passage 4. Mary Shelley, *Frankenstein*

There was a considerable difference between the ages of my parents, but this circumstance seemed to unite them only closer in bonds of devoted affection. There was a sense of justice in my father's upright mind which rendered it necessary that he should approve highly to love strongly. Perhaps during former years he had suffered from the late-discovered unworthiness of one beloved and so was disposed to set a greater value on tried worth. There was a show of gratitude and worship in his attachment to my mother, differing wholly from the doting fondness of age, for it was inspired by reverence for her virtues and a desire to be the means of, in some degree, recompensing her for the sorrows she had endured, but which gave inexpressible grace to his behaviour to her. Everything was made to yield to her wishes and her convenience. He strove to shelter her, as a fair exotic is sheltered by the gardener, from every rougher wind and to surround her with all that could tend to excite pleasurable emotion in her soft and benevolent mind. Her health, and even the tranquillity of her hitherto constant spirit, had been shaken by what she had gone through. During the two years that had elapsed previous to their marriage my father had gradually relinquished all his public functions; and immediately after their union they sought the pleasant climate of Italy, and the change of scene and interest attendant on a tour through that land of wonders, as a restorative for her weakened frame.

From Italy they visited Germany and France. I, their eldest child, was born at Naples, and as an infant accompanied them in their rambles. I remained for several years their only child. Much as they were attached to each other, they seemed to draw inexhaustible stores of affection from a very mine of love to bestow them upon me. My mother's tender caresses and my father's smile of benevolent pleasure while regarding me are my first recollections. I was their plaything and their idol, and something better—their child, the innocent and helpless creature bestowed on them by heaven, whom to bring up to good, and whose future lot it was in their hands to direct to happiness or misery, according as they fulfilled their duties towards me. With this deep consciousness of what they owed towards the being to which they had given life, added to the active spirit of tenderness that animated both, it may be imagined that while during every hour of my infant life I received a lesson of patience, of charity, and of self-control, I was so guided by a silken cord that all seemed but one train of enjoyment to me. For a long time I was their only care. My mother had much desired to have a daughter, but I continued their single offspring. When I was about five years old, while making an excursion beyond the frontiers of Italy, they passed a week on the shores of the Lake of Como. Their benevolent disposition often made them enter the cottages of the poor. This, to my mother, was more than a duty; it was a necessity, a passion—remembering what she had suffered, and how she had been relieved—for her to act in her turn the guardian angel to the afflicted. During one of their walks a poor cot in the foldings of a vale attracted their notice as being singularly disconsolate, while the number of half-clothed children gathered about it spoke

of penury in its worst shape. One day, when my father had gone by himself to
Milan, my mother, accompanied by me, visited this abode. She found a peas-
ant and his wife, hard working, bent down by care and labour, distributing a   45
scanty meal to five hungry babes. Among these there was one which attracted my
mother far above all the rest. She appeared of a different stock. The four others
were dark-eyed, hardy little vagrants; this child was thin and very fair. Her hair
was the brightest living gold, and despite the poverty of her clothing, seemed
to set a crown of distinction on her head. Her brow was clear and ample, her   50
blue eyes cloudless, and her lips and the moulding of her face so expressive of
sensibility and sweetness that none could behold her without looking on her as
of a distinct species, a being heaven-sent, and bearing a celestial stamp in all her
features.

201. The passage implies that the father's behavior and attitude toward the
mother is due to all of the following *except*

(A) the desire to be useful
(B) the mother's reverential virtues
(C) the considerable difference between their ages
(D) the mother's frailty
(E) his habit of loving unconditionally

202. In line 8, "it" refers to

(A) "doting"
(B) "his attachment"
(C) "a show of gratitude and worship"
(D) "fondness of age"
(E) "my mother"

203. The mother is presented as all of the following *except*

(A) virtuous
(B) generous
(C) importunate
(D) convalescent
(E) enervated

204. The simile in line 12 characterizes

(A) the mother as distinct
(B) the mother as distinguished
(C) the father as nurturing
(D) the mother as a child
(E) the father as officious

205. What is the relationship between the first and second paragraphs?

(A) The first asks questions that the second answers.

(B) The first poses theories that the second explores.

(C) The second belies assumptions made in the first.

(D) The first provides background for comprehension of the second.

(E) The first sparks curiosity that the second satiates.

206. The metaphor in lines 22–24 ("Much as they were...upon me") gives particular emphasis to

(A) the parents' infinite capacity to love

(B) the parents' industriousness

(C) the parents' economic class

(D) the speaker's importance in the family

(E) the hierarchy within the family

207. The word "idol" in line 26 implies that

(A) the parents saw religious power in their child

(B) the child is like a prophet

(C) the parents admire their child

(D) the speaker is arrogant

(E) the parents worship their child

208. The one train of enjoyment" (33) is illustrated by use of

(A) an allegory

(B) a periodic sentence

(C) a developed anecdote

(D) a series of dependent clauses

(E) hyperbole

209. The word "penury" in line 43 most likely means

(A) destitution

(B) itinerancy

(C) sadness

(D) vagrancy

(E) selfishness

210. The girl described in lines 46–54 is characterized as

    I. conspicuous
   II. otherworldly
 III. evocative

(A) I only
(B) I and II only
(C) II only
(D) I and III only
(E) I, II, and III

211. The description of the girl in lines 46–54 contains all of the following devices *except*

(A) allusion
(B) simile
(C) alliteration
(D) hyperbole
(E) polysyndeton

212. The tone of the passage can be described as

(A) grave
(B) factual
(C) earnest
(D) resentful
(E) objective

213. The main purpose of the passage as a whole is

(A) to characterize the speaker's mother
(B) to characterize the speaker
(C) to characterize the father
(D) to describe the setting
(E) to characterize the speaker's family

Passage 5. Jonathan Swift, *Gulliver's Travels*

One morning, about a fortnight after I had obtained my liberty, Reldresal, principal secretary (as they style him) for private affairs, came to my house, attended only by one servant. He ordered his coach to wait at a distance, and desired I would give him an hour's audience; which I readily consented to, on account of his quality and personal merits, as well as of the many good offices he had done me during my solicitations at court. I offered to lie down, that he might the more conveniently reach my ear; but he chose rather to let me hold him in my hand during our conversation.

5

He began with compliments on my liberty; said he might pretend to some
merit in it. But however, added, that if it had not been for the present situation   10
of things at court, perhaps I might not have obtained it so soon. For, said he, as
flourishing a condition as we may appear to be in to foreigners, we labor under
two mighty evils: a violent faction at home, and the danger of an invasion, by a
most potent enemy, from abroad. As to the first, you are to understand, that, for
above seventy moons past, there have been two struggling parties in this empire,   15
under the names of *Tramecksan* and *Slamecksan*, from the high and low heels of
their shoes, by which they distinguish themselves. It is alleged, indeed, that the
high heels are most agreeable to our ancient constitution; but, however this may
be, his majesty hath determined to make use only of low heels in the administration of the government, and all offices in the gift of the crown, as you cannot   20
but observe: and particularly, that his majesty's imperial heels are lower, at least
by a *drurr*, than any of his court (*drurr* is a measure about the fourteenth part
of an inch). The animosities between these two parties run so high, that they
will neither eat nor drink nor talk with each other. We compute the *Tramecksan*,
or high heels, to exceed us in number; but the power is wholly on our side. We   25
apprehend his imperial highness, the heir to the crown, to have some tendency
towards the high heels; at least, we can plainly discover that one of his heels is
higher than the other, which gives him a hobble in his gait. Now, in the midst
of these intestine disquiets, we are threatened with an invasion from the island
of Blefuscu, which is the other great empire of the universe, almost as large and   30
powerful as this of his majesty. For, as to what we have heard you affirm, that
there are other kingdoms and states in the world, inhabited by human creatures
as large as yourself, our philosophers are in much doubt, and would rather conjecture that you dropped from the moon or one of the stars, because it is certain,
that an hundred mortals of your bulk would, in a short time, destroy all the   35
fruits and cattle of his majesty's dominions. Besides, our histories of six thousand
moons make no mention of any other regions than the two great empires of
Lilliput and Blefuscu. Which two mighty powers have, as I was going to tell you,
been engaged in a most obstinate war for six-and-thirty moons past. It began
upon the following occasion: It is allowed on all hands, that the primitive way   40
of breaking eggs, before we eat them, was upon the larger end; but his present
majesty's grandfather, while he was a boy, going to eat an egg, and breaking it
according to the ancient practice, happened to cut one of his fingers. Whereupon
the emperor, his father, published an edict, commanding all his subjects, upon
great penalties, to break the smaller end of their eggs. The people so highly   45
resented this law, that our histories tell us, there have been six rebellions raised
on that account, wherein one emperor lost his life, and another his crown. These
civil commotions were constantly fomented by the monarchs of Blefuscu; and
when they were quelled, the exiles always fled for refuge to that empire. It is com-
puted, that eleven thousand persons have, at several times, suffered death, rather   50
than submit to break their eggs at the smaller end. Many hundred large volumes
have been published upon this controversy, but the books of the Big-endians have

been long forbidden, and the whole party rendered incapable, by law, of holding employments. During the course of these troubles, the Emperors of Blefuscu did frequently expostulate, by their ambassadors, accusing us of making a schism in religion, by offending against a fundamental doctrine of our great prophet Lustrog, in the fifty-fourth chapter of the *Blundecral* (which is their *Alcoran*). This, however, is thought to be a mere strain upon the text; for the words are these: *That all true believers break their eggs at the convenient end.* And which is the convenient end, seems, in my humble opinion, to be left to every man's conscience, or, at least, in the power of the chief magistrate to determine. Now, the Big-endian exiles have found so much credit in the emperor of Blefuscu's court, and so much private assistance and encouragement from their party here at home, that a bloody war hath been carried on between the two empires for six-and-thirty moons, with various success; during which time we have lost forty capital ships, and a much greater number of smaller vessels, together with thirty thousand of our best seamen and soldiers; and the damage received by the enemy is reckoned to be somewhat greater than ours. However, they have now equipped a numerous fleet, and are just preparing to make a descent upon us; and his imperial majesty, placing great confidence in your valor and strength, hath commanded me to lay this account of his affairs before you.

214. The first paragraph implies that the speaker is all of the following *except*

(A) grateful
(B) recently emancipated
(C) obsequious
(D) gracious
(E) large

215. The phrase "pretend to some merit in it" (9–10) indicates that

(A) Reldresal's compliments are not genuine
(B) Reldresal is demonstrating guile
(C) the speaker's freedom was hard won
(D) the speaker's freedom was unwarranted
(E) Reldresal believes there were weightier factors involved

216. In lines 11–12, the speaker of the passage changes

(A) from the speaker of the first paragraph to the principal secretary
(B) from gracious to severe
(C) from first person to second person
(D) from the speaker of the first paragraph to his majesty
(E) without warning

217. In lines 15–22, ("there have been...his court"), the speaker discusses the empire's problem of

(A) his majesty's shoes
(B) prejudice in their community
(C) the ancient constitution
(D) his majesty's partiality
(E) his majesty's impartiality

218. The speaker of lines 22–25 is a member of

I. the high heels
II. *Tramecksan*
III. *Slamecksan*

(A) I only
(B) II only
(C) III only
(D) I and III only
(E) I, II, and III

219. The heir's "hobble" (28) is worrying because

(A) he is in need of convalescence
(B) it suggests his potential defection
(C) it is unsightly
(D) it suggests he is partial to the *Slamecksan* party
(E) it suggests he and his father are estranged

220. In line 29, the phrase "intestine disquiets" most likely means

(A) physical illness
(B) municipal politics
(C) political treason
(D) domestic strife
(E) the speaker's inner turmoil

221. Based on lines 31–36, it can be interpreted that the addressee's claims are viewed as fallible due to

(A) the philosophers' logical reasoning
(B) the philosophers' research-based claims
(C) the existence of fruit and cattle
(D) overwhelming evidence
(E) the philosophers' convenient denial

222. The word "fomented" in line 48 most nearly means

    (A) goaded
    (B) quelled
    (C) dispelled
    (D) formed
    (E) derided

223. The "*Alcoran*" (58) is

    (A) the Blundecral
    (B) the holy text of Big-endians
    (C) the holy text of the *Slamecksan*
    (D) the holy text of the *Tramecksan*
    (E) the holy text of Lilliput

224. The argument between Blefuscu and Lilliput described in lines 53–60 is most similar to

    (A) physical sparring
    (B) familial spats
    (C) altercations about facts
    (D) arguments about semantics
    (E) ad hominem attacks

225. The passage's style most closely resembles the style of

    (A) a historical novel
    (B) a Gothic novel
    (C) a fable
    (D) an epic
    (E) a lampoon

226. In the passage, the words "*Slamecksan*," "*Tramecksan*," "*drurr*," "*Alcoran*," and "*Blundecral*" are all written in italics to indicate

    (A) that they are the names of renowned people and places
    (B) that they are important
    (C) that they are words from this world's argot
    (D) a lack of respect
    (E) emphasis

227. The passage suggests that the imperial majesty expects the speaker of the first paragraph to assist him because

    I. he has recently been acquitted
   II. he is large
  III. he is doughty

(A) I only
(B) II only
(C) I and II only
(D) II and III only
(E) I, II, and III

228. The speaker of lines 11–71, as opposed to the passage as a whole, carries a tone of

(A) gravity
(B) irony
(C) absurdity
(D) amicability
(E) neutrality

Passage 6. Oscar Wilde, *The Picture of Dorian Gray*

The studio was filled with the rich odour of roses, and when the light summer wind stirred amidst the trees of the garden, there came through the open door the heavy scent of the lilac, or the more delicate perfume of the pink-flowering thorn.

From the corner of the divan of Persian saddle-bags on which he was lying,   5
smoking, as was his custom, innumerable cigarettes, Lord Henry Wotton could just catch the gleam of the honey-sweet and honey-coloured blossoms of a laburnum, whose tremulous branches seemed hardly able to bear the burden of a beauty so flamelike as theirs; and now and then the fantastic shadows of birds in flight flitted across the long tussore-silk curtains that were stretched in front of   10
the huge window, producing a kind of momentary Japanese effect, and making him think of those pallid, jade-faced painters of Tokyo who, through the medium of an art that is necessarily immobile, seek to convey the sense of swiftness and motion. The sullen murmur of the bees shouldering their way through the long unmown grass, or circling with monotonous insistence round the dusty gilt horns   15
of the straggling woodbine, seemed to make the stillness more oppressive. The dim roar of London was like the bourdon note of a distant organ. In the centre of the room, clamped to an upright easel, stood the full-length portrait of a young man of extraordinary personal beauty, and in front of it, some little distance away, was sitting the artist himself, Basil Hallward, whose sudden disappearance   20
some years ago caused, at the time, such public excitement and gave rise to so many strange conjectures.

As the painter looked at the gracious and comely form he had so skillfully mirrored in his art, a smile of pleasure passed across his face, and seemed about to linger there. But he suddenly started up, and closing his eyes, placed his fingers 25 upon the lids, as though he sought to imprison within his brain some curious dream from which he feared he might awake. "It is your best work, Basil, the best thing you have ever done," said Lord Henry languidly. "You must certainly send it next year to the Grosvenor. The Academy is too large and too vulgar. Whenever I have gone there, there have been either so many people that I have not 30 been able to see the pictures, which was dreadful, or so many pictures that I have not been able to see the people, which was worse. The Grosvenor is really the only place."

"I don't think I shall send it anywhere," he answered, tossing his head back in that odd way that used to make his friends laugh at him at Oxford. "No, I 35 won't send it anywhere." Lord Henry elevated his eyebrows and looked at him in amazement through the thin blue wreaths of smoke that curled up in such fanciful whorls from his heavy, opium-tainted cigarette. "Not send it anywhere? My dear fellow, why? Have you any reason? What odd chaps you painters are! You do anything in the world to gain a reputation. As soon as you have one, 40 you seem to want to throw it away. It is silly of you, for there is only one thing in the world worse than being talked about, and that is not being talked about. A portrait like this would set you far above all the young men in England, and make the old men quite jealous, if old men are ever capable of any emotion."

229. Lines 1–16 contain

   I. at least one simile
  II. passive voice
 III. compound sentences

(A) I only
(B) II only
(C) III only
(D) I and III only
(E) I, II, and III

230. The "momentary Japanese effect" in line 11 sets up

(A) a parallel between London and Tokyo
(B) a contrast between movement and stillness
(C) Lord Henry Wotton's preference for European art over Asian art
(D) an emphasis on the pleasure offered by the setting
(E) an attack on Japanese painters

231. In line 9, "theirs" refers to
    (A) innumerable cigarettes
    (B) a laburnum's blossoms
    (C) a laburnum's branches
    (D) Persian saddle-bags
    (E) birds' shadows

232. From the description of the setting in the first and second paragraphs, we can infer all of the following *except* that
    (A) Lord Henry would rather be somewhere else
    (B) the characters are familiar with the art of foreign countries
    (C) the characters are wealthy
    (D) the abundance in nature is symbolic of the abundance of riches in the room
    (E) the mood is one of lethargy

233. The comparison to "a bourdon note of a distant organ" (17) is intended to serves as
    (A) a reminder of the pollution and noise of London
    (B) a visual of the culture the city has to offer
    (C) an indication that Lord Henry prefers London to his current setting
    (D) an emphasis of the "oppressive stillness" of the current setting
    (E) an objective way to indicate the proximity of the current setting to the city of London

234. Lord Henry's speech is notable for its use of all of the following *except*
    (A) wit
    (B) irony
    (C) epigrams
    (D) cliché
    (E) exhortation

235. From the passage we can infer all of the following about Basil Hallward *except* that
    (A) he is a notable painter
    (B) he is well educated
    (C) he is insecure about his work
    (D) he has been the subject of idle talk
    (E) he likes his painting

236. The dialogue in the passage serves primarily to

    (A) contrast Lord Henry with his environment
    (B) demonstrate the characters' level of education
    (C) develop Lord Henry's viewpoint
    (D) draw a correlation between wealth and intellect
    (E) criticize old men

237. A question that remains unanswered by the passage is

    (A) Why is there a stillness in the room?
    (B) Why is Basil determined not to send his painting anywhere?
    (C) Why is Lord Henry amazed?
    (D) What is Basil's painting of?
    (E) How does Lord Henry view artists?

238. The passage as a whole serves primarily to

    (A) present Basil Hallward as a talented artist
    (B) show the friendship between Lord Henry and Basil Hallward
    (C) critique London's high society
    (D) introduce main characters and the central motif of art
    (E) demonstrate highly ornate descriptions of a natural setting

Passage 7. Virginia Woolf, "An Unwritten Novel"

Such an expression of unhappiness was enough by itself to make one's eyes slide above the paper's edge to the poor woman's face–insignificant without that look, almost a symbol of human destiny with it. Life's what you see in people's eyes; life's what they learn, and, having learnt it, never, though they seek to hide it, cease to be aware of–what? That life's like that, it seems. Five faces oppo-   5
site–five mature faces–and the knowledge in each face. Strange, though, how people want to conceal it! Marks of reticence are on all those faces: lips shut, eyes shaded, each one of the five doing something to hide or stultify his knowledge. One smokes; another reads; a third checks entries in a pocket book; a fourth stares at the map of the line framed opposite; and the fifth–the terrible thing   10
about the fifth is that she does nothing at all. She looks at life. Ah, but my poor, unfortunate woman, do play the game–do, for all our sakes, conceal it!

As if she heard me, she looked up, shifted slightly in her seat and sighed. She seemed to apologise and at the same time to say to me, "If only you knew!" Then she looked at life again. "But I do know," I answered silently, glancing   15
at the *Times* for manners' sake. "I know the whole business. 'Peace between Germany and the Allied Powers was yesterday officially ushered in at Paris– Signor Nitti, the Italian Prime Minister–a passenger train at Doncaster was in collision with a goods train...' We all know–the *Times* knows–but we pretend we don't." My eyes had once more crept over the paper's rim. She shuddered,   20

twitched her arm queerly to the middle of her back and shook her head. Again I
dipped into my great reservoir of life. "Take what you like," I continued, "births,
death, marriages, Court Circular, the habits of birds, Leonardo da Vinci, the
Sandhills murder, high wages and the cost of living–oh, take what you like," I
repeated, "it's all in the *Times!*" Again with infinite weariness she moved her head   25
from side to side until, like a top exhausted with spinning, it settled on her neck.

The *Times* was no protection against such sorrow as hers. But other human
beings forbade intercourse. The best thing to do against life was to fold the
paper so that it made a perfect square, crisp, thick, impervious even to life. This
done, I glanced up quickly, armed with a shield of my own. She pierced through   30
my shield; she gazed into my eyes as if searching any sediment of courage at
the depths of them and damping it to clay. Her twitch alone denied all hope,
discounted all illusion.

239. According to the narrator, the "expression" referred to in line 1 is hard to
avoid because

(A) the woman is intrusive
(B) there are no distractions
(C) its sadness is overwhelming
(D) the narrator is obsessed with sorrow
(E) the narrator is confined on a train

240. The narrator defines "life" as

(A) knowledge reluctantly gained from experience
(B) that which people learn, seek to hide, and then disregard
(C) experiences that appear in the news
(D) that which is learned through living
(E) shared experiences

241. Based on the first paragraph, it can be inferred that the "fifth" person
opposite is distinct in that she

(A) plays the game
(B) is older than the others
(C) has a mark of reticence
(D) conceals life
(E) attempts to engage

242. The other four passengers are primarily characterized as

(A) garrulous
(B) tenaciously secretive
(C) cruelly indifferent
(D) apathetic
(E) observing custom

243. In line 12 (last sentence of first paragraph), "it" refers primarily to

(A) the game
(B) the woman
(C) life
(D) hope
(E) a secret

244. The author makes use of all of the following devices to develop the characterization of the woman *except*

(A) dialogue
(B) simile
(C) auditory imagery
(D) visual imagery
(E) subjective point of view

245. In the second paragraph, what does the narrator repeatedly imply she, and others, "knows"?

(A) the events, details, and emotions that make up life
(B) the specific cause of the woman's unhappiness
(C) the details of the woman's life story
(D) that the woman is hoping for conversation
(E) the secret to happiness

246. The *Times* is portrayed as all of the following *except*

(A) a reservoir
(B) a shield
(C) a crutch
(D) impenetrable
(E) exhaustive

247. The narrator's point of view is developed primarily through

(A) exclamations
(B) third-person narration
(C) interior monologue
(D) personification
(E) dialogue

248. Over the course of the passage, the narrator experiences

(A) curiosity, pity, compulsion, hope, and resignation
(B) desperation, anger, resentment, fear, and hope
(C) certainty, disgust, power, weakness, and regret
(D) audacity, concern, annoyance, surrender, and hope
(E) desperation, antipathy, empathy, and resolution

249. The figurative language in the last paragraph implies that, to the narrator, the woman appears as

(A) a vulnerable citizen
(B) a redoubtable foe
(C) a calculating leader
(D) a formidable ally
(E) a pathetic inferior

250. The narrator's primary hope in the passage is best summarized as

(A) she wishes to avoid further interaction with any passengers
(B) she wishes others would reveal their life experiences
(C) she wishes that the *Times* would protect her from engaging with strangers
(D) she wishes to learn the cause of the woman's unhappiness
(E) she wishes the woman would conceal her unhappiness

251. The excerpt ends on a note of

(A) ambivalence
(B) denial
(C) optimism
(D) capitulation
(E) renunciation

American Fiction

Passage 1. Louisa May Alcott, "An Old-fashioned Girl"

"It's time to go to the station, Tom."

"Come on, then."

"Oh, I'm not going; it's too wet. Shouldn't have a crimp left if I went out such a day as this; and I want to look nice when Polly comes."

"You don't expect me to go and bring home a strange girl alone, do you?" 5
And Tom looked as much alarmed as if his sister had proposed to him to escort
the wild woman of Australia.

"Of course I do. It's your place to go and get her; and if you wasn't a bear,
you'd like it."

"Well, I call that mean! I supposed I'd got to go; but you said you'd go, too. 10
Catch me bothering about your friends another time! No, *sir!* " And Tom rose
from the sofa with an air of indignant resolution, the impressive effect of which
was somewhat damaged by a tousled head, and the hunched appearance of his
garments generally.

"Now, don't be cross; and I'll get mamma to let you have that horrid Ned 15
Miller, that you are so fond of, come and make you a visit after Polly's gone," said
Fanny, hoping to soothe his ruffled feelings.

"How long is she going to stay?" demanded Tom, making his toilet by a promiscuous shake.

"A month or two, maybe. She's ever so nice; and I shall keep her as long as 20
she's happy."

"She won't stay long then, if I can help it," muttered Tom, who regarded girls as a very unnecessary portion of creation. Boys of fourteen are apt to think so, and perhaps it is a wise arrangement; for, being fond of turning somersaults, they have an opportunity of indulging in a good one, metaphorically speaking, when, three or four years later, they become the abject slaves of "those bothering girls." 25

"Look here! how am I going to know the creature? I never saw her, and she never saw me. You'll have to come too, Fan," he added, pausing on his way to the door, arrested by the awful idea that he might have to address several strange girls before he got the right one. 30

"You'll find her easy enough; she'll probably be standing round looking for us. I dare say she'll know *you*, though I'm not there, because I've described you to her."

"Guess she won't, then;" and Tom gave a hasty smooth to his curly pate and a glance at the mirror, feeling sure that his sister hadn't done him justice. Sisters 35 never do, as "we fellows" know too well.

"Do go along, or you'll be too late; and then, what *will* Polly think of me?" cried Fanny, with the impatient poke which is peculiarly aggravating to masculine dignity.

"She'll think you cared more about your frizzles than your friends, and she'll 40 be about right, too."

Feeling that he said rather a neat and cutting thing, Tom sauntered leisurely away, perfectly conscious that it *was* late, but bent on not being hurried while in sight, though he ran himself off his legs to make up for it afterward.

"If I was the President, I'd make a law to shut up all boys till they were 45 grown; for they certainly are the most provoking toads in the world," said Fanny, as she watched the slouchy figure of her brother strolling down the street. She might have changed her mind, however, if she had followed him, for as soon as he turned the corner, his whole aspect altered; his hands came out of his pockets, he stopped whistling, buttoned his jacket, gave his cap a pull, and went off at a 50 great pace.

The train was just in when he reached the station, panting like a race-horse, and as red as a lobster with the wind and the run.

"Suppose she'll wear a top-knot and a thingumbob, like everyone else; and however shall I know her? Too bad of Fan to make me come alone!" thought 55 Tom, as he stood watching the crowd stream through the depot, and feeling rather daunted at the array of young ladies who passed. As none of them seemed looking for any one, he did not accost them, but eyed each new batch with the air of a martyr. "That's her," he said to himself, as he presently caught sight of a girl in gorgeous array, standing with her hands folded, and a very small hat 60 perched on the top of a very large "chig-non," as Tom pronounced it. "I suppose I've got to speak to her, so here goes;" and, nerving himself to the task, Tom slowly approached the damsel, who looked as if the wind had blown her clothes into rags, such a flapping of sashes, scallops, ruffles, curls, and feathers was there.

"I say, if you please, is your name Polly Milton?" meekly asked Tom, pausing 65 before the breezy stranger.

"No, it isn't," answered the young lady, with a cool stare that utterly quenched him.

252. The humor in lines 11–14 ("And Tom rose . . . generally") is primarily created by
(A) the indignant resolution
(B) Tom's antipathy toward Fanny
(C) Tom's biting comments about Fanny's friends
(D) the dissonance between what Tom does and how he appears
(E) Tom's tousled head

253. Which of the following lines indicates the narrator has access to the characters' points of view?
 I. "hoping to soothe his ruffled feelings" (17)
 II. "And Tom rose from the sofa . . . generally" (11–14)
 III. "who regarded girls as a very unnecessary portion of creation" (22–23)
 IV. "Boys of fourteen are apt to think so" (23)
(A) I and III only
(B) I, II, and III only
(C) II and IV only
(D) III and IV only
(E) I, II, III, and IV

254. The author uses the word "somersaults" (24) in this context

    (A) literally and figuratively
    (B) arrogantly
    (C) sarcastically
    (D) regretfully
    (E) didactically

255. In context, the phrase "abject slaves" (26) is intended as

    (A) a comment on the servile nature of boys
    (B) ridicule for boys who change their minds about girls
    (C) a somber description of male-female dynamics
    (D) a literal description of the male-female relationship
    (E) an exaggeration of boys' about-face

256. The phrases "we fellows" (36) and "those bothering girls" (26) are in quotation marks to indicate

    (A) sarcasm
    (B) dialogue
    (C) the views of an expert
    (D) specialized terms
    (E) a distinct voice

257. Tom's "hasty smooth" and "glance at the mirror" (34–35) are actions that are meant to

    (A) confirm Fanny's opinion
    (B) belie Fanny's opinion
    (C) reveal Tom's superficiality
    (D) suggest Tom's arrogance
    (E) indicate Tom's distrust

258. Fanny appears to be primarily concerned with

    (A) her brother's willfulness
    (B) vexing her brother
    (C) looking better than Polly
    (D) pleasing Polly
    (E) her hair

259. The narration in lines 42–44 reveals that Tom communicates with his sister with

   (A) hesitation
   (B) anger
   (C) posturing
   (D) frankness
   (E) refusal

260. The details provided in lines 49–51 ("his hands . . . at a great pace") provide a contrast to the details provided in which of the following lines?

   (A) "he ran himself off his legs to make up for it afterward" (44)
   (B) "Tom gave a hasty smooth to his curly pate" (34)
   (C) "Tom sauntered leisurely away" (42–43)
   (D) "hoping to soothe his ruffled feathers" (17)
   (E) "feeling sure that his sister hadn't done him justice" (35)

261. The reference to "chig-non" is a detail that is intended to develop

   (A) Tom's unfamiliarity and awkwardness around the opposite sex
   (B) Tom's laughable naiveté and ignorance
   (C) Tom's uncultured background
   (D) Tom's unique form of expression
   (E) the colloquial pronunciation and vocabulary of the time period

262. The function of the figurative language in lines 52–53 ("The train ... run") is best described by which of the following?

   (A) Personification presents the obstacle Tom faces as forbidding.
   (B) Visual imagery reveals Tom's posturing.
   (C) A metaphor compares Tom's behavior to Fanny's expectations of him.
   (D) Two similes dramatize Tom's actual intention as opposed to his feigned intention.
   (E) Two similes highlight Tom's behaviors as animalistic.

263. The passage implies that Tom is most apprehensive about

   (A) following orders
   (B) interacting with girls
   (C) antagonizing Fanny
   (D) appearing to be a gentleman
   (E) pleasing girls

264. In context, the phrase "utterly quenched him" is meant to emphasize

(A) the deep anxiety Tom feels when approaching females
(B) how unwarranted and misplaced Tom's reaction is
(C) the cruel and powerful influence young ladies have on young men
(D) Tom's relief that the young lady is not Polly
(E) Tom's frustration that the young lady is not Polly

265. The relationship between the siblings in the passage is best described by which of the following?

(A) They are friends who delight in annoying each other.
(B) They fight but actually want to please each other.
(C) Each is unconcerned with the other's needs.
(D) They tolerate each other only because they have to.
(E) They tease each other but are actually quite close.

Passage 2. Kate Chopin, "The Kiss"

It was still quite light out of doors, but inside with the curtains drawn and the smouldering fire sending out a dim, uncertain glow, the room was full of deep shadows.

Brantain sat in one of these shadows; it had overtaken him and he did not mind. The obscurity lent him courage to keep his eyes fastened as ardently as he liked upon the girl who sat in the firelight. 5

She was very handsome, with a certain fine, rich coloring that belongs to the healthy brune type. She was quite composed, as she idly stroked the satiny coat of the cat that lay curled in her lap, and she occasionally sent a slow glance into the shadow where her companion sat. They were talking low, of indifferent 10 things which plainly were not the things that occupied their thoughts. She knew that he loved her—a frank, blustering fellow without guile enough to conceal his feelings, and no desire to do so. For two weeks past he had sought her society eagerly and persistently. She was confidently waiting for him to declare himself and she meant to accept him. The rather insignificant and unattractive Brantain 15 was enormously rich; and she liked and required the entourage which wealth could give her.

During one of the pauses between their talk of the last tea and the next reception the door opened and a young man entered whom Brantain knew quite well. The girl turned her face toward him. A stride or two brought him to her side, 20 and bending over her chair—before she could suspect his intention, for she did not realize that he had not seen her visitor—he pressed an ardent, lingering kiss upon her lips.

Brantain slowly arose; so did the girl arise, but quickly, and the newcomer stood between them, a little amusement and some defiance struggling with the 25 confusion in his face.

"I believe," stammered Brantain, "I see that I have stayed too long. I—I had no idea—that is, I must wish you good-by." He was clutching his hat with both hands, and probably did not perceive that she was extending her hand to him, her presence of mind had not completely deserted her; but she could not have trusted herself to speak.   30

"Hang me if I saw him sitting there, Nattie! I know it's deuced awkward for you. But I hope you'll forgive me this once—this very first break. Why, what's the matter?"

"Don't touch me; don't come near me," she returned angrily. "What do you   35
mean by entering the house without ringing?"

"I came in with your brother, as I often do," he answered coldly, in self-justification. "We came in the side way. He went upstairs and I came in here hoping to find you. The explanation is simple enough and ought to satisfy you that the misadventure was unavoidable. But do say that you forgive me,   40
Nathalie," he entreated, softening.

"Forgive you! You don't know what you are talking about. Let me pass. It depends upon—a good deal whether I ever forgive you."

At that next reception which she and Brantain had been talking about she approached the young man with a delicious frankness of manner when she saw   45
him there.

"Will you let me speak to you a moment or two, Mr. Brantain?" she asked with an engaging but perturbed smile. He seemed extremely unhappy; but when she took his arm and walked away with him, seeking a retired corner, a ray of hope mingled with the almost comical misery of his expression. She was   50
apparently very outspoken.

"Perhaps I should not have sought this interview, Mr. Brantain; but—but, oh, I have been very uncomfortable, almost miserable since that little encounter the other afternoon. When I thought how you might have misinterpreted it, and believed things"—hope was plainly gaining the ascendancy over misery in   55
Brantain's round, guileless face—"Of course, I know it is nothing to you, but for my own sake I do want you to understand that Mr. Harvy is an intimate friend of long standing. Why, we have always been like cousins—like brother and sister, I may say. He is my brother's most intimate associate and often fancies that he is entitled to the same privileges as the family. Oh, I know it is absurd, uncalled   60
for, to tell you this; undignified even," she was almost weeping, "but it makes so much difference to me what you think of—of me." Her voice had grown very low and agitated. The misery had all disappeared from Brantain's face.

"Then you do really care what I think, Miss Nathalie? May I call you Miss Nathalie?" They turned into a long, dim corridor that was lined on either side   65
with tall, graceful plants. They walked slowly to the very end of it. When they turned to retrace their steps Brantain's face was radiant and hers was triumphant.

Harvy was among the guests at the wedding; and he sought her out in a rare moment when she stood alone.

"Your husband," he said, smiling, "has sent me over to kiss you."   70

A quick blush suffused her face and round polished throat. "I suppose it's natural for a man to feel and act generously on an occasion of this kind. He tells me he doesn't want his marriage to interrupt wholly that pleasant intimacy which has existed between you and me. I don't know what you've been telling him," with an insolent smile, "but he has sent me here to kiss you." 75

She felt like a chess player who, by the clever handling of his pieces, sees the game taking the course intended. Her eyes were bright and tender with a smile as they glanced up into his; and her lips looked hungry for the kiss which they invited.

"But, you know," he went on quietly, "I didn't tell him so, it would have 80 seemed ungrateful, but I can tell you. I've stopped kissing women; it's dangerous." Well, she had Brantain and his million left. A person can't have everything in this world; and it was a little unreasonable of her to expect it.

266. The imagery in the opening paragraph creates what type of atmosphere?

    (A) matrimonial
    (B) tender
    (C) morose
    (D) solemn
    (E) surreptitious

267. Brantain, as opposed to Harvy, is

    (A) a philanderer
    (B) penurious
    (C) libidinous
    (D) meek
    (E) astute

268. Lines 15–17 uncover Nathalie's

    (A) indifference
    (B) ardor
    (C) frankness
    (D) opportunism
    (E) venality

269. The phrase "'deuced awkward'" (32) is an example of

    (A) an oxymoron
    (B) a paradox
    (C) a colloquialism
    (D) a malapropism
    (E) slander

270. In context, Nathalie's "delicious frankness" of manner (45) implies

(A) she is extremely frank
(B) she is amorous for Brantain
(C) she is ambivalent about Braintain
(D) she is genuinely remorseful
(E) she is more wily than frank

271. The "privileges" mentioned in line 60 are meant to refer to

(A) friendship
(B) affection
(C) familial intimacy
(D) material comforts
(E) marriage

272. Nathalie's speech to Brantain is notable for its use of all of the following *except*

(A) a logical explanation
(B) an admittance of her own wrongdoing
(C) a tactful evasion to prevent Brantain's embarrassment
(D) a display of intense emotion
(E) an appeal to Brantain's ego

273. In context, the word "triumphant" (67) contributes most to

(A) the passage's imagery
(B) the characterization of Nathalie
(C) the passage's tone
(D) the characterization of Brantain
(E) the passage's mood

274. The phrase "Her eyes were bright and tender with a smile … " (77) suggests that Nathalie

(A) is still thinking about Brantain
(B) is torn between her love for Brantain and for Harvy
(C) is interested primarily in Harvy's riches
(D) is guileful in her interactions with all men
(E) may have a genuinely romantic interest in Harvy

275. The simile in lines 76–77 coincides most with which other phrase?

(A) "Brantain's face was radiant and hers was triumphant" (67)

(B) "She was very handsome" (7)

(C) "'Don't touch me; don't come near me'" (35)

(D) "'but it makes so much difference to me what you think of—of me'" (61–62)

(E) "Her voice had grown very low and agitated" (62–63)

276. In the phrase "A person can't have everything in this world" (82–83), the word "everything" refers to

(A) unrequited affection

(B) having every man's attention

(C) kissing Harvy

(D) having her emotional and financial needs met

(E) "Brantain and his million"

277. The narrative perspective in lines 82–83 is best described as that of

(A) an objective narrator

(B) a removed narrator

(C) most women of the time

(D) an omniscient narrator

(E) Nathalie

Passage 3. Nathaniel Hawthorne, *The Scarlet Letter*

A throng of bearded men, in sad-coloured garments and grey steeple-crowned hats, inter-mixed with women, some wearing hoods, and others bareheaded, was assembled in front of a wooden edifice, the door of which was heavily timbered with oak, and studded with iron spikes.

The founders of a new colony, whatever Utopia of human virtue and happiness they might originally project, have invariably recognised it among their earliest practical necessities to allot a portion of the virgin soil as a cemetery, and another portion as the site of a prison. In accordance with this rule it may safely be assumed that the forefathers of Boston had built the first prison-house somewhere in the Vicinity of Cornhill, almost as seasonably as they marked out the first burial-ground, on Isaac Johnson's lot, and round about his grave, which subsequently became the nucleus of all the congregated sepulchres in the old churchyard of King's Chapel. Certain it is that, some fifteen or twenty years after the settlement of the town, the wooden jail was already marked with weather-stains and other indications of age, which gave a yet darker aspect to its beetle-browed and gloomy front. The rust on the ponderous iron-work of its oaken door looked more antique than anything else in the New World. Like all that pertains to crime, it seemed never to have known a youthful era. Before this ugly

edifice, and between it and the wheel-track of the street, was a grass-plot, much
overgrown with burdock, pig-weed, apple-pern, and such unsightly vegetation,   20
which evidently found something congenial in the soil that had so early borne
the black flower of civilised society, a prison. But on one side of the portal, and
rooted almost at the threshold, was a wild rose-bush, covered, in this month of
June, with its delicate gems, which might be imagined to offer their fragrance
and fragile beauty to the prisoner as he went in, and to the condemned criminal   25
as he came forth to his doom, in token that the deep heart of Nature could pity
and be kind to him.

    This rose-bush, by a strange chance, has been kept alive in history; but
whether it had merely survived out of the stern old wilderness, so long after the
fall of the gigantic pines and oaks that originally overshadowed it, or whether, as   30
there is fair authority for believing, it had sprung up under the footsteps of the
sainted Ann Hutchinson[1] as she entered the prison-door, we shall not take upon
us to determine. Finding it so directly on the threshold of our narrative, which is
now about to issue from that inauspicious portal, we could hardly do otherwise
than pluck one of its flowers, and present it to the reader. It may serve, let us   35
hope, to symbolise some sweet moral blossom that may be found along the track,
or relieve the darkening close of a tale of human frailty and sorrow.

278. The mood of the opening paragraph is best described as

    (A) somber and oppressive
    (B) claustrophobic and religious
    (C) peaceful and placid
    (D) misogynistic and domineering
    (E) religious and meditative

279. In line 6, "it" refers to

    (A) soil
    (B) cemetery
    (C) the allotment
    (D) the new colony
    (E) Utopia

---

1. Ann Hutchinson (1591–1643) was a pioneer settler in Massachusetts, Rhode Island, and
New Netherlands and the unauthorized minister of a dissident church discussion group.
After a trial before a jury of officials and clergy, she was banished from the Massachusetts Bay
Colony.

280. In context, "nucleus" (12) means

(A) the first prison-house
(B) Vicinity of Cornhill
(C) all the congregated sepulchres
(D) the old churchyard of King's Chapel
(E) Isaac Johnson's lot

281. The description of the prison primarily focuses on

(A) its precise location
(B) its history
(C) its origin
(D) its denizens
(E) its appearance

282. In line 34, "that inauspicious portal" refers to

(A) the prison door
(B) the sepulchres
(C) the rose bush
(D) the wilderness
(E) the throng

283. The narrator most likely mentions Ann Hutchinson to

(A) explicitly deplore the colonies' disenfranchisement of its citizens
(B) sympathize with Puritan leaders
(C) provide potentially useful background
(D) denigrate the symbol
(E) introduce the main character of the story

284. The narrator offers readers a rose because of

I. its convenient location
II. its symbolic value
III. its potential function
IV. its significance to the main character of the tale

(A) I and II only
(B) I and III only
(C) I, II, and III only
(D) II, III, and IV only
(E) I, II, III, and IV

285. The final paragraph does all of the following *except*

    (A) introduces a metaphor
    (B) speculates
    (C) anticipates
    (D) offers solace
    (E) establishes a cynical tone

286. The passage as a whole

    (A) presents a historical account of the settlement of the new colonies
    (B) introduces a tragic account
    (C) upbraids the penal system
    (D) serves as a panegyric of the human spirit
    (E) deplores human weakness

287. The narrator's attitude toward the society being described is

    (A) objective
    (B) critical
    (C) bewildered
    (D) reverential
    (E) dispassionate

288. The purpose of the passage is to

    (A) lambaste the New World
    (B) create an eerie atmosphere
    (C) introduce the main characters of a story
    (D) establish motivation for a crime
    (E) set up the mood, setting, and symbols of a story

Passage 4. Nathaniel Hawthorne, *The Scarlet Letter*

It may seem marvellous that, with the world before her—kept by no restrictive clause of her condemnation within the limits of the Puritan settlement, so remote and so obscure—free to return to her birth-place, or to any other European land, and there hide her character and identity under a new exterior, as completely as if emerging into another state of being—and having also the passes of the dark, inscrutable forest open to her, where the wildness of her nature might assimilate itself with a people whose customs and life were alien from the law that had condemned her—it may seem marvellous that this woman should still call that place her home, where, and where only, she must needs be the type of shame. But there is a fatality, a feeling so irresistible and inevitable that it has the force of doom, which almost invariably compels human beings to linger around and haunt, ghost-like, the spot where some great and marked event has given the colour to their lifetime; and, still the more irresistibly, the darker the tinge that saddens it. Her sin, her ignominy, were the roots which she had struck into the soil. It was as if a new birth, with stronger assimilations than the first, had converted the forest-land, still so uncongenial to every other pilgrim and wanderer, into Hester Prynne's wild and dreary, but life-long home. All other scenes of earth—even that village of rural England, where happy infancy and stainless maidenhood seemed yet to be in her mother's keeping, like garments put off long ago—were foreign to her, in comparison. The chain that bound her here was of iron links, and galling to her inmost soul, but could never be broken. 20

It might be, too—doubtless it was so, although she hid the secret from herself, and grew pale whenever it struggled out of her heart, like a serpent from its hole—it might be that another feeling kept her within the scene and pathway that had been so fatal. There dwelt, there trode, the feet of one with whom she deemed herself connected in a union that, unrecognised on earth, would bring them together before the bar of final judgment, and make that their marriage-altar, for a joint futurity of endless retribution. Over and over again, the tempter of souls had thrust this idea upon Hester's contemplation, and laughed at the passionate and desperate joy with which she seized, and then strove to cast it from her. She barely looked the idea in the face, and hastened to bar it in its dungeon. What she compelled herself to believe—what, finally, she reasoned upon as her motive for continuing a resident of New England—was half a truth, and half a self-delusion. Here, she said to herself had been the scene of her guilt, and here should be the scene of her earthly punishment; and so, perchance, the torture of her daily shame would at length purge her soul, and work out another purity than that which she had lost: more saint-like, because the result of martyrdom.

289. In context, "marvellous" (1) means

    (A) grand
    (B) hyperbolic
    (C) farcical
    (D) appropriate
    (E) impressive

290. The afterthoughts expressed in lines 1–10 serve primarily to

    (A) distract the reader from the subject of the sentence
    (B) present a character as unstable
    (C) cast doubt upon the reliability of the narrator
    (D) elucidate the alternative possibilities to a problem
    (E) explain the reasons for a character's choice

291. The speaker immediately follows up on the idea expressed in lines 1–10 with

(A) skepticism
(B) a personal anecdote
(C) a generality about human nature
(D) irrefutable counter-evidence
(E) increased uncertainty

292. For Hester, the "fatality" mentioned in line 10 is later suggested to be

(A) the sighting of a ghost
(B) her transgression
(C) the death of her child
(D) her choice to live in "that place"
(E) doom

293. The figurative language in lines 14–21 provides

  I. an explanation of why Hester Prynne desires to remain in "that place"
  II. a unique perspective on sin
  III. a comparison of two homes

(A) I and II only
(B) I and III only
(C) II and III only
(D) III only
(E) I, II, and III

294. The second paragraph differs from the first in that it introduces Hester's

(A) fatality
(B) sin
(C) predicament
(D) chosen setting
(E) probable justification

295. In the phrase "the feet of one" in line 25, "one" refers to

(A) Hester's child
(B) Hester's mother
(C) the tempter of souls
(D) Hester's husband
(E) Hester's accomplice

296. The second paragraph suggests that Hester Prynne stays in New England because

    (A) she has been exiled from her home

    (B) she is ambivalent

    (C) it is better than her birth-place

    (D) she longs for eventual absolution

    (E) it has been the most important place in her life

297. The laughable secret described in the second paragraph is best summarized as

    (A) Hester's sincere atonement for her crime

    (B) Hester's twisted attempt at a kind of marriage with her accomplice

    (C) Hester's expectation that she will be forgiven if she remains at the site of her crime

    (D) Hester's sense that her punishment is unwarranted

    (E) Hester's hope that she can escape and return to her birth-place

298. Based on the context of the passage, the narrator's point of view is best stated as

    (A) limited to that of Hester's

    (B) third person and objective

    (C) third person and judgmental

    (D) omniscient and sensitive

    (E) omniscient and indifferent

299. The narrator's attitude towards Hester can best be described as

    (A) condescending

    (B) pejorative

    (C) hagiographic

    (D) intrigued

    (E) aloof

Passage 5. Henry James, *The Turn of the Screw*

I remember the whole beginning as a succession of flights and drops, a little
seesaw of the right throbs and the wrong. After rising, in town, to meet his
appeal, I had at all events a couple of very bad days—found myself doubtful
again, felt indeed sure I had made a mistake. In this state of mind I spent the
long hours of bumping, swinging coach that carried me to the stopping place at   5
which I was to be met by a vehicle from the house. This convenience, I was told,
had been ordered, and I found, toward the close of the June afternoon, a commodious fly in waiting for me. Driving at that hour, on a lovely day, through a
country to which the summer sweetness seemed to offer me a friendly welcome,
my fortitude mounted afresh and, as we turned into the avenue, encountered a   10
reprieve that was probably but a proof of the point to which it had sunk. I suppose I had expected, or had dreaded, something so melancholy that what greeted
me was a good surprise. I remember as a most pleasant impression the broad,
clear front, its open windows and fresh curtains and the pair of maids looking
out; I remember the lawn and the bright flowers and the crunch of my wheels on   15
the gravel and the clustered treetops over which the rooks circled and cawed in
the golden sky. The scene had a greatness that made it a different affair from my
own scant home, and there immediately appeared at the door, with a little girl
in her hand, a civil person who dropped me as decent a curtsy as if I had been
the mistress or a distinguished visitor. I had received in Harley Street a narrower   20
notion of the place, and that, as I recalled it, made me think the proprietor still
more of a gentleman, suggested that what I was to enjoy might be something
beyond his promise.

I had no drop again till the next day, for I was carried triumphantly through
the following hours by my introduction to the younger of my pupils. The little   25
girl who accompanied Mrs. Grose appeared to me on the spot a creature so
charming as to make it a great fortune to have to do with her. She was the most
beautiful child I had ever seen, and I afterward wondered that my employer had
not told me more of her. I slept little that night—I was too much excited; and
this astonished me, too, I recollect, remained with me, adding to my sense of the   30
liberality with which I was treated. The large, impressive room, one of the best
in the house, the great state bed, as I almost felt it, the full, figured draperies,
the long glasses in which, for the first time, I could see myself from head to foot,
all struck me—like the extraordinary charm of my small charge—as so many
things thrown in. It was thrown in as well, from the first moment, that I should   35
get on with Mrs. Grose in a relation over which, on my way, in the coach, I fear
I had rather brooded. The only thing indeed that in this early outlook might
have made me shrink again was the clear circumstance of her being so glad to see
me. I perceived within half an hour that she was so glad—stout, simple, plain,
clean, wholesome woman—as to be positively on her guard against showing it   40
too much. I wondered even then a little why she should wish not to show it, and
that, with reflection, with suspicion, might of course have made me uneasy.

300. Lines 1–4 describe the speaker's state of mind as

    (A) tenacious
    (B) penitent
    (C) reserved
    (D) impatient
    (E) anxious

301. The "convenience" mentioned in line 6 refers to

    (A) a spacious means of conveyance
    (B) an insect
    (C) "the bumping swinging coach"
    (D) the stopping-place
    (E) the nice June weather

302. The word "fortitude" in line 10 most likely means

    (A) contentment
    (B) amicability
    (C) mental and emotional strength
    (D) senses
    (E) terror

303. The speaker's reaction upon arriving at the residence is attributed to all of the following *except*

    (A) a surprisingly reverential reception
    (B) the stateliness of the residence
    (C) low expectations
    (D) the temperate climate
    (E) Mrs. Grose's forthrightness

304. Which of the following enhances the speaker's excitement in lines 11–16?

    (A) imagery, polysyndeton, and onomatopoeia
    (B) simile, metaphor, and onomatopoeia
    (C) imagery, hyperbole, and simile
    (D) understatement, allusion, and imagery
    (E) allusion, irony, and figurative language

305. From the first paragraph, we can infer that the speaker is

    (A) a precocious girl
    (B) not upper class
    (C) a distinguished visitor
    (D) the overseer
    (E) the proprietor

306. The "drop" in line 24 refers to

    (A) the rain
    (B) a fall
    (C) doubts
    (D) sustenance
    (E) excitement

307. What "remained" with the speaker in line 30?

    (A) her employer's reticence
    (B) the beautiful child
    (C) her excitement
    (D) the generosity of her hosts
    (E) Mrs. Grose

308. The second paragraph differs from the first in its

    (A) mention of the speaker's multiple emotions
    (B) focus on characters
    (C) reflective tone
    (D) focus on setting
    (E) narrative point of view

309. Overall, the speaker feels she has been treated

    (A) gregariously
    (B) servilely
    (C) irreverently
    (D) munificently
    (E) suspiciously

310. The speaker's impression of Mrs. Grose can be interpreted as both

    (A) objective and erroneous
    (B) prejudicial and delusional
    (C) relieved and hesitant
    (D) ecstatic and relieved
    (E) anxious and suspicious

Passage 6. Sinclair Lewis, *Babbitt*

He was busy, from March to June. He kept himself from the bewilderment
of thinking. His wife and the neighbors were generous. Every evening he played
bridge or attended the movies, and the days were blank of face and silent.

In June, Mrs. Babbitt and Tinka went East, to stay with relatives, and Babbitt
was free to do—he was not quite sure what.   5

All day long after their departure he thought of the emancipated house in
which he could, if he desired, go mad and curse the gods without having to keep
up a husbandly front. He considered, "I could have a reg'lar party to-night; stay
out till two and not do any explaining afterwards. Cheers!" He telephoned to
Vergil Gunch, to Eddie Swanson. Both of them were engaged for the evening,   10
and suddenly he was bored by having to take so much trouble to be riotous.

He was silent at dinner, unusually kindly to Ted and Verona, hesitating but
not disapproving when Verona stated her opinion of Kenneth Escott's opinion
of Dr. John Jennison Drew's opinion of the opinions of the evolutionists. Ted
was working in a garage through the summer vacation, and he related his daily   15
triumphs: how he had found a cracked ball-race, what he had said to the Old
Grouch, what he had said to the foreman about the future of wireless telephony.

Ted and Verona went to a dance after dinner. Even the maid was out. Rarely
had Babbitt been alone in the house for an entire evening. He was restless. He
vaguely wanted something more diverting than the newspaper comic strips   20
to read. He ambled up to Verona's room, sat on her maidenly blue and white
bed, humming and grunting in a solid-citizen manner as he examined her
books: Conrad's "Rescue," a volume strangely named "Figures of Earth," poetry
(quite irregular poetry, Babbitt thought) by Vachel Lindsay, and essays by
H. L. Mencken—highly improper essays, making fun of the church and all the   25
decencies. He liked none of the books. In them he felt a spirit of rebellion against
niceness and solid-citizenship. These authors—and he supposed they were
famous ones, too—did not seem to care about telling a good story which would
enable a fellow to forget his troubles. He sighed. He noted a book, "The Three
Black Pennies," by Joseph Hergesheimer. Ah, that was something like it! It would   30
be an adventure story, maybe about counterfeiting—detectives sneaking up on
the old house at night. He tucked the book under his arm, he clumped down-
stairs and solemnly began to read, under the piano-lamp …

311. The first paragraph implies that Babbitt's life from March to June is

    (A) intellectually stimulating
    (B) perfunctory
    (C) reclusive
    (D) onerous
    (E) pensive

312. In context, the phrase "blank of face and silent" (3) is an example of

    (A) hyperbole
    (B) simile
    (C) personification
    (D) understatement
    (E) irony

313. The primary function of the second paragraph is to

    (A) highlight a key characteristic of Babbitt that will be developed throughout the passage
    (B) characterize Babbitt's relationship with his wife
    (C) stress the importance of the new characters mentioned
    (D) present Babbitt as independent
    (E) contrast Babbitt with others

314. In context, the word "emancipated" (6) suggests that

    (A) Mrs. Babbitt is unrelenting
    (B) Babbitt's home life is regulated
    (C) the house is forsaken
    (D) Babbitt is lost without his routine
    (E) Babbitt is suffering from ennui

315. The tone of lines 12–14, "He was silent . . . evolutionists," is best described as

    (A) vitriolic
    (B) offended
    (C) sardonic
    (D) splenetic
    (E) sympathetic

316. The word "vaguely" in line 20 implies that Babbitt

    (A) abhors comics
    (B) is tenacious
    (C) is frenetic
    (D) is ambivalent
    (E) is apathetic

317. Based on Babbitt's thoughts about the books, we can infer all of the following *except* that
   (A) he is discomfited by their spirit
   (B) he wants them to offer him an escape
   (C) he is quick to judge them
   (D) he dislikes their antisocial themes
   (E) his interests are congruous with Verona's

318. It can be inferred that Babbitt ordinarily responds to Verona's opinions with
   (A) kindness
   (B) concordance
   (C) antagonism
   (D) openness
   (E) dismissal

319. The sentence "Ah, that was something like it!" (30) is an example of what narrative technique?
   (A) stream of consciousness
   (B) third person
   (C) first person
   (D) free indirect style
   (E) first person plural

320. The final paragraph primarily characterizes Babbitt as
   (A) desperately seeking escape
   (B) reveling in solitude
   (C) admiringly conservative
   (D) perpetually unsatisfied
   (E) seeking a mild diversion

Passage 7. Upton Sinclair, *The Jungle*

Jurgis had made some friends by this time, and he sought one of them and asked what this meant. The friend, who was named Tamoszius Kuszleika, was a sharp little man who folded hides on the killing beds, and he listened to what Jurgis had to say without seeming at all surprised. They were common enough, he said, such cases of petty graft. It was simply some boss who proposed to add a little to his income. After Jurgis had been there awhile he would know that the plants were simply honeycombed with rottenness of that sort—the bosses grafted off the men, and they grafted off each other; and some day the superintendent would find out about the boss, and then he would graft off the boss. Warming to the subject, Tamoszius went on to explain the situation. Here was Durham's, 10

for instance, owned by a man who was trying to make as much money out of
it as he could, and did not care in the least how he did it; and underneath him,
ranged in ranks and grades like an army, were managers and superintendents and
foremen, each one driving the man next below him and trying to squeeze out
of him as much work as possible. And all the men of the same rank were pitted   15
against each other; the accounts of each were kept separately, and every man
lived in terror of losing his job, if another made a better record than he. So from
top to bottom the place was simply a seething caldron of jealousies and hatreds;
there was no loyalty or decency anywhere about it, there was no place in it where
a man counted for anything against a dollar. And worse than there being no   20
decency, there was not even any honesty. The reason for that? Who could say? It
must have been old Durham in the beginning; it was a heritage which the self-
made merchant had left to his son, along with his millions.

Jurgis would find out these things for himself, if he stayed there long enough;
it was the men who had to do all the dirty jobs, and so there was no deceiving   25
them; and they caught the spirit of the place, and did like all the rest. Jurgis
had come there, and thought he was going to make himself useful, and rise and
become a skilled man; but he would soon find out his error—for nobody rose
in Packingtown by doing good work. You could lay that down for a rule—if you
met a man who was rising in Packingtown, you met a knave. That man who had   30
been sent to Jurgis' father by the boss, he would rise; the man who told tales and
spied upon his fellows would rise; but the man who minded his own business
and did his work—why, they would "speed him up" till they had worn him out,
and then they would throw him into the gutter.

Jurgis went home with his head buzzing. Yet he could not bring himself to   35
believe such things—no, it could not be so. Tamoszius was simply another of the
grumblers. He was a man who spent all his time fiddling; and he would go to
parties at night and not get home till sunrise, and so of course he did not feel like
work. Then, too, he was a puny little chap; and so he had been left behind in the
race, and that was why he was sore. And yet so many strange things kept coming   40
to Jurgis' notice every day!

321. The word "this" in line 2 is later suggested to mean

    (A) Jurgis's low wages
    (B) the attaching of one thing to another
    (C) an incident involving unethical behavior
    (D) Tamoszius's job
    (E) the superintendent's behavior

322. The word "simply" in line 5 implies

    (A) the narrator's skepticism of Tamoszius's account
    (B) Tamoszius's dismay at the corruption around him
    (C) the obvious and overwhelming amount of graft in the company
    (D) Jurgis's realization of the company's true nature
    (E) the minor nature of the problems of the company

323. In the first paragraph, the image provided by the phrase "honeycombed with rotteness" is apt because

    I. the author intends to liken the workers to bees
    II. the boss functions similarly to a queen bee
    III. the incidents of graft are ubiquitous and interconnected
    IV. there is a kind of sweetness to the unscrupulous structure of the factory

    (A) I and II only
    (B) II and III only
    (C) I and IV only
    (D) I, II, and III only
    (E) I, II, III, and IV

324. The phrase "like an army" (line 13) is used to portray

    (A) the severity of the discipline in the plants
    (B) the fierce patriotism of the workers in the plants
    (C) the fortitude necessary for survival in the plants
    (D) the significance of the hierarchical structure evident in the plants
    (E) the conscripted labor of the workers in the plants

325. The state of Durham's is attributed to all of the following causes *except*

    (A) inheritance of an unprincipled management system
    (B) desperation for advancement
    (C) disregard for humanity
    (D) ubiquitous venality
    (E) appreciation of a scrupulous work ethic

326. In the second paragraph, the word "knave" most likely means

    (A) a person who is law abiding
    (B) a person who minds his own business
    (C) a person who is industrious
    (D) a skilled man
    (E) a charlatan

327. The phrase *speed him up* (second paragraph) is in quotation marks because

    I. the implied speaker is mocking the bosses' euphemistic command
    II. the phrase is part of a dialogue
    III. the phrase is distinct from the implied speaker's voice

    (A) I only
    (B) II only
    (C) I and II only
    (D) I and III only
    (E) I, II, and III only

328. Tamoszius's account of how Packingtown works (first paragraph beginning "It was") makes use of all of the following *except*

    (A) metaphor and simile
    (B) anaphora
    (C) rhetorical questions
    (D) examples
    (E) speculation

329. What is the predominant narrative voice in the third paragraph?

    (A) Jurgis's, and it begins with, "no, it could not be so" (36)
    (B) Tamoszius's, and it begins with, "and then they would throw him into the gutter" (34)
    (C) Jurgis's, and it begins with, "he was a puny little chap" (39)
    (D) The objective narrator's, and it begins with, "Jurgis went home with his head buzzing." (35)
    (E) The objective narrator's, and it begins with, "he could not bring himself to believe such things" (35–36)

330. Jurgis's response to Tamoszius's assessment of the company is most like the response of

    (A) someone who is firm in his or her beliefs
    (B) someone who has successfully been disabused of his or her initial perceptions
    (C) someone who is skeptical about new information
    (D) someone corrupt
    (E) someone in complete denial

331. The last sentence of the passage suggests that the next paragraph might

    (A) belie the three paragraphs in the passage

    (B) corroborate the details given in the first and second paragraphs

    (C) detail the hardships incurred by Jurgis

    (D) present Tamoszius as dubious

    (E) validate the company's behavior

332. According to the passage as a whole, the company being described seems to value workers who are

    (A) skilled, useful men

    (B) fast

    (C) fastidious

    (D) candid

    (E) unprincipled

CHAPTER 6

World Fiction

Passage 1. Miguel de Cervantes, *Don Quixote*

These preliminaries settled, he did not care to put off any longer the execution of his design, urged on to it by the thought of all the world was losing by his delay, seeing what wrongs he intended to right, grievances to redress, injustices to repair, abuses to remove, and duties to discharge. So, without giving notice of his intention to anyone, and without anybody seeing him, one morning before 5 the dawning of the day (which was one of the hottest of the month of July) he donned his suit of armour, mounted Rocinante with his patched-up helmet on, braced his buckler, took his lance, and by the back door of the yard sallied forth upon the plain in the highest contentment and satisfaction at seeing with what ease he had made a beginning with his grand purpose. But scarcely did he find 10 himself upon the open plain, when a terrible thought struck him, one all but enough to make him abandon the enterprise at the very outset. It occurred to him that he had not been dubbed a knight, and that according to the law of chivalry he neither could nor ought to bear arms against any knight; and that even if he had been, still he ought, as a novice knight, to wear white armour, without a 15 device upon the shield until by his prowess he had earned one. These reflections made him waver in his purpose, but his craze being stronger than any reasoning, he made up his mind to have himself dubbed a knight by the first one he came across, following the example of others in the same case, as he had read in the books that brought him to this pass. As for white armor, he resolved, on the first 20 opportunity, to scour his until it was whiter than an ermine; and so comforting himself he pursued his way, taking that which his horse chose, for in this he believed lay the essence of adventures.

Thus setting out, our new-fledged adventurer paced along, talking to himself and saying, "Who knows but that in time to come, when the veracious history 25 of my famous deeds is made known, the sage who writes it, when he has to set forth my first sally in the early morning, will do it after this fashion? 'Scarce had the rubicund Apollo spread o'er the face of the broad spacious earth the golden threads of his bright hair, scarce had the little birds of painted plumage attuned their notes to hail with dulcet and mellifluous harmony the coming of the 30 rosy Dawn, that, deserting the soft couch of her jealous spouse, was appearing to mortals at the gates and balconies of the Manchegan horizon, when the

⟨ **97**

renowned knight Don Quixote of La Mancha, quitting the lazy down, mounted
his celebrated steed Rocinante and began to traverse the ancient and famous
Campo de Montiel;'" which in fact he was actually traversing. "Happy the age,   35
happy the time," he continued, "in which shall be made known my deeds of
fame, worthy to be molded in brass, carved in marble, limned in pictures, for
a memorial for ever. And thou, O sage magician, whoever thou art, to whom
it shall fall to be the chronicler of this wondrous history, forget not, I entreat
thee, my good Rocinante, the constant companion of my ways and wanderings."   40
Presently he broke out again, as if he were love-stricken in earnest, "O Princess
Dulcinea, lady of this captive heart, a grievous wrong hast thou done me to drive
me forth with scorn, and with inexorable obduracy banish me from the presence
of thy beauty. O lady, deign to hold in remembrance this heart, thy vassal, that
thus in anguish pines for love of thee."   45

333. The "terrible thought" (11) that Don Quixote had refers to

(A) his leaving home without telling anyone
(B) his not knowing where he was going
(C) the wrongs that his lady had done him
(D) his status not being quite legitimate
(E) his ambitions being too great

334. According to the narrator, Don Quixote was able to overcome his initial
hesitation because

(A) he was unable to reason coherently
(B) his fantasizing was resourceful
(C) he had a tenuous grasp on reality
(D) he had faith in his good fortune
(E) he was unwilling to return home

335. Don Quixote's use of the expression "veracious history" in line 25 can best
be described as

(A) scrupulous
(B) droll
(C) ironic
(D) disingenuous
(E) emphatic

336. The tone of the sentence in lines 27–35, "'Scarce had the rubicund Apollo … Campo de Montiel,'" can best be described as

(A) ridiculous
(B) sarcastic
(C) sophisticated
(D) grandiloquent
(E) provincial

337. It can be interpreted that the addressee in the sentence in lines 38–40 ("And thou, O sage magician . . . and wanderings") is likely a reference to

(A) Don Quixote himself
(B) Dulcinea
(C) someone imaginary
(D) the narrator
(E) a renowned chronicler

338. In line 43, the word "obduracy" most likely means

(A) cruelty
(B) durability
(C) unpredictability
(D) stubbornness
(E) loudness

339. The genre of the narrative as a whole can best be described as

(A) romance
(B) epic
(C) tragedy
(D) ode
(E) farce

340. According to Don Quixote's chivalric code, a knight is not meant to do any of the following *except*

(A) travel directly and purposefully
(B) speak plainly and succinctly
(C) maintain a supercilious attitude about himself
(D) avoid romantic entanglement
(E) disregard unreasonable rules

341. The passage's tone is primarily established through

    (A) the protagonist's unwarranted and exaggerated hubris

    (B) the imminent failure of the protagonist's adventure

    (C) the sincerity of the protagonist's hallucinatory experiences

    (D) the lowly status of the aspirational protagonist

    (E) the lofty language

342. The narrator's attitude toward the protagonist can best be described as

    (A) magnanimous

    (B) sardonic

    (C) acrimonious

    (D) sympathetic

    (E) dispassionate

Passage 2. Fyodor Dostoyevsky, *Crime and Punishment*

On an exceptionally hot evening early in July a young man came out of the garret in which he lodged in S. Place and walked slowly, as though in hesitation, towards K. bridge.

He had successfully avoided meeting his landlady on the staircase. His garret was under the roof of a high, five-storied house and was more like a cupboard than a room. The landlady who provided him with garret, dinners, and attendance, lived on the floor below, and every time he went out he was obliged to pass her kitchen, the door of which invariably stood open. And each time he passed, the young man had a sick, frightened feeling, which made him scowl and feel ashamed. He was hopelessly in debt to his landlady, and was afraid of meeting her.

This was not because he was cowardly and abject, quite the contrary; but for some time past he had been in an overstrained irritable condition, verging on hypochondria. He had become so completely absorbed in himself, and isolated from his fellows that he dreaded meeting, not only his landlady, but anyone at all. He was crushed by poverty, but the anxieties of his position had of late ceased to weigh upon him. He had given up attending to matters of practical importance; he had lost all desire to do so. Nothing that any landlady could do had a real terror for him. But to be stopped on the stairs, to be forced to listen to her trivial, irrelevant gossip, to pestering demands for payment, threats and complaints, and to rack his brains for excuses, to prevaricate, to lie—no, rather than that, he would creep down the stairs like a cat and slip out unseen.

This evening, however, on coming out into the street, he became acutely aware of his fears.

"I want to attempt a thing like that and am frightened by these trifles," he thought, with an odd smile. "Hm ... yes, all is in a man's hands and he lets it all slip from cowardice, that's an axiom. It would be interesting to know what it is men are most afraid of. Taking a new step, uttering a new word is what they fear most... . But I am talking too much. It's because I chatter that I do nothing. Or perhaps it is that I chatter because I do nothing. I've learned to chatter this last month, lying for days together in my den thinking ... of Jack the Giant-killer. Why am I going there now? Am I capable of that? Is that serious? It is not serious at all. It's simply a fantasy to amuse myself; a plaything! Yes, maybe it is a plaything."

30

The heat in the street was terrible: and the airlessness, the bustle and the plaster, scaffolding, bricks, and dust all about him, and that special Petersburg stench, so familiar to all who are unable to get out of town in summer—all worked painfully upon the young man's already overwrought nerves. The insufferable stench from the pot-houses, which are particularly numerous in that part of the town, and the drunken men whom he met continually, although it was a working day, completed the revolting misery of the picture. An expression of the profoundest disgust gleamed for a moment in the young man's refined face. He was, by the way, exceptionally handsome, above the average in height, slim, well-built, with beautiful dark eyes and dark brown hair. Soon he sank into deep thought, or more accurately speaking into a complete blankness of mind; he walked along not observing what was about him and not caring to observe it. From time to time, he would mutter something, from the habit of talking to himself, to which he had just confessed. At these moments he would become conscious that his ideas were sometimes in a tangle and that he was very weak; for two days he had scarcely tasted food.

35

40

45

50

343. The primary function of the last sentence of the second paragraph is

    (A) to repeat key information
    (B) to speculate
    (C) to answer a question
    (D) to provide context
    (E) to characterize the landlady

344. The third paragraph differs from the second in that

    (A) the third paragraph refutes the analysis introduced in the second paragraph
    (B) the third paragraph responds to a question raised in the second paragraph
    (C) the third paragraph focuses on characterizing the protagonist's emotional state
    (D) the third paragraph mentions a character that the second does not
    (E) the third paragraph's tone is melancholy

345. The protagonist's avoidance of his landlady is eventually attributed (in the third paragraph) to

(A) his abject poverty
(B) the terror the landlady inspires
(C) his poor health
(D) his self-absorption
(E) his crippling fear

346. Lines 25–34 imply that the narrator's inaction is due to all of the following *except*

(A) temerity
(B) fear
(C) thinking
(D) deliberating
(E) vacillation

347. What is the "axiom" the protagonist refers to in line 27?

(A) that men lose their minds because of their cowardice
(B) that a man's cowardice causes him to squander opportunities
(C) careful consideration of consequences leads to intelligent action
(D) his conjecture that doing nothing causes him to chatter
(E) his conjecture that chatter prevents him from doing things

348. The two sentences in lines 29–30 ("It's because I chatter that I do nothing. Or perhaps it is that I chatter because I do nothing") are

(A) chiastic and reveal the protagonist's self-doubt
(B) axiomatic and reveal an eternal truth
(C) veracious and provide commentary on the times
(D) hyperbolic and suggest the tone is satirical
(E) delusional and characterize the protagonist as absurd

349. The words "there," "that," and "It" in line 32 do all of the following *except*

(A) provoke curiosity
(B) characterize the protagonist's reluctance and fear
(C) elucidate the protagonist's desires
(D) create a sense of mystery
(E) hide the protagonist's actual fantasy from the reader

350. The description of the setting serves to

    I. provide justification for the protagonist's feelings
   II. develop the overall tone of misery
  III. critique the government of "Petersburg"

(A) I only
(B) I and II only
(C) II and III only
(D) I and III
(E) III only

351. In the final paragraph, a contrast is established between

(A) beauty and ugliness
(B) rich and poor
(C) cleanliness and filth
(D) good and evil
(E) hunger and satiation

352. The protagonist is described as all of the following *except*

(A) emotionally detached
(B) distinctive
(C) petulant
(D) destitute
(E) intrepid

353. The narrator's tone can best be described as

(A) observant
(B) curious
(C) intrusive
(D) pitiful
(E) empathetic

354. The passage provides answers to all of the following questions *except*

(A) Why does the protagonist avoid his landlady?
(B) Why is the protagonist physically weak?
(C) What precisely is the protagonist fearful of doing?
(D) How does the protagonist feel about his environment?
(E) How does the protagonist look?

Passage 3. Gustave Flaubert, *Madame Bovary*

We were in class when the head-master came in, followed by a "new fellow," not wearing the school uniform, and a school servant carrying a large desk. Those who had been asleep woke up, and every one rose as if just surprised at his work.

The head-master made a sign to us to sit down. Then, turning to the class-master, he said to him in a low voice: 5

"Monsieur Roger, here is a pupil whom I recommend to your care; he'll be in the second. If his work and conduct are satisfactory, he will go into one of the upper classes, as becomes his age."

The "new fellow," standing in the corner behind the door so that he could hardly be seen, was a country lad of about fifteen, and taller than any of us. His 10 hair was cut square on his forehead like a village chorister's; he looked reliable, but very ill at ease. Although he was not broad-shouldered, his short school jacket of green cloth with black buttons must have been tight about the armholes, and showed at the opening of the cuffs red wrists accustomed to being bare. His legs, in blue stockings, looked out from beneath yellow trousers, drawn tight by 15 braces. He wore stout, ill-cleaned, hobnailed boots.

We began repeating the lesson. He listened with all his ears, as attentive as if at a sermon, not daring even to cross his legs or lean on his elbow; and when at two o'clock the bell rang, the master was obliged to tell him to fall into line with the rest of us. 20

When we came back to work, we were in the habit of throwing our caps on the floor so as to have our hands more free; we used from the door to toss them under the form, so that they hit against the wall and made a lot of dust: it was "the thing."

But, whether he had not noticed the trick, or did not dare to attempt it, the 25 "new fellow" was still holding his cap on his knees even after prayers were over. It was one of those head-gears of composite order, in which we find traces of the bearskin, shako, billycock hat, sealskin cap, and cotton nightcap; one of those poor things, in fine, whose dumb ugliness has depths of expression, like an imbecile's face. Oval, stiffened with whalebone, it began with three round knobs; then 30 came in succession lozenges of velvet and rabbit-skin separated by a red band; after that a sort of bag that ended in a cardboard polygon covered with complicated braiding, from which hung, at the end of a long, thin cord, small twisted gold threads in the manner of a tassel. The cap was new; its peak shone.

355. The passage implies that the speaker and his peers view their time at school as

(A) wasteful
(B) essential
(C) a privilege
(D) a right
(E) habitual

356. The speaker most likely describes the new fellow's attire (12–16) to emphasize

    (A) that he does not want to be there
    (B) how he does not fit in
    (C) how varied the available school uniforms are
    (D) how apprehensive the "new fellow" is
    (E) that he appears to have academic potential

357. The clause in lines 19–20 ("the master was obliged . . . rest of us") implies

    (A) the new boy is misbehaving
    (B) the new boy is recalcitrant
    (C) the new boy is rapt
    (D) the new boy is an outcast
    (E) the speaker is belittling the new boy

358. The phrase "'the thing'" (24) is in quotation marks because

    (A) it is part of a dialogue
    (B) it is an idiomatic expression
    (C) it is sarcastic
    (D) it is ironic
    (E) it is being mocked

359. The detailed description of the new boy's cap (25–34)

    (A) highlights similarities between the boy and others
    (B) reveals it is symbolic of the boy himself
    (C) emphasizes the boy's piety
    (D) is intended purely to ridicule the boy
    (E) is a motif throughout the passage

360. The last two sentences of the passage can be described as

    (A) creating sentence variety
    (B) paradoxes
    (C) contradictions
    (D) redundant
    (E) run-ons

361. The overall tone of the passage is

    (A) attentive
    (B) regretful
    (C) sentimental
    (D) detached
    (E) informal

362. The primary purpose of the passage as a whole is

    I. to portray the culture of a specific school
   II. to provide insight into class differences
  III. to portray a character through others' observations

  (A) I and III only
  (B) II and III only
  (C) III only
  (D) I and II only
  (E) I, II, and III

363. The narrator of the passage is best described as

  (A) an unreliable witness
  (B) a charming raconteur
  (C) a sanctimonious moralizer
  (D) an unfair biographer
  (E) a subjective onlooker

364. The new boy differs from the speaker in all of the following ways *except*

  (A) his attire
  (B) his height
  (C) his deportment
  (D) his environs
  (E) his interests

Passage 4. Hermann Hesse, *Siddhartha*

    In the shade of the house, in the sunshine of the riverbank near the boats, in
the shade of the Salwood forest, in the shade of the fig tree is where Siddhartha
grew up, the handsome son of the Brahman, the young falcon, together with
his friend Govinda, son of a Brahman. The sun tanned his light shoulders by
the banks of the river when bathing, performing the sacred ablutions, the sacred   5
offerings. In the mango grove, shade poured into his black eyes, when playing
as a boy, when his mother sang, when the sacred offerings were made, when
his father, the scholar, taught him, when the wise men talked. For a long time,
Siddhartha had been partaking in the discussions of the wise men, practicing
debate with Govinda, practicing with Govinda the art of reflection, the service of   10
meditation. He already knew how to speak the Om silently, the word of words,
to speak it silently into himself while inhaling, to speak it silently out of himself
while exhaling, with all the concentration of his soul, the forehead surrounded
by the glow of the clear-thinking spirit. He already knew to feel Atman in the
depths of his being, indestructible, one with the universe.   15

Joy leapt in his father's heart for his son who was quick to learn, thirsty for knowledge; he saw him growing up to become a great wise man and priest, a prince among the Brahmans.

Bliss leapt in his mother's breast when she saw him, when she saw him walking, when she saw him sit down and get up, Siddhartha, strong, handsome,   20 he who was walking on slender legs, greeting her with perfect respect.

Love touched the hearts of the Brahmans' young daughters when Siddhartha walked through the lanes of the town with the luminous forehead, with the eye of a king, with his slim hips.

But more than all the others he was loved by Govinda, his friend, the son of   25 a Brahman. He loved Siddhartha's eye and sweet voice, he loved his walk and the perfect decency of his movements, he loved everything Siddhartha did and said and what he loved most was his spirit, his transcendent, fiery thoughts, his ardent will, his high calling. Govinda knew: he would not become a common Brahman, not a lazy official in charge of offerings; not a greedy merchant with magic spells;   30 not a vain, vacuous speaker; not a mean, deceitful priest; and also not a decent, stupid sheep in the herd of the many. No, and he, Govinda, as well did not want to become one of those, not one of those tens of thousands of Brahmans. He wanted to follow Siddhartha, the beloved, the splendid. And in days to come, when Siddhartha would become a god, when he would join the glorious, then   35 Govinda wanted to follow him as his friend, his companion, his servant, his spear-carrier, his shadow.

Siddhartha was thus loved by everyone. He was a source of joy for everybody, he was a delight for them all.

365. The first sentence of the passage can be described as

    I. redundant
   II. containing repetition
  III. containing metaphor

  (A) II only
  (B) I and II only
  (C) II and III only
  (D) I and III only
  (E) I, II, and III

366. The word "ablutions" (5) most likely means

  (A) forgiveness
  (B) prayers
  (C) rituals
  (D) religious cleansings
  (E) devotions

367. The dominant technique in the first paragraph is

(A) parallel structures
(B) personification
(C) hyperbole
(D) allusion
(E) metaphor

368. We can infer that "Om" is

(A) a sedative
(B) like an opiate
(C) a prayer
(D) a meditative recitation
(E) a routine

369. Siddhartha's parents are impressed by all of the following *except*

(A) his impudence
(B) his reverence
(C) his thirst for knowledge
(D) his ecclesiastical potential
(E) his litheness

370. Which of the following line(s) provides evidence for the assertion that Siddhartha is coveted?

(A) "Govinda knew: he would not become a common Brahman" (29)
(B) "For a long time, Siddhartha had been partaking in the discussions of the wise men" (8–9)
(C) "No, and he, Govinda, as well did not want to become one of those, not one of those tens of thousands of Brahmans" (32–33)
(D) "Love touched the hearts of the Brahmans' young daughters...hips" (22–24)
(E) "He already knew to feel Atman in the depths of his being, indestructible, one with the universe" (14–15)

371. Govinda's admiration for Siddhartha is

(A) partly self-serving
(B) partially unwarranted
(C) mostly exaggerated
(D) likely disingenuous
(E) self-deprecating

372. According to the passage, many Brahmans are

    I. supercilious
   II. venal
  III. banal

(A) I only
(B) II only
(C) III only
(D) I and III only
(E) I, II, and III

373. The tone of the passage as a whole is

(A) idyllic
(B) slanderous
(C) wistful
(D) nationalistic
(E) exalted

374. The passage's primary purpose is to

(A) portray a culture through a glimpse of its people and dominant religion
(B) characterize Siddhartha through the perceptions of others
(C) introduce Siddhartha objectively
(D) characterize Siddhartha through descriptions of his setting
(E) characterize Siddhartha through figurative language

Passage 5. James Joyce, "The Dead"

Lily, the caretaker's daughter, was literally run off her feet. Hardly had she brought one gentleman into the little pantry behind the office on the ground floor and helped him off with his overcoat than the wheezy hall-door bell clanged again and she had to scamper along the bare hallway to let in another guest. It was well for her she had not to attend to the ladies also. But Miss Kate and Miss Julia had thought of that and had converted the bathroom upstairs into a ladies' dressing-room. Miss Kate and Miss Julia were there, gossiping and laughing and fussing, walking after each other to the head of the stairs, peering down over the banisters and calling down to Lily to ask her who had come.

It was always a great affair, the Misses Morkan's annual dance. Everybody who knew them came to it, members of the family, old friends of the family, the members of Julia's choir, any of Kate's pupils that were grown up enough, and even some of Mary Jane's pupils too. Never once had it fallen flat. For years and years it had gone off in splendid style, as long as anyone could remember; ever since Kate and Julia, after the death of their brother Pat, had left the house in

5

10

15

Stoney Batter and taken Mary Jane, their only niece, to live with them in the
dark, gaunt house on Usher's Island, the upper part of which they had rented
from Mr. Fulham, the corn-factor on the ground floor. That was a good thirty
years ago if it was a day. Mary Jane, who was then a little girl in short clothes, was
now the main prop of the household, for she had the organ in Haddington Road. 20
She had been through the Academy and gave a pupils' concert every year in the
upper room of the Ancient Concert Rooms. Many of her pupils belonged to the
better-class families on the Kingstown and Dalkey line. Old as they were, her
aunts also did their share. Julia, though she was quite grey, was still the leading
soprano in Adam and Eve's, and Kate, being too feeble to go about much, gave 25
music lessons to beginners on the old square piano in the back room. Lily, the
caretaker's daughter, did housemaid's work for them. Though their life was modest, they believed in eating well; the best of everything: diamond-bone sirloins,
three-shilling tea and the best bottled stout. But Lily seldom made a mistake in
the orders, so that she got on well with her three mistresses. They were fussy, that 30
was all. But the only thing they would not stand was back answers.

Of course, they had good reason to be fussy on such a night. And then it was
long after ten o'clock and yet there was no sign of Gabriel and his wife. Besides
they were dreadfully afraid that Freddy Malins might turn up screwed. They
would not wish for worlds that any of Mary Jane's pupils should see him under 35
the influence; and when he was like that it was sometimes very hard to manage
him. Freddy Malins always came late, but they wondered what could be keeping
Gabriel: and that was what brought them every two minutes to the banisters to
ask Lily had Gabriel or Freddy come.

375. The structure of the second sentence of the passage

  (A) obfuscates meaning
  (B) juxtaposes conflicting ideas
  (C) complements the harried state it describes
  (D) contrasts Lily's emotional state
  (E) corresponds to that of the first sentence of the paragraph

376. The imagery of the first paragraph provides

  (A) spacial and auditory details
  (B) metaphoric and ironic descriptions
  (C) exaggerated and comic details
  (D) a sympathetic and regretful tone
  (E) a partiality towards one character

377. In the context of the second paragraph, the sentence in line 13 ("Never once had it fallen flat") is distinct in which of the following ways?

(A) Its simplicity and proximity to compound sentences allow it to emphasize an essential point.
(B) It repeats information from previous and upcoming sentences, which creates a sense of monotony.
(C) It is markedly short to create anxiety.
(D) It is redundant and serves no ultimate purpose.
(E) It is passive in order to highlight the agency of the characters.

378. The mood in the house is predominantly

(A) pacific
(B) patient
(C) indulgent
(D) anxious
(E) fearful

379. The phrase "main prop" (20) reveals that

(A) the two aunts view Mary Jane as servile
(B) Mary Jane is the sole supporter of the household
(C) the two aunts use Mary Jane for their financial survival
(D) Mary Jane is the main provider in the family
(E) Mary Jane is objectified

380. The phrases "if it was a day" (19), "They were fussy ... back answers" (30–31), "turn up screwed" (34), and "wish for worlds" (35) have what in common?

  I. They are examples of the characters' vernacular.
 II. They are examples of free indirect style.
III. They are examples of malapropisms.

(A) I only
(B) I and II only
(C) I and III only
(D) II and III only
(E) I, II, and III

381. From the passage as a whole, we can infer that the three women (Julia, Kate, and Mary Jane) are all of the following *except*
   (A) discerning
   (B) musically inclined
   (C) not upper class
   (D) overly demanding
   (E) finicky

382. The second paragraph of the passage differs from the first in that
   (A) the second contains Lily's perspective
   (B) the first sets up a problem that the second solves
   (C) the first sets the scene, and the second provides background
   (D) the first contains simple sentences, and the second does not
   (E) the first mentions characters that the second does not

383. The passage's closing sentence intends to provide
   (A) the aunts' preference for specific guests
   (B) a resolution that eases the anxiety of the scene
   (C) a weak justification of a character's behavior
   (D) a clarification of the aunts' preoccupation
   (E) a parallel between Freddy and Gabriel

384. The passage provides answers to all of the following questions about the two aunts *except*
   (A) What are some of their interests?
   (B) Why are they eager for Gabriel's arrival?
   (C) How do they know Lily and Mary Jane?
   (D) What are their vocations?
   (E) How did they come to live in this house?

Passage 6. Franz Kafka, "Metamorphosis"

One morning, when Gregor Samsa woke from troubled dreams, he found himself transformed in his bed into a horrible vermin.[2] He lay on his armor-like back, and if he lifted his head a little he could see his brown belly, slightly domed and divided by arches into stiff sections. The bedding was hardly able to cover it and seemed ready to slide off any moment. His many legs, pitifully thin com-pared with the size of the rest of him, waved about helplessly as he looked.   5

"What's happened to me?" he thought. It wasn't a dream. His room, a proper human room although a little too small, lay peacefully between its

_____

2. Modern translations indicate that the transformation is into a bug or insect, very likely a cockroach.

four familiar walls. A collection of textile samples lay spread out on the table— Samsa was a travelling salesman—and above it there hung a picture that he had recently cut out of an illustrated magazine and housed in a nice, gilded frame. It showed a lady fitted out with a fur hat and fur boa who sat upright, raising a heavy fur muff that covered the whole of her lower arm towards the viewer.

Gregor then turned to look out the window at the dull weather. Drops of rain could be heard hitting the pane, which made him feel quite sad. "How about if I sleep a little bit longer and forget all this nonsense," he thought, but that was something he was unable to do because he was used to sleeping on his right, and in his present state couldn't get into that position. However hard he threw himself onto his right, he always rolled back to where he was. He must have tried it a hundred times, shut his eyes so that he wouldn't have to look at the floundering legs, and only stopped when he began to feel a mild, dull pain there that he had never felt before.

"Oh, God," he thought, "what a strenuous career it is that I've chosen! Travelling day in and day out. Doing business like this takes much more effort than doing your own business at home, and on top of that there's the curse of travelling, worries about making train connections, bad and irregular food, contact with different people all the time so that you can never get to know anyone or become friendly with them. It can all go to Hell!" He felt a slight itch up on his belly; pushed himself slowly up on his back towards the headboard so that he could lift his head better; found where the itch was, and saw that it was covered with lots of little white spots which he didn't know what to make of; and when he tried to feel the place with one of his legs he drew it quickly back because as soon as he touched it he was overcome by a cold shudder.

He slid back into his former position. "Getting up early all the time," he thought, "it makes you stupid. You've got to get enough sleep. Other travelling salesmen live a life of luxury. For instance, whenever I go back to the guest house during the morning to copy out the contract, these gentlemen are always still sitting there eating their breakfasts. I ought to just try that with my boss; I'd get kicked out on the spot. But who knows, maybe that would be the best thing for me. If I didn't have my parents to think about I'd have given in my notice a long time ago, I'd have gone up to the boss and told him just what I think, tell him everything I would, let him know just what I feel. He'd fall right off his desk! And it's a funny sort of business to be sitting up there at your desk, talking down at your subordinates from up there, especially when you have to go right up close because the boss is hard of hearing. Well, there's still some hope; once I've got the money together to pay off my parents' debt to him—another five or six years I suppose—that's definitely what I'll do. That's when I'll make the big change. First of all though, I've got to get up, my train leaves at five."

385. The main purpose of the first paragraph is to

(A) display figurative language
(B) upset the reader
(C) pique interest by setting up a problem
(D) introduce the setting
(E) characterize Gregor Samsa

386. The second paragraph differs from the first in that

(A) it contains a metaphor
(B) it characterizes Gregor through description of his personal items
(C) it distracts from the main concern
(D) it changes the mood from eerie to peaceful
(E) it further complicates the situation

387. In the context of the passage as a whole, Gregor's actions in the third paragraph are likely indicative of

(A) the futility of his daily efforts in the workplace
(B) the severity of an insect's life
(C) the intensity of the problem Gregor is facing
(D) the ease with which Gregor gives up on problems
(E) the hopelessness that characterizes the society of the time

388. The inclusion of Gregor's thoughts in lines 23–28 serves to

(A) belittle Gregor's choice of career
(B) introduce a symbol
(C) reveal Gregor's primary preoccupation
(D) emphasize Gregor's frustration with his transformation into an insect
(E) divert our attention from his physical transformation

389. In context, the word "'stupid'" (35) most likely means

(A) disabled
(B) ignorant
(C) pointless
(D) stuporous
(E) without luxury

390. The primary purpose of the last paragraph is to

(A) display Gregor's vernacular

(B) incite distaste for the main character

(C) critique the modern working world

(D) introduce the problems with Gregor's job

(E) further develop the symbolic meaning of Gregor's metamorphosis

391. The narrative tone is

(A) clear and straightforward

(B) scientific

(C) arabesque

(D) cryptic

(E) passionate

392. In the last sentence of the passage the author seeks to interest us in the subject by

(A) confounding us with Gregor's priority

(B) impressing us with Gregor's fastidiousness

(C) dumbfounding us with Gregor's denial

(D) infuriating us with Gregor's tenacity

(E) distancing us from Gregor's situation

393. Gregor's tone contrasts with the narrator's in its

(A) frustration

(B) didacticism

(C) astonishment

(D) compassion

(E) sentimentality

394. The passage portrays Gregor as all of the following *except*

(A) desiring vengeance against his employer

(B) resentful towards his predicament

(C) sincerely motivated by his fealty to his parents

(D) crippled by a lack of agency

(E) buoyed by impressive fortitude

395. The passage is developed primarily through

(A) an extended metaphor
(B) relationships among characters
(C) a sarcastic tone
(D) complex sentence structure
(E) allusions

CHAPTER 7

Drama

Passage 1. Hannah Cowley, "The Belle's Strategem"

Enter Courtall *singing.*

SAVILLE.   Ha, Courtall!—Bid him keep the horses in motion, and then
enquire at all the chambers round.

                                                           [*Exit servant.*]

What the devil brings you to this part of the town?—Have any of   5
the Long Robes, handsome wives, sisters or chambermaids?

COURTALL.   Perhaps they have;—but I came on a different errand; and, had thy
good fortune brought thee here half an hour sooner, I'd have given
thee such a treat, ha! ha! ha!

SAV.   I'm sorry I miss'd it: what was it?   10

COURT.   I was informed a few days since, that my cousins Fallow were
come to town, and desired earnestly to see me at their lodgings in
Warwick-Court, Holborn. Away drove I, painting them all the way
as so many Hebes. They came from the farthest part of Northumberland, had never been in town, and in course were made up of   15
rusticity, innocence, and beauty.

SAV.   Well!

COURT.   After waiting thirty minutes, during which there was a violent
bustle, in bounced five fallow damsels, four of them maypoles;—
the fifth, Nature, by way of variety, had bent in the Æsop style.—   20
But they all opened at once, like hounds on a fresh scent:—"Oh,
cousin Courtall!—How do you do, cousin Courtall! Lord, cousin,
I am glad you are come! We want you to go with us to the Park,
and the Plays, and the Opera, and Almack's, and all the fine
places!"——The devil, thought I, my dears, may attend you, for I   25
am sure I won't.—However, I heroically stayed an hour with them,
and discovered, the virgins were all come to town with the hopes
of leaving it—Wives:—their heads full of Knight-Baronights,
Fops, and adventures.

SAV.   Well, how did you get off?   30

COURT.   Oh, pleaded a million engagements.——However, conscience
         twitched me; so I breakfasted with them this morning, and
         afterwards 'squired them to the gardens here, as the most private
         place in town; and then took a sorrowful leave, complaining of
         my hard, hard fortune, that obliged me to set off immediately for   35
         Dorsetshire, ha! ha! ha!

SAV.   I congratulate your escape!—Courtall at Almack's, with five
         aukward country cousins! ha! ha! ha!—Why, your existence, as a
         Man of Gallantry, could never have survived it.

COURT.   Death, and fire! had they come to town, like the rustics of the   40
         last age, to see Paul's, the Lions, and the Wax-work—at their
         service;—but the cousins of our days come up Ladies—and, with
         the knowledge they glean from magazines and pocket-books, Fine
         Ladies; laugh at the bashfulness of their grandmothers, and boldly
         demand their *entrées* in the first circles.   45

396. In context, Courtall's phrase "painting them" (13) is best paraphrased as

    (A) disparaging them
    (B) imagining them
    (C) designing them
    (D) creating them
    (E) avoiding them

397. In context, Courtall's use of the term "Hebes" is meant

    (A) positively
    (B) malevolently
    (C) ignorantly
    (D) lovingly
    (E) derisively

398. Which of the following lines provides the biggest contrast to Courtall's initial expectations of his cousins ("They came from . . . beauty")?

    I. "boldly demand their *entrées* in the first circles"

   II. "I breakfasted with them this morning, and afterwards 'squired them to the gardens here"

  III. "five fallow damsels, four of them maypoles"

  (A) I only

  (B) I and II only

  (C) III only

  (D) II and III only

  (E) I and III only

399. In context of the passage as a whole, Courtall's use of the word "fallow" in reference to his cousins can be interpreted to mean both

  (A) virginal and moral

  (B) lustful and uncouth

  (C) spirited and disciplined

  (D) unmarried and rustic

  (E) unrefined and dirty

400. In the passage as a whole, Courtall's cousins are characterized as all of the following *except*

  (A) opportunistic

  (B) country dwellers

  (C) reticent

  (D) aspirational

  (E) audacious

401. All of the following contribute to the characterization of Courtall's cousins *except*

  (A) contrasts

  (B) repetition

  (C) polysyndeton

  (D) simile

  (E) periodic sentences

402. Courtall's statement, "The devil, thought I, my dears, may attend you, for I am sure I won't" reveals his

(A) distaste for sightseeing
(B) disapproval of his cousins' visit
(C) suspicion of his cousins' chosen destinations
(D) condemnation of his cousins' matrimonial ambitions
(E) annoyance of his cousins' arrival

403. It can be interpreted that "Almack's" must be

(A) a casual gathering space for everyone in town
(B) a secluded place in the country
(C) a city place perfect for visitors from the country
(D) an exclusive and refined place
(E) a tourist trap

404. Which of the following phrases suggests insincerity?

  I. "Man of Gallantry"
 II. "my hard, hard fortune"
III. "Fine Ladies"

(A) I only
(B) II only
(C) I and II only
(D) III only
(E) I, II, and III

405. In contrast to the places mentioned in line 24 ("the Park, and the Plays, and the Opera, and Almack's"), the places mentioned in lines 41 ("Paul's . . .") are most likely preferred by Courtall because

(A) they are easy to get to
(B) they have free admission
(C) they are better suited to rustic visitors
(D) they are public places
(E) they are tourist traps

406. An example of Courtall's sincerity is found in which of the following phrases?

(A) "I'd have given thee such a treat"
(B) "I heroically stayed an hour"
(C) "took a sorrowful leave"
(D) "pleaded a million engagements"
(E) "conscience twitched me"

407. Courtall most likely chooses "the most private place in town" because

    (A) he prefers privacy

    (B) he knows his cousins will prefer an isolated setting

    (C) he does not want his cousins to meet men in the city

    (D) he is concerned for his reputation

    (E) he is concerned about safety

408. Based on Courtall's comparison between "cousins of our day" and "rustics of the last age," Courtall has a clear preference for

    (A) social mobility

    (B) "Fine Ladies"

    (C) cosmopolitanism

    (D) sightseeing

    (E) timidity

409. Which of the following best articulates the primary source of humor in the scene?

    (A) Courtall and Saville's joint distaste for rustic girls

    (B) Courtall's commentary on "rustics of the last age"

    (C) Courtall's depictions of his gauche cousins

    (D) the cousins' country background

    (E) Courtall's successful escape

410. Saville's role in the conversation is most similar to that of

    (A) a concerned friend

    (B) a commiserating acquaintance

    (C) an intimidating peer

    (D) a toadying admirer

    (E) a pitying relative

Passage 2. Euripides, *Medea*

MEDEA.   From the house I have come forth, Corinthian ladies, for fear lest
you be blaming me; for well I know that amongst men many by
showing pride have gotten them an ill name and a reputation for
indifference, both those who shun men's gaze and those who move
amid the stranger crowd, and likewise they who choose a quiet   5
walk in life. For there is no just discernment in the eyes of men, for
they, or ever they have surely learnt their neighbour's heart, loathe
him at first sight, though never wronged by him; and so a stranger
most of all should adopt a city's views; nor do I commend that
citizen, who, in the stubbornness of his heart, from churlishness   10
resents the city's will.

But on me hath fallen this unforeseen disaster, and sapped my life;
ruined I am, and long to resign the boon of existence, kind friends,
and die. For he who was all the world to me, as well thou knowest,
hath turned out the worst of men, my own husband. Of all things   15
that have life and sense we women are the most hapless creatures;
first must we buy a husband at a great price, and o'er ourselves a
tyrant set which is an evil worse than the first; and herein lies the
most important issue, whether our choice be good or bad. For
divorce is not honourable to women, nor can we disown our lords.   20
Next must the wife, coming as she does to ways and customs new,
since she hath not learnt the lesson in her home, have a diviner's
eye to see how best to treat the partner of her life. If haply we
perform these tasks with thoroughness and tact, and the husband
live with us, without resenting the yoke, our life is a happy one; if   25
not, 'twere best to die. But when a man is vexed with what he finds
indoors, he goeth forth and rids his soul of its disgust, betaking
him to some friend or comrade of like age; whilst we must needs
regard his single self.

And yet they say we live secure at home, while they are at the   30
wars, with their sorry reasoning, for I would gladly take my stand
in battle array three times o'er, than once give birth. But enough!
this language suits not thee as it does me; thou hast a city here, a
father's house, some joy in life, and friends to share thy thoughts,
but I am destitute, without a city, and therefore scorned by my   35
husband, a captive I from a foreign shore, with no mother, brother,
or kinsman in whom to find a new haven of refuge from this
calamity. Wherefore this one boon and only this I wish to win
from thee, thy silence, if haply I can some way or means devise
to avenge me on my husband for this cruel treatment, and on the   40
man who gave to him his daughter, and on her who is his wife.
For though woman be timorous enough in all else, and as regards

courage, a coward at the mere sight of steel, yet in the moment she finds her honour wronged, no heart is filled with deadlier thoughts than hers.

45

411. According to the first paragraph, Medea has come out of her house

(A) because she is fearless
(B) to criticize the lack of justice among men
(C) to show her pride
(D) to mitigate the people's judgment of her
(E) because she fears the town's wrath

412. According to Medea, why is there "no just discernment in the eyes of men" (6)?

  I. because people hold grudges against those who have wronged them
 II. because people resent the city's will
III. because people form immutable opinions of people they may not even know

(A) I only
(B) II only
(C) III only
(D) I and III only
(E) I, II, and III

413. How does the second paragraph differ from the first?

(A) The first is addressed to women and the second to men.
(B) The first introduces the topic that the second develops.
(C) The first poses a question that the second attempts to answer.
(D) The first is general, and the second is specific.
(E) The first excoriates, and the second justifies.

414. Which of the following best describes the structure of Medea's commentary on womens' lives?

(A) a list of complaints in no logical order
(B) a side-by-side comparison of the experiences of men and women
(C) a thesis statement, followed by reasons, examples, a counter-argument, and a rebuttal
(D) hyperbolic descriptions of hardship tempered by optimism
(E) a catalogue of misfortunes listed in order of importance

415. According to Medea, marital bliss would likely depend mostly on

(A) a woman's skill in pleasing her finicky husband
(B) the support of friends and family
(C) societal approval of divorce
(D) fate
(E) true love

416. What does Medea suggest are the differences between the lives of men and women?

 I. Men have easy access to camaraderie but women do not
 II. Men do not have to suffer as much physical pain as women
 III. Men have authority while women are expected to be servile

(A) I only
(B) I and III only
(C) II only
(D) II and III only
(E) I, II, and III

417. In context, the word "yoke" (25) most likely means

(A) egg
(B) husband
(C) life
(D) situation
(E) burden

418. Medea cites all of the following as examples of women being "hapless" (16) *except*

(A) their forced isolation from "some friend or comrade of like age"
(B) the fact that they have to "buy a husband"
(C) the fact that they have to raise children
(D) their submission to their husbands
(E) the fact that they cannot be unfettered

419. The function of the phrase "And yet" (30) is

(A) it anticipates a counter-argument that will be addressed
(B) it indicates a digression
(C) it signals a rebuttal
(D) it foreshadows a qualifier for the previous argument
(E) it disrupts the flow of the otherwise coherent argument

420. The phrase "But enough!" (32) can best be paraphrased as

(A) Sorry to have wasted your time!
(B) Do not disagree!
(C) Let me get to my main point!
(D) But I digress!
(E) Stop distracting me!

421. Medea distinguishes herself from the other women by

(A) describing their families
(B) comparing their husbands
(C) insisting on their silence
(D) assuming they have all that she lacks
(E) listing what she has that they lack

422. The passage indicates that Medea is seeking vengeance on

(A) her former husband only
(B) her former husband and his new wife
(C) her former husband, his new wife, and his wife's father
(D) her former husband, his new wife, and the king
(E) Corinthian men, specifically her husband

423. According to Medea, when a woman "finds her honour wronged" (44), she

(A) relinquishes her honor
(B) is overcome with resilience
(C) fears the sight of steel
(D) questions her values
(E) is consumed by thoughts of revenge

424. The passage closes on a note of

(A) hopelessness
(B) optimism
(C) cruelty
(D) moralism
(E) indecision

425. Based on the passage, all of the following describe how Medea views herself
except
(A) not responsible for her current predicament
(B) innately courageous
(C) worthy of sympathy
(D) victimized
(E) alienated

Passage 3. Euripides, *Medea*

MEDEA.   Ill hath it been done on every side. Who will gainsay it? but these
things are not in this way, do not yet think it. Still is there a con-
test for those lately married, and to those allied to them no small
affliction. For dost thou think I ever would have fawned upon this
man, if I were not to gain something, or form some plan? I would   5
not even have addressed him. I would not even have touched him
with my hands. But he hath arrived at such a height of folly, as
that, when it was in his power to have crushed my plans, by banishing me from this land, he hath granted me to stay this day in
which three of mine enemies will I put to death, the father, the   10
bride, and my husband. But having in my power many resources
of destruction against them, I know not, my friends, which I shall
first attempt. Whether shall I consume the bridal house with fire,
or force the sharpened sword through her heart having entered the
chamber by stealth where the couch is spread? But one thing is   15
against me; if I should be caught entering the house and prosecut-
ing my plans, by my death I shall afford laughter for my foes. Best
then is it to pursue the straight path, in which I am most skilled,
to take them off by poison. Let it be so. And suppose them dead:
what city will receive me? What hospitable stranger affording a   20
land of safety and a faithful home will protect my person? There
is none. Waiting then yet a little time, if any tower of safety shall
appear to us, I will proceed to this murder in treachery and silence.
But if ill fortune that leaves me without resource force me, I myself
having grasped the sword, although I should die, will kill them,   25
and will rush to the extreme height of daring. For never, I swear
by my mistress whom I revere most of all, and have chosen for my
assistant, Hecate, who dwells in the inmost recesses of my house,
shall any one of them wring my heart with grief with impunity.

Bitter and mournful to them will I make these nuptials, and bitter   30
this alliance, and my flight from this land. But come, spare none
of these sciences in which thou art skilled, Medea, deliberating and
plotting. Proceed to the deed of terror: now is the time of resolution: seest thou what thou art suffering? Ill doth it become thee to
incur ridicule from the race of Sisyphus, and from the nuptials of   35
Jason, who art sprung from a noble father, and from the sun. And
thou art skilled. Besides also we women are, by nature, to good
actions of the least capacity, but the most cunning inventors of
every ill.

426. In the phrase "he hath granted me," (9) "he" refers to

(A) "the father" (10)
(B) "those lately married" (3)
(C) "thou" (4)
(D) "this man" (4–5)
(E) "mine enemies" (10)

427. The lines from "But having in my power …" to "rush to the extreme height of daring," (11–26) consist, in order, of

(A) illogical reasoning and faulty conclusions
(B) questioning, reasoning logically, drawing conclusions, and considering alternatives
(C) hypotheses, theories, experiment, and conclusions
(D) venting irrationally, reasoning rationally, and drawing conclusions
(E) rhetorical questioning, weighing of consequences, and indecision

428. According to Medea's reasoning in lines 11–26, her primary obstacle is indicated by which of the following line(s)?

(A) "laughter for my foes" (17)
(B) "crushed my plans, by banishing me from these lands" (8–9)
(C) "There is none" (21–22)
(D) "Waiting then yet a little time" (22)
(E) "wring my heart with grief and impunity" (29)

429. What does Medea appear to dread most from her foes?

(A) vengeance
(B) pity
(C) emotional control
(D) derision
(E) wrath

430. In context, "Hecate" is best interpreted as

(A) a mentor figure adept in vengeance and treachery
(B) a spiritual manifestation of Medea herself
(C) a mortal friend who will serve as Medea's accomplice
(D) a figurative moral compass who counsels Medea on healthy grieving
(E) a close friend who will do as Medea desires

431. Line 31 marks a change from

(A) Medea addressing herself to addressing others, to garner support
(B) Medea speaking in first person to second person, to rally herself to action
(C) a public address to a private aside, to deliberate further
(D) a private aside to a public address, to declare her plan
(E) deliberation to determination, as a result of guidance from others

432. Medea's tone is

   I. proud
  II. tenacious
 III. rational

(A) I only
(B) I and II only
(C) II and III only
(D) II only
(E) I, II, and III

Passage 4. Zora Neale Hurston and Langston Hughes, "Mule Bone: A Comedy of Negro Life"

(The noise of cane-chewing is heard again. Enter JOE LINDSAY left with a gun over his shoulder and the large leg bone of a mule in the other hand. He approaches the step wearily.)

HAMBO: Well, did you git any partridges, Joe?

JOE: (Resting his gun and seating himself) Nope, but I made de feathers fly.   5

HAMBO: I don't see no birds.

JOE: Oh, the feathers flew off on de birds.

LIGE: I don't see nothin but dat bone. Look lak you done kilt a cow and et 'im raw out in de woods.   10

JOE: Don't y'all know dat hock-bone?

WALTER: How you reckon we gointer know every hock-bone in Orange County sight unseen?

JOE: (Standing the bone up on the floor of the porch) Dis is a hock-bone of Brazzle's ole yaller mule. (General pleased interest. Everybody wants to touch it.)   15

BRAZZLE: (Coming forward) Well, sir! (Takes bone in both hands and looks up and down the length of it) If 'tain't my ole mule! This sho was one hell of a mule, too. He'd fight every inch in front of de plow.... he'd turn over de mowing machine . . . run away wid de wagon... 20
and you better not look like you wanter ride 'im!

LINDSAY: (Laughing) Yeah, I 'member seein' you comin' down de road just so... (He limps wid one hand on his buttocks) one day.

BRAZZLE: Dis mule was so evil he used to try to bite and kick when I'd go in de stable to feed 'im. 25

WALTER: He was too mean to git fat. He was so skinny you could do a week's washing on his ribs for a washboard and hang 'em up on his hip-bones to dry.

LIGE: I member one day, Brazzle, you sent yo' boy to Winter Park after some groceries wid a basket. So here he went down de road ridin 30
dis mule wid dis basket on his arm.... Whut you reckon dat ole contrary male done when he got to dat crooked place in de road going round Park Lake? He turnt right round and went through de handle of dat basket ... wid de boy still up on his back. (General laughter) 35

BRAZZLE: Yeah, he up and died one Sat'day just for spite...but he was too contrary to lay down on his side like a mule orter and die decent. Naw, he made out to lay down on his narrer contracted back and die wid his feets sticking straight up in de air just so. (He gets down on his back and illustrates.) We drug him out to de swamp 40
wid 'im dat way, didn't we, Hambo?

JOE CLARK: I God, Brazzle, we all seen it. Didn't we all go to de draggin' out? More folks went to yo' mule's draggin' out than went to last school closing . . . Bet there ain't been a thing right in mule-hell for four years. 45

HAMBO: Been dat long since he been dead?

CLARK: I God, yes, He died de week after I started to cuttin' dat new ground. (The bone is passing from hand to hand. At last a boy about twelve takes it. He has just walked up and is proudly handling the bone when a woman's voice is heard off stage right.) 50

433. Based on the passage as a whole, Joe most likely expects the others to recognize the bone because

(A) they have extensive experience with hunting
(B) of the mule's infamy
(C) it is physically distinctive
(D) it is a "hock-bone"
(E) of its familiarity

434. Brazzle's response to seeing the bone is developed through

I. exclamation
II. equivocation
III. reflection
IV. physicality

(A) I and II only
(B) I, III, and IV only
(C) III and IV only
(D) I, II, and III only
(E) I, II, III, and IV

435. It can be inferred that the limping alluded to in line 23 is intended as

(A) an example of Lindsay's biting humor
(B) a visual of Brazzle's inadequate strength
(C) evidence of the mule's aversion to carrying a rider
(D) a reference to Joe's valor in successfully hunting the stubborn mule
(E) comic relief in the scene

436. Brazzle uses the word "evil" (24) in which of the following ways?

(A) regretfully
(B) lightheartedly
(C) literally
(D) metaphorically
(E) symbolically

437. Lige's anecdote is notable for all of the following reasons *except*

(A) its visual imagery
(B) the reaction it incites
(C) its shock value
(D) its ability to captivate
(E) its fallibility

438. Joe Clark's assertion in lines 44–45 ("Bet there ain't . . . four years") is best summarized as

(A) no other mules have died since Brazzle's mule died
(B) Brazzle's mule has been sorely missed since he died
(C) Brazzle's mule is probably causing strife in his after-life
(D) things have not been quite right since Brazzle's mule died
(E) Brazzle's mule is where he belongs now

439. Based on the passage as a whole, which of the following is the mule's most defining attribute?

(A) its size and weight
(B) its sense of humor
(C) its cruelty
(D) its intractability
(E) its mode of dying

440. The overall tone of the passage is best described as

(A) historical
(B) comic
(C) dirgelike
(D) ironic
(E) biting

441. Which of the following is most indicative of the characters' fellowship?

(A) "dat hock-bone"
(B) "Brazzle's ole yaller mule"
(C) Brazzle and Hambo's friendship
(D) "de draggin out"
(E) Lige's anecdote

442. The diction and language in the passage can be described as all of the following *except*

(A) vernacular
(B) colloquial
(C) exaggerated
(D) figurative
(E) culturally specific

Passage 5. Sophocles, *Oedipus the King*

OEDIPUS.   My children, fruit of Cadmus' ancient tree
            New springing, wherefore thus with bended knee
            Press ye upon us, laden all with wreaths
            And suppliant branches? And the city breathes
            Heavy with incense, heavy with dim prayer   5
            And shrieks to affright the Slayer.—Children, care
            For this so moves me, I have scorned withal
            Message or writing: seeing 'tis I ye call,
            'Tis I am come, world-honoured Oedipus.

            Old Man, do thou declare—the rest have thus   10
            Their champion—in what mood stand ye so still,
            In dread or sure hope? Know ye not, my will
            Is yours for aid 'gainst all? Stern were indeed
            The heart that felt not for so dire a need.

PRIEST.   O Oedipus, who holdest in thy hand   15
            My city, thou canst see what ages stand
            At these thine altars; some whose little wing
            Scarce flieth yet, and some with long living
            O'erburdened; priests, as I of Zeus am priest,
            And chosen youths: and wailing hath not ceased   20
            Of thousands in the market-place, and by
            Athena's two-fold temples and the dry
            Ash of Ismênus' portent-breathing shore.

            For all our ship, thou see'st, is weak and sore
            Shaken with storms, and no more lighteneth   25
            Her head above the waves whose trough is death.
            She wasteth in the fruitless buds of earth,
            In parchèd herds and travail without birth
            Of dying women: yea, and midst of it
            A burning and a loathly god hath lit   30
            Sudden, and sweeps our land, this Plague of power;
            Till Cadmus' house grows empty, hour by hour,
            And Hell's house rich with steam of tears and blood.

            O King, not God indeed nor peer to God
            We deem thee, that we kneel before thine hearth,   35
            Children and old men, praying; but of earth
            A thing consummate by thy star confessed
            Thou walkest and by converse with the blest;
            Who came to Thebes so swift, and swept away
            The Sphinx's song, the tribute of dismay,   40

That all were bowed beneath, and made us free.
A stranger, thou, naught knowing more than we,
Nor taught of any man, but by God's breath
Filled, thou didst raise our life. So the world saith;
So we say.   45

Therefore now, O Lord and Chief,
We come to thee again; we lay our grief
On thy head, if thou find us not some aid.

443. The passage begins with

    (A) a command
    (B) a rhetorical question
    (C) an invocation
    (D) an inquiry
    (E) an aside

444. In context, the word "us" (3) refers to

    (A) Oedipus
    (B) Cadmus
    (C) the tree
    (D) the land's people
    (E) the rulers

445. In lines 4–6, personification is used to present the city as

    (A) macabre
    (B) diabolical
    (C) desperate
    (D) alive
    (E) pious

446. In lines 7–9 and lines 12–14, Oedipus characterizes himself as

    I. venerable
    II. concerned primarily for his citizens
    III. preoccupied

    (A) I only
    (B) II only
    (C) I and II only
    (D) I and III only
    (E) I, II, and III

447. The passage implies that Oedipus has decided to appear in person because

    (A) it is his obligation as King
    (B) it is the custom of the time
    (C) he was summoned
    (D) he is deeply concerned for his people
    (E) he is concerned for his image

448. In line 7, "this" refers to

    (A) breathing, shrieks, and prayer
    (B) care
    (C) the Slayer
    (D) the city
    (E) children

449. The people appeal to Oedipus for help primarily because

    (A) he is filled with God's breath
    (B) he has rescued them previously
    (C) he is a peer to God
    (D) he knows more than they know
    (E) rumors of his accomplishments have reached them

450. According to the priest, the city has been harmed by

    (A) a shipwreck
    (B) a disease
    (C) dying women
    (D) deadly waves
    (E) a ruthless scourge

451. The metaphor in lines 24–26

    (A) compares a ship to the city and the sea to death
    (B) emphasizes the futility of fighting back
    (C) highlights the people's resilience
    (D) contrasts life and death
    (E) compares a ship to the priest; the sea to the gods

452. The word "house" in lines 32 and 33 functions primarily as

    (A) a metaphor that compares people to furniture
    (B) a literal description of where the people are located
    (C) part of an internal rhyme that contributes to the mournful tone
    (D) a metaphor that emphasizes the depths of the people's victimization
    (E) a symbol of both heaven and hell

453. In context, "we" (35) refers to

  (A) the priest and his friends
  (B) all the citizens
  (C) all men
  (D) the young and senescent
  (E) the clergy

454. Which of the following provides the best summary of the priest's final lines?

  (A) We have faith in your ability to bring us aid.
  (B) Please liberate us as you have done before.
  (C) You will be responsible if our turmoil does not end.
  (D) Your help is invaluable to us.
  (E) We will be utterly disappointed in you if you do not provide aid.

455. The priest's tone differs from Oedipus's in that it is

  (A) grave as opposed to compassionate
  (B) bitter as opposed to reverent
  (C) pitiful as opposed to patriotic
  (D) elegiac as opposed to remorseful
  (E) laudatory as opposed to loving

456. We can infer from the passage that Cadmus (1, 32) is

  (A) the founder of Thebes
  (B) the current king
  (C) their God
  (D) the city's name
  (E) an ancient tree

Expository Prose

Passage 1. Charles Darwin, *On the Origin of Species*

I have now recapitulated the chief facts and considerations which have thoroughly convinced me that species have been modified, during a long course of descent, by the preservation or the natural selection of many successive slight favourable variations. I cannot believe that a false theory would explain, as it seems to me that the theory of natural selection does explain, the several large classes of facts above specified. I see no good reason why the views given in this volume should shock the religious feelings of any one. A celebrated author and divine has written to me that "he has gradually learnt to see that it is just as noble a conception of the Deity to believe that He created a few original forms capable of self-development into other and needful forms, as to believe that He required a fresh act of creation to supply the voids caused by the action of His laws."

Why, it may be asked, have all the most eminent living naturalists and geologists rejected this view of the mutability of species? It cannot be asserted that organic beings in a state of nature are subject to no variation; it cannot be proved that the amount of variation in the course of long ages is a limited quantity; no clear distinction has been, or can be, drawn between species and well-marked varieties. It cannot be maintained that species when intercrossed are invariably sterile, and varieties invariably fertile; or that sterility is a special endowment and sign of creation. The belief that species were immutable productions was almost unavoidable as long as the history of the world was thought to be of short duration; and now that we have acquired some idea of the lapse of time, we are too apt to assume, without proof, that the geological record is so perfect that it would have afforded us plain evidence of the mutation of species, if they had undergone mutation.

But the chief cause of our natural unwillingness to admit that one species has given birth to other and distinct species, is that we are always slow in admitting any great change of which we do not see the intermediate steps. The difficulty is the same as that felt by so many geologists, when Lyell first insisted that long lines of inland cliffs had been formed, and great valleys excavated, by the slow action of the coast-waves. The mind cannot possibly grasp the full meaning of the term of a hundred million years; it cannot add up and perceive the full effects of many slight variations, accumulated during an almost infinite number of generations.

457. The first sentence in this passage does which of the following?

    (A) summarizes points made in previous paragraphs
    (B) proves the writer's main point
    (C) provides evidence of previous points
    (D) emphasizes the writer's authority
    (E) provides a counterargument to opponents' points

458. The "false theory" (4) most likely refers to

    (A) the immutability of species
    (B) divine intervention
    (C) spontaneous generation
    (D) natural selection
    (E) gaps in the geological record

459. It can be inferred from the question starting in line 12 that the writer

    (A) discounts the opinion of geologists
    (B) agrees with the opinion of geologists
    (C) does not respect the opinion of geologists
    (D) understands the opinion of geologists
    (E) defers to the opinion of geologists

460. The word "mutability" (13) most nearly means

    (A) variability
    (B) silence
    (C) persistence
    (D) life
    (E) death

461. In order to emphasize his point of view, the author uses which of the following devices in lines 13–19?

    (A) vivid imagery
    (B) uncommon verbs
    (C) hyperbole
    (D) appeal to emotion
    (E) anaphora

462. The tone of the passage is

(A) pedantic
(B) droll
(C) exasperated
(D) caustic
(E) expository

463. According to the passage, what are we "too apt to assume" (21)?

(A) the omniscience of God
(B) the origin of the species will remain contestable
(C) the mutability of the species would be reflected in easily observable evidence
(D) the immutability of the species would be reflected in easily observable evidence
(E) the history of the world is quite short

464. According to the passage, natural selection is all of the following *except*

(A) theoretical
(B) falsifiable
(C) directly observable
(D) compatible with religion
(E) coherent

465. In lines 29–30, the writer asserts that the "mind cannot possibly grasp the full meaning of the term of a hundred million years," in large part because

   I. few variations are slight
  II. changes accumulate over generations
 III. human perception is limited

(A) I only
(B) III only
(C) I and III only
(D) I, II, and III
(E) II and III only

466. The writer assumes that the reader's attitude toward the theory of natural selection is one of

(A) incredulity
(B) accordance
(C) refraction
(D) skepticism
(E) intolerance

467. The references to "a celebrated author and divine" and "Lyell" are intended to

(A) show agreement with the author's theory
(B) interrogate the claims made in the passage
(C) highlight the inconsistencies of opposing points of view
(D) assuage common skepticism and hesitance about the theory
(E) expose weaknesses in the argument, which are subsequently addressed

Passage 2. Thomas Hobbes, *Leviathan*

Whatsoever therefore is consequent to a time of Warre, where every man is Enemy to every man; the same is consequent to the time, wherein men live without other security, than what their own strength, and their own invention shall furnish them withall. In such condition, there is no place for Industry; because the fruit thereof is uncertain; and consequently no Culture of the Earth; no   5
Navigation, nor use of the commodities that may be imported by Sea; no commodious Building; no Instruments of moving, and removing such things as require much force; no Knowledge of the face of the Earth; no account of Time; no Arts; no Letters; no Society; and which is worst of all, continuall feare, and danger of violent death; And the life of man, solitary, poore, nasty, brutish, and short.   10

It may seem strange to some man, that has not well weighed these things; that Nature should thus dissociate, and render men apt to invade, and destroy one another: and he may therefore, not trusting to this Inference, made from the Passions, desire perhaps to have the same confirmed by Experience. Let him therefore consider with himselfe, when taking a journey, he armes himselfe, and seeks   15
to go well accompanied; when going to sleep, he locks his dores; when even in his house he locks his chests; and this when he knows there bee Lawes, and publike Officers, armed, to revenge all injuries shall bee done him; what opinion he has of his fellow subjects, when he rides armed; of his fellow Citizens, when he locks his dores; and of his children, and servants, when he locks his chests. Does he not   20
there as much accuse mankind by his actions, as I do by my words? But neither of us accuse mans nature in it. The Desires, and other Passions of man, are in themselves no Sin. No more are the Actions, that proceed from those Passions, till they know a Law that forbids them; which till Lawes be made they cannot know: nor can any Law be made, till they have agreed upon the Person that shall make it.   25

It may peradventure be thought, there was never such a time, nor condition of warre as this; and I believe it was never generally so, over all the world: but there are many places, where they live so now. For the savage people in many places of America, except the government of small Families, the concord whereof dependeth on naturall lust, have no government at all; and live at this day in that 30 brutish manner, as I said before. Howsoever, it may be perceived what manner of life there would be, where there were no common Power to feare; by the manner of life, which men that have formerly lived under a peacefull government, use to degenerate into, in a civill Warre.

But though there had never been any time, wherein particular men were in 35 a condition of warre one against another; yet in all times, Kings, and persons of Soveraigne authority, because of their Independency, are in continuall jealousies, and in the state and posture of Gladiators; having their weapons pointing, and their eyes fixed on one another; that is, their Forts, Garrisons, and Guns upon the Frontiers of their Kingdomes; and continuall Spyes upon their neighbours; 40 which is a posture of War. But because they uphold thereby, the Industry of their Subjects; there does not follow from it, that misery, which accompanies the Liberty of particular men.

468. The "condition" referred to in line 4 is one in which

    I.   there is no purpose to work
   II. men are independent
 III. the state is tyrannical

(A) I only
(B) III only
(C) I and II only
(D) II and III only
(E) I, II, and III

469. The "some man" in line 11 refers to

(A) a known opponent
(B) the writer's alter ego
(C) the implied audience
(D) a hypothetical objector
(E) the writer's patron

470. The writer exhorts "some man" to "consider with himselfe" (11–15)

(A) his own experiences that will call into question that which he views as strange

(B) the writer's experiences that will assuage the man's skepticism

(C) incontrovertible evidence of "these things" (11)

(D) his own hypocrisy and ignorance

(E) the benefits provided by an absolute monarch

471. The argument that the writer makes in lines 11–17 is best described as

(A) apodictic

(B) empirical

(C) a priori

(D) deductive

(E) ad absurdum

472. The writer asserts in lines 22–23 that harmful "Desires" and "Actions" of man are "no Sin" under the following conditions *except*

(A) ignorance of the law

(B) a state of anarchy

(C) the installment of a legitimate sovereign

(D) the outbreak of civil war

(E) forgiveness from the church

473. The purpose of the first sentence of the second and third paragraphs is to

(A) anticipate counterarguments

(B) demonstrate the writer's skepticism

(C) undermine authoritative accounts

(D) cast doubt on the argument

(E) establish an ironic tone

474. In the third paragraph of the passage, the writer mentions Native Americans as an example of

(A) the effectiveness of small government

(B) people in an unnatural state

(C) the ideal of the noble savage

(D) people lacking an authority

(E) a society that values family

475. In the last paragraph of the passage, the writer asserts that "Kings" are "in the state and posture of Gladiators," and their "Subjects" are not

(A) independent
(B) under scrutiny
(C) protected
(D) neighborly
(E) productive

476. The purpose of the passage as a whole is to

(A) elaborate on the natural state of man
(B) legitimize absolute monarchy
(C) cast aspersions on native savages
(D) question the reader's integrity
(E) argue against the value of liberty

477. It can be inferred from the passage that the writer's attitude toward humanity is most likely one of

(A) aplomb
(B) cynicism
(C) contempt
(D) idealism
(E) realism

478. According to the passage, "a time of Warre" (1) and "the Liberty of particular men" (42–43) share all of the following features *except*

(A) an atmosphere of fear
(B) a motivation for industry
(C) an absence of knowledge
(D) constraints on movement
(E) a general state of misery

Passage 3. Friedrich Nietzsche, *Beyond Good and Evil* (Translated by Helen Zimmern)

Inasmuch as in all ages, as long as mankind has existed, there have also been human herds (family alliances, communities, tribes, peoples, states, churches), and always a great number who obey in proportion to the small number who command—in view, therefore, of the fact that obedience has been most practiced and fostered among mankind hitherto, one may reasonably suppose that, gener- 5 ally speaking, the need thereof is now innate in every one, as a kind of FORMAL CONSCIENCE which gives the command "Thou shalt unconditionally do something, unconditionally refrain from something," in short, "Thou shalt." This need tries to satisfy itself and to fill its form with a content, according to its strength, impatience, and eagerness, it at once seizes as an omnivorous appetite 10 with little selection, and accepts whatever is shouted into its ear by all sorts of commanders—parents, teachers, laws, class prejudices, or public opinion. The extraordinary limitation of human development, the hesitation, protractedness, frequent retrogression, and turning thereof, is attributable to the fact that the herd-instinct of obedience is transmitted best, and at the cost of the art of com- 15 mand. If one imagine this instinct increasing to its greatest extent, commanders and independent individuals will finally be lacking altogether, or they will suffer inwardly from a bad conscience, and will have to impose a deception on themselves in the first place in order to be able to command just as if they also were only obeying. This condition of things actually exists in Europe at present—I 20 call it the moral hypocrisy of the commanding class. They know no other way of protecting themselves from their bad conscience than by playing the role of executors of older and higher orders (of predecessors, of the constitution, of justice, of the law, or of God himself), or they even justify themselves by max- ims from the current opinions of the herd, as "first servants of their people," or 25 "instruments of the public weal." On the other hand, the gregarious European man nowadays assumes an air as if he were the only kind of man that is allow- able, he glorifies his qualities, such as public spirit, kindness, deference, industry, temperance, modesty, indulgence, sympathy, by virtue of which he is gentle, endurable, and useful to the herd, as the peculiarly human virtues. In cases, 30 however, where it is believed that the leader and bell-wether cannot be dispensed with, attempt after attempt is made nowadays to replace commanders by the summing together of clever gregarious men. All representative constitutions, for example, are of this origin. In spite of all, what a blessing, what a deliverance from a weight becoming unendurable, is the appearance of an absolute ruler for 35 these gregarious Europeans—of this fact the effect of the appearance of Napoleon was the last great proof. The history of the influence of Napoleon is almost the history of the higher happiness to which the entire century has attained in its worthiest individuals and periods.

479. According to the passage, the most salient feature of "formal conscience" (6–7) is that

(A) its ends justify its means
(B) specific precepts are inconsequential
(C) its appetite is easily sated
(D) it contributes to sound rule
(E) prohibitions are often unconditional

480. The writer uses the word "something" (8) in order to

(A) emphasize the wide applicability of his point
(B) obscure a potential flaw in his reasoning
(C) communicate the irrelevance of being specific in this context
(D) remain general about a complex point
(E) show the ludicrous nature of the commands people must follow

481. The simile in line 10 compares

(A) a need to an appetite
(B) a desire to satisfy to a desire to devour
(C) a follower to an omnivore
(D) content to an appetite
(E) a need to a content

482. According to the writer, the inevitable consequence of the "herd-instinct of obedience" (15) is

(A) a dearth of strong leadership
(B) constitutional representation
(C) tyrants such as Napoleon
(D) persistent class conflict
(E) cohesive public opinion

483. According to the passage, human herds are all of the following *except*

(A) reprehensible
(B) obdurate
(C) autocratic
(D) self-perpetuating
(E) transitory

484. The expression "moral hypocrisy of the commanding class" (21) refers to

(A) leaders calling leadership a form of service
(B) the illegitimacy of the divine right of kings
(C) rulers taking advantage of their position
(D) the notion that might makes right
(E) herds lacking the need for guidance

485. According to the writer, European leaders "[protect] themselves from their bad conscience" (22) by all of the following *except*

(A) celebrating self-effacing virtues
(B) embracing public opinion
(C) vilifying rulers such as Napoleon
(D) encouraging collegiality
(E) respecting consensus

486. The writer's tone when describing democratic institutions can best be stated as

(A) apathetic
(B) idealistic
(C) sanguine
(D) skeptical
(E) sarcastic

487. The writer mentions Napoleon (36) as an example of

(A) herd instinct gone awry
(B) command that requires no justification
(C) the corrupting influence of power
(D) a check on democratic institutions
(E) the difficulty in serving the common good

488. The tone of the passage is

(A) ironic
(B) apologetic
(C) apodictic
(D) polemical
(E) expository

489. The purpose of the passage as a whole is to

(A) justify the desire to disobey
(B) expose the hypocrisy of leaders
(C) celebrate the power of the collective
(D) criticize group behavior
(E) make a case against democracy

Passage 4. Zhuangzi

His cook was cutting up an ox for the ruler Wen Hui. Whenever he applied his hand, leaned forward with his shoulder, planted his foot, and employed the pressure of his knee, in the audible ripping off of the skin, and slicing operation of the knife, the sounds were all in regular cadence. Movements and sounds proceeded as in the dance of "the Mulberry Forest" and the blended notes of "the King Shou." 5

The ruler said, "Ah! Admirable! That your art should have become so perfect!"

(Having finished his operation), the cook laid down his knife, and replied to the remark, "What your servant loves is the method of the Dao, something 10 in advance of any art. When I first began to cut up an ox, I saw nothing but the (entire) carcass. After three years I ceased to see it as a whole. Now I deal with it in a spirit-like manner, and do not look at it with my eyes. The use of my senses is discarded, and my spirit acts as it wills. Observing the natural lines, (my knife) slips through the great crevices and slides through the great cavities, tak- 15 ing advantage of the facilities thus presented. My art avoids the ligaments and tendons, and much more the great bones. A good cook changes his knife every year; (it may have been injured) in cutting—an ordinary cook changes his every month—(it may have been) broken. Now my knife has been in use for nineteen years; it has cut up several thousand oxen, and yet its edge is as sharp as if it 20 had newly come from the whetstone. There are the interstices of the joints, and the edge of the knife has no (appreciable) thickness; when that which is so thin enters where the interstice is, how easily it moves along! The blade has more than room enough. Nevertheless, whenever I come to a complicated joint, and see that there will be some difficulty, I proceed attentively and with caution, not allowing 25 my eyes to wander from the place, and moving my hand slowly. Then by a very slight movement of the knife, the part is quickly separated, and drops like (a clod of) earth to the ground. Then standing up with the knife in my hand, I look all round, and in a leisurely manner, with an air of satisfaction, wipe it clean, and put it in its sheath." 30

The ruler Wen Hui said, "Excellent! I have heard the words of my cook, and learned from them the nourishment of (our) life."

490. Based on the ruler Wen Hui's responses to the cook, we can infer that Wen Hui is

(A) intrusive
(B) tolerant
(C) enlightened
(D) sarcastic
(E) permissive

491. According to the cook, the "method of the Dao" is "in advance of any art" (10–11) because

(A) it is entirely mechanistic
(B) it transcends conscious effort
(C) it is in harmony with the ruler
(D) it requires only simple technology
(E) it makes work easier

492. When the cook says that he deals with the ox carcass "in a spirit-like manner" (13), the reader can infer that

(A) he goes into a hypnotic trance
(B) his mastery is unconscious
(C) he is in a state of heightened sensitivity
(D) he defers to the ruler's wishes
(E) he relies entirely on instinct

493. In line 19, the cook claims that he has had no need to replace his knife for nineteen years because

(A) the knife has magical properties
(B) he sharpens the knife regularly
(C) he leaves the carcasses intact
(D) his method prevents blunting
(E) he always proceeds slowly

494. Through comparisons between himself and other cooks, the cook in the passage views himself as

  I. unparalleled
 II. dexterous
III. plodding

(A) I only
(B) I and II only
(C) II and III only
(D) I and III only
(E) I, II, and III

495. The cook's description of his final action ("Then standing up ... sheath") emphasizes

(A) his effortless success
(B) the simplicity with which he views his task
(C) the pride he takes in his carefully practiced endeavor
(D) his expectation that others are watching and admiring
(E) his arrogance over his exceptional skill

496. The cook's attitude toward the ox is best described as

(A) irreverent
(B) venerating
(C) religious
(D) animistic
(E) courteous

497. The passage makes use of all of the following *except*

(A) allegory
(B) simile
(C) sarcasm
(D) hyperbole
(E) exclamation

498. According to the passage, the cook's method is none of the following *except*

(A) ambidextrous
(B) overwrought
(C) maladroit
(D) fractious
(E) meticulous

499. The tone of the passage is

(A) insincere
(B) sincere
(C) ironic
(D) instructive
(E) ecstatic

500. The writer's attitude toward butchering meat is best interpreted as one of

(A) caution
(B) indifference
(C) pragmatism
(D) avidity
(E) aversion

ANSWERS

Chapter 1: British Poetry

Passage 1. Elizabeth Barrett Browning, "Sonnet 32"

1. (D) While the sun is equated with the excitement of their "oath" of love, the speaker mentions the moon only in the context of hoping for its arrival because of its power to "slacken all those bonds which seemed too soon/ And quickly tied to make a lasting troth." The moon is not blocked or hindered (A), it is not menacing or threatening (C), and it is not calculating (intending harm, strategizing) (E). A moon is generally associated with brightness so it cannot be said to be gloomy, especially in this context since the speaker anticipates its arrival (B). The context of the poem reveals that the moon is longed for because of its ability to loosen the bonds/promises that may have been made only in haste and not in truth.

2. (C) If read as prose, the sentence in lines 1–4 says, "The first time that the sun rose on thine oath to love me, I looked forward to the moon to slacken all those bonds which seemed too soon and quickly tied to make a lasting troth." The clause "which seemed too soon and quickly tied" is referring to "those bonds," which themselves refer to "thine oath to love me." The "lasting troth" is not quickly tied; rather, the speaker is indicating that she worries a lasting troth (truth, loyalty) may not be realistic, given how hastily the oath was made.

3. (A) The speaker communicates her initial worry that her partner declared his oath of love so rashly that he would be likely to change his mind. By using the word "quick" in two different contexts, she draws a parallel between being quick to love or to profess love and quick to change one's mind drastically (loathe). Fickle means "inconstant, wavering, vacillating."

4. (E) The speaker's initial assumption is signaled by the phrase, "The first time …" (1). She goes on to say that she "thought" that "Quick-loving hearts … may quickly loath" and that, "looking on myself, I seemed not one/ For such man's love." The speaker's initial fear is that her partner will realize she is not worthy of his love and that he may "Quickly loathe" her. Line 11 reveals a contrast to this initial thought. She realizes that she "placed a wrong on" her partner, that she underestimated his potential to love someone less masterful than himself.

5. (A) The speaker's **simile** is in lines 6–10: "And looking on myself, I seemed not one/ For such man's love;–more like an out-of-tune/ Worn viol, a good singer would be wroth/ To spoil his song with, and which, snatched in haste,/ Is laid down at the first ill-sounding note." She compares herself ("myself," "I") to an out-of-tune instrument to illustrate her own insecurity about being worthy of her partner's love and attention. She worries that her partner, compared in the simile to "a good singer," would lay down the out-of-tune instrument (herself) that was "snatched in haste" (he professed his love too quickly, without careful consideration) at the "first ill-sounding note" (evidence of her inadequacies).

6. (B) In the **simile** discussed in questions 4 and 5, the "good singer" is the speaker's mate, who snatches (quickly grabs) an out-of-tune instrument (the speaker). She worries he will put her down once she "spoils his song." In this comparison, the good singer's song would then be symbolic of what she fears she is not worthy of—his estimable love.

7. (A) In the **simile** discussed in questions 4 and 5, the "ill-sounding note" is symbolic of the speaker's insecurity about being worthy of her impressive mate's love. This idea is clearly expressed in lines 6–7: "I seemed not one/ For such man's love!"

8. (E) The speaker never explicitly charges her mate with being disingenuous in his oath to love her (B); rather, she merely articulates her worry that his love may quickly change to "loathe." (C) is incorrect because the speaker does not ascribe any blame solely to herself for rushing into an oath. (D) is incorrect because the tone of the word "procrastinate" implies delaying due to indifference or apathy. She does not wish they delayed their oath out of disinterest. (A) is incorrect because the speaker implies that her own vows were genuine, as she views her mate as a "good singer" whom she may not be worthy of. The speaker does explicitly express the wish for the oath and bonds that were "too soon/ And quickly tied" to be "slackened" by the moon so that the "Quick-loving hearts" would not "quickly loathe" and that the good singer's song would not be spoiled by an ill-sounding instrument that was grabbed in haste. Her worry about the effects of their rash commitment would have been assuaged if their commitment had been made over time.

9. (D) In these lines, the speaker explains that her initial concerns about her and her mate's "quickly tied" bonds were misguided because she "placed a wrong on *thee* [her mate]," meaning she wrongly assumed he, like the "good singer" in the **simile**, would quickly put down the inadequate instrument (herself) once he realized it was not as it seemed. She goes on to explain her reasoning for why she was initially wrong: "For perfect strains (a good song, true love) may float/ 'Neath master-hands (like her mate's), from instruments defaced,–(the speaker)/ And great souls (her mate), at one stroke (a quickly-tied bond), may do and dote (give genuine love)." When she says she placed a wrong on her addressee, she is saying she underestimated his potential for being genuine and loyal, despite his speedy oath. She now realizes that "master-hands" like his have the ability to make perfect music (true love) even with inadequate instruments (herself). (A) is incorrect because she states that she was not wrong about her views of herself: "I did not wrong myself so, but I placed/ A wrong on *thee*."

10. (B) The repeated references to the comparisons of her mate to a good singer, his love to a song, and herself to an out-of-tune viol are instrumental in communicating the poem's central idea that a strong oath of love can be made without long deliberation and that a genuinely loving mate is likely to remain steadfast in his love for his partner, regardless of her own insecurities or inadequacies. The comparison is first signaled by the word "like" in line 7, indicating it is a **simile**, but the comparison is drawn out for a few more lines and then picked up again in the final lines of the poem, making it an **extended metaphor**.

11. (A) The speaker does refer to her initial worries and fear (C) but this fear is later revealed to be misplaced and "wrong." The question asks us to identify what the speaker experiences <u>throughout</u> the poem, and reflection (A) is the speaker's state of mind for all 14 lines. In lines 1–10, she thinks back to "The first time" their oath was made and reflects on her reaction and emotions at that time. She moves on in line 11 to reflect on her misguided assumption.

Passage 2. Gerard Manley Hopkins, "God's Grandeur"

12. (A) The word "It" refers to "the grandeur of God" from line 1. Lines 2 and 3 elaborate on this grandeur, describing it as flaming and gathering. The other answers mention nouns that are merely stated nearby but are not the nouns that the speaker is describing as flaming and gathering to a greatness.

13. (A) The abundance of **alliteration** in the first three lines ("*g*randeur of *G*od," "*g*athers to a *g*reatness," "*fl*ame out like *sh*ining from *sh*ook *f*oil," "*oo*ze and *oi*l") creates a mellifluous (soothing) sound to mirror the praise the speaker feels for "God's grandeur." This sound changes, however, in the fourth line, where alliteration is mixed with **assonance** and different vowel sounds to create a cacophonous (harsh) and confusing sound, making the clause actually difficult to pronounce: "Why do men then now not reck his rod?" Alliteration is evident in "*n*ow *n*ot" and "*r*eck his *r*od." This otherwise soothing alliteration is then marred (spoiled) by the combination of assonance ("m*e*n th*e*n") and the similar but different sounds of "reck and rod."

14. (D) The words in line 4 are difficult to pronounce (see question 13) perhaps because they are describing behavior of men that the speaker finds hard to understand. After all, he *is* asking a question: How is it that men do not acknowledge God's magnificent power? He finds their obliviousness confusing and unwarranted considering how magnificent he thinks God is.

15. (B) The speaker repeats that "Generations have trod, have trod, have trod." The following clauses further clarify his point: "And all is seared with trade; bleared and smeared with toil;/ And wears man's smudge and shares man's smell: the soil/ Is bare now, nor can foot feel, being shod." The speaker is describing the numbing and tiring effects that modern industry, production, and technology have had on man. The "soil," which represents the natural world created by "God's grandeur," is "bare" because of man's folly. The repetition of "trod" emphasizes the repeated mistakes of man. Humanity persists habitually (inexorably) in its mistaken path rather than progressing. (E) does not work because the dissatisfaction is the speaker's and not necessarily man's. (D) does not work because the speaker's repetition indicates that man continues to prefer industry over God; this is not temporary. (A) and (E) are opposites of the answer.

16. (E) Line 6 contains **internal rhyme** (I) ("bleared" rhymes with "seared" *within* the same line), as does line 7 ("wears" rhymes with "shares"). Line 6 contains a **parallel structure** (II) ("seared with" and "smeared with") as does line 7 ("wears man's" and "shares man's"). Line 6 contains negative **imagery** (III) with words like "seared," "bleared," and "smeared with toil." Line 7 also contains negative sensory imagery with words like "smudge" and "smell." The reader can smell the damaging industry of man all over the Earth.

17. (C) The **alliteration** in the first three lines (see question 13) helps emphasize the speaker's admiration for and wonder at "God's grandeur." He is in awe (C) of God's "shining," oozing, great, flaming grandeur. This tone changes, however, in the next four lines, when the speaker focuses more on man's obliviousness to God's magnificence (see question 15).

Man has toiled, "trod," worked in industry, and neglected God and the natural world. As a result, he is "seared with trade; bleared, smeared with toil." He smells and cannot feel his feet on the soil. The tone here is dirgelike (like a funeral song) because there is a steady rhythm to the descriptions of man's persistent and injurious mistakes. (E) is a close answer, but the tone of lines 4–8 is not as much pitiful as it is reproachful (disapproving, critical) and dirgelike.

18. (C) A **sonnet** always contains 14 lines, but a Shakespearean sonnet will end in a **couplet** (the last two lines will have end rhymes). This sonnet does not end in a couplet, so it must be a Petrarchan sonnet. Further evidence is that there is a clear change from the first eight lines to the last six lines (the separation of the **octave** from the **sestet**). Questions that ask for identification of a poetic form are rare on the exam, but they occasionally appear. The Shakespearean sonnet is perhaps the most recognizable form for students at this level.

19. (E) Alliteration is abundant in the opening three lines (see question 13) and dominates again in the final six lines. In the opening lines, the alliteration coincides with the grand diction emphasizing God's brilliance, so when the alliteration returns in the final six lines, so does the description of God's grandeur, his eminence—I. The speaker also conveys confidence—II—in the resilience of nature: "for all this [man's desecration of the soil and earth], nature is never spent." The speaker is assured that God still loves and protects the world "with warm breast and with ah! bright wings." In these lines, the alliteration also coincides with the portrayal of God as in harmony with the world. God loves and protects the world, so "nature is never spent." The mellifluous (soothing) sounds of the alliteration in "with warm breast and with ah! bright wings" complement the harmonious partnership between God and the world—III.

20. (D) The first eight lines express dismay at why men do not acknowledge God's power when he, in fact, is so grand. The speaker actually asks the same question in line 4 after detailing how magnificent God is. The final six lines, however, provide some reassurance that even though men have spoiled and damaged the earth with their trodding and smearing and toil, God will still protect and care for the world. "[N]ature is never spent ... Because the Holy Ghost over the bent/ World broods with warm breast and with ah! bright wings." In these last six lines God is not portrayed as any less powerful than in the opening lines (B); the focus is not on man; it is still on God (C); the speaker is not skeptical; he is in awe of God's generosity and love (E). The sound created by the **assonance** and **alliteration** is similar to the sounds in the opening three lines (A) (see question 13).

21. (C) The word "broods" refers to the Holy Ghost from line 13, which is bent over the world with its "warm breast" and "bright wings." The diction and **imagery** indicate a paternal, or fatherly, tone to the word "broods." The word also conjures an image of a hen sitting on her eggs, incubating and protecting them. While "broods" can also mean dwelling on an issue, obsessing over a subject with morbid persistence, making (A) and (B) tempting choices, the surrounding details do not support this meaning.

22. (D) The overall theme of the poem can be expressed most closely by the phrase "nature is never spent" because this phrase encompasses the **octave**, in which the speaker explains that man has "spent" nature (he has toiled and emptied the soil, smeared and bleared with his modern industry and production), and the sestet, which explains that even though man has done this, nature is never actually ruined because God protects the world. The other answer choices encompass only parts of the poem's message and not the entire theme.

23. (B) By the close of the poem, the speaker is very reassured that God will protect and nurture the world despite the damage man has done with his modern industry and production. The **sestet** begins with "And for all this [damage caused by man] nature is never spent." We can still see "the dearest freshness" deep down inside things "[b]ecause the Holy Ghost [God] over the bent/ World broods with warm breast and with ah! bright wings." The exclamation point especially shows the speaker's unrestrained awe at God's munificence (generosity). There are no details to suggest that the hope expressed by the speaker is qualified or restrained (D). He is in wonder at God's power, but bemusement implies that he is perplexed by it (A). He is definitely not criticizing God (E).

Passage 3. Andrew Marvell, "To His Coy Mistress"

24. (D) The first stanza contains verbs like "had," "would," and "should" to indicate conditional and hypothetical situations and actions. The speaker says that he *would* be more than willing to be patient and wait centuries for his addressee to "show her heart," if they actually had that much time (1).

25. (E) Throughout the first stanza, the speaker is making the point to his addressee that if there were plenty of time, it would be fine to delay their physical expressions of love. Since they do not, however, actually have a "hundred years" (13), he implies that the addressee's modesty ("coyness," hesitance, prudery, shyness) is a crime.

26. (A) The speaker flatters his addressee when he imagines her by the Indian Ganges finding rubies. He places her in (what is to them) an exotic locale with connotations of rare riches while he is back in England (the Humber). He intends to impress her with his intelligence by making biblical references to the Flood and the Jews. The point of this stanza is to compliment her and make her think she would be worth waiting an eternity for if they had an eternity.

27. (E) The speaker compares his love to vegetables, which grow slowly over time. He uses this **metaphor** to emphasize how strong and interminable (never ending) his love is for his addressee.

28. (B) Throughout the first stanza, the speaker attempts to convince his addressee that he would be happy for them to slowly express their love and passion over centuries if they had that amount of time. Beginning in line 12, he details how much time he would spend adoring her specific features (eyes, forehead, each breast) and then apportions "thirty thousand to the rest;/ An age at least to every part," which we can take to mean her remaining physical characteristics and other qualities.

29. (E) The **imagery** in the first stanza is libidinous (lustful, passionate) because the speaker wants his addressee to be convinced of his enduring passion for her—I. He conjures up images of endless infatuation and amorousness. He will adore her forehead, eyes, and breasts for hundreds and thousands of years. The second stanza, however, contains much more morbid, dark imagery—I—as the speaker now tries to emphasize the fact that they do not have thousands of years to wait; rather, they will soon face death ("marble vault") and faded beauty (25, 26). Their love will turn to "dust" (29) and "ashes" (30)—I. The tone does change from the first to the second stanza, but it is not quite a change from arrogance to desperation because the tone of the second stanza is not quite desperate— II; rather, the speaker here seems more grave (serious, intense) than in the first stanza because the imagery is of death and decay. The compliments are noticeably missing from the second stanza, especially in contrast to the incessant flattery provided in the first—III.

30. (C) The phrase essentially means "time flies." In fact, the speaker characterizes time as actually flying in his "winged" chariot. The phrase is also in the context of emphasizing how little time we have on earth, how we must "seize the day" and indulge in our desires.

31. (E) The focus of the second stanza is on the bleak reality of time passing, the inevitability of death, and the temporal nature of youth and beauty. In this context, the speaker qualifies his addressee's "honour" with the word "quaint" to emphasize the inappropriateness of her "coyness" (2) and choice to delay physical expressions of passion, given the circumstances (time is flying). According to the speaker, her modesty and prudence are not admirable; rather, this "honour" is merely charming and ultimately out of place, unsuited to the reality of their situation.

32. (B) By comparing his addressee's youth to "morning dew" on her skin, the speaker is emphasizing the ephemeral (short-lived) nature of her youth and beauty. Morning dew exists only in the morning; it does not even last more than a few hours. Dew also connotes freshness, virginity, and purity, which also describe the youthful and modest addressee. The speaker is trying to make the point that, as dew lasts only a short time, so will the addressee's youth.

33. (E) The speaker uses a **simile** to compare himself and his addressee to "am'rous birds of prey" who, instead of being eaten by time's "slow-chapp'd power" (chaps are jaws—time slowly eats away at our youth), will devour time itself by seizing the day and indulging in their amorous desires.

34. (C) Alliteration permeates (fills) the last two lines: "*Th*us, *th*ough … *s*un/ *s*tand *s*till … *w*e *w*ill." The speaker uses alliteration in the first stanza, abandons it in the second, and returns to it with a flourish at the end, indicating that the alliteration helps communicate his passion and energy since the first and final stanzas focus on consummating desire—II. The ending words of each of the final two lines rhyme with each other ("sun" and "run")—I. The speaker attributes human actions to the sun (**personification**), like running and standing still (III). There are no instances of **oxymoron** in these two lines (IV).

35. (D) The speaker's argument follows the structure of a **syllogism**, which is a logical argument consisting of a major premise ("If … " in stanza one), minor premise ("But … " in stanza two) and conclusion ("Now therefore … " in stanza three). The speaker's argument does not culminate in a logical, airtight conclusion, but he mimics the syllogism's style, perhaps to create the appearance and sound of a foolproof argument.

Passage 4. Christina Rossetti, "Winter: My Secret"

36. (C) The question "I tell my secret?" and the subsequent response "No indeed, not I" (1) imply that someone has just asked the speaker if she will tell her secret or stated that she

would. The question "You would not peck?" and the subsequent response "I thank you ... "
(21) also imply that someone has just told the speaker they would not "peck." Both these
questions are written as restatements and responses to another's comment or question. (A),
(B), and (D) describe common reasons for asking questions, but overlook the context and
tone of the quoted questions from the poem. (E) is incorrect because the speaker is not at
all communicating hope when she asks, "I tell my secret?"

37. (A) In line 6, the speaker responds to the addressee's plea to hear her secret with,
" ... well/ Only, my secret's mine, and I won't tell." The tone here is certainly juvenile. The
reader can imagine a child responding this way, and the rhyme helps to communicate that
sing-song, teasing tone. (B–E) are too extreme for the lighthearted and coy teasing and
playful rhyme that dominate the poem.

38. (A) The first stanza introduces a dilemma, a predicament, that the poem will continue
to develop. The quandary is that the implied addressee would like to know the speaker's
secret, but she is purposely withholding it while also suggesting she may reveal it under
certain circumstances. The specific setting is never actually developed in the poem, though
seasons are alluded to. The references to the seasons and environment are symbolic and
not descriptions of the actual setting (B). While a reader may view the speaker's teasing
about her secret as indicative of her enjoying the power she wields over her addressee,
that characterization would develop over the course of the poem (not in the first stanza
alone) (D). While the first stanza does introduce the relationship between the speaker
and her addressee (he wants something she is not readily supplying), it does not *develop*
the relationship (E). The first stanza does have a regular **rhyme scheme**, but its particular
rhyme scheme is not carried into the remaining stanzas. Also, the rhyme scheme is a device
and stylistic choice that helps to communicate the purpose; the rhyme would not be the
purpose itself (B).

39. (D) The wraps and clothing are symbolic of the speaker's protection from those who
incessantly inquire after her secret (symbolically). The word "wraps" does rhyme with "taps"
in line 13 (A), but the question asks about the main purpose of the word.

40. (C) The word "hall" rhymes with "all," creating an instance of **end rhyme**. Line 15
contains two words that rhyme ("bounding and surrounding") as does line 17 ("nipping
and clipping"), both instances of **internal rhyme**. Lines 15 and 16 both begin with the
same word ("Come"), an example of **anaphora**. As described in question 39, the weather
(draughts, winds) is symbolic of overzealous people who are interested in the speaker's secret.
The figurative language in these lines serves to dramatize the winds/people as threatening.
The speaker has to wear "wraps" to protect herself (her secret), but the winds would still
manage to nip and clip through them if she were to open her door.

41. (D) Capricious means fickle and unpredictable. The speaker does not "trust/
March ... Nor April with its rainbow-crowned brief showers,/ Nor even May, whose
flowers" may wither with just one frost. The weather in spring is too inconstant to be
trustworthy. Winter, however, is consistently overbearing with its biting, nipping, clipping, and whistling. Summer is consistently warm, languid, and still. (A), (B), and (E)
more closely describe winter and summer. There are no details to support that spring
is never-ending (C).

42. (D) The winter winds are symbolic of the meddlers who intrude and pester the speaker about her secret. She wears "wraps" and shuts her door because this burdensome meddling makes her want to protect her secret even more. She even asserts to her addressee in the first stanza that he's "too curious," which is keeping her from revealing her secret to him. In spring, however, she considers it more, but there are still instances of rain and frost, so there are still those who pry into her private matters and pester her. Summer, however, may be ideal, since the "warm wind is neither still nor loud" (32). The meddlers have retreated and quieted down. Under these conditions, when people stop harassing her or expressing incessant interest, "Perhaps [her] secret [she] may say,/ Or [he] may guess" (33–34).

43. (D) The speaker mentions her addressee is "Too curious" (too eager, overzealous) as part of her response to his implied request to hear her secret, making (A) correct. She also teases the addressee by suggesting that "perhaps there's none" (7), making (B) correct. The figurative descriptions of the nipping and clipping and whistling winter draughts make the speaker depend on her "wraps" to protect her from the pecking of "every wind that blows." The descriptions of the wind serve as believable descriptions of intrusive secret-seekers, and she wears her "wraps" and does not "ope to everyone that taps" (13) to impede their intrusion. All of these details provide sufficient support to interpret the speaker is concerned about the potential reaction and so does not reveal her secret, making (C) correct. The playful tone and word choice indicate the speaker enjoys the exclusivity of her secret and the power she wields over her addressee who has asked to know it. This reveling is most evident in lines 7–9: "Or, after all, perhaps there's none:/ Suppose there is no secret after all,/ But only just my fun," making (E) correct. The poem does not, however, include details that imply the speaker is worried specifically that the secret will spread uncontrollably. The figurative descriptions of the winter weather carry a tone of wildness, but those whistling winds are symbolic of overly-inquisitive visitors, pecking at her to reveal her secret. She does not want to reveal her secret to "everyone that taps," but that could be due to reasons other than a fear that the secret would spread uncontrollably, making (D) the only incorrect reason (and the correct answer).

44. (A) The juvenile tone of line 6 (see question 37), the playful rhyming, teasing, and coyness all reveal the speaker's attitude toward her addressee is one of mild amusement. She is enjoying dangling her secret just out of reach, of leading her addressee to think she will reveal it and then suddenly switching to suggesting there might actually not be a secret at all. She is playing a game and literally says that perhaps this is "just my fun" (9). While (D) is true—the speaker does appear willing to engage with the addressee—this is not as specific as (A) in describing her *main* attitude.

45. (E) The weather symbolizes those who are intrusive and overzealously interested in the speaker's secret. Like wind, they bite and nip, they whistle and bound and astound her. They are relentless, so she must stay indoors and not "ope" her house's door "to everyone who taps." Here, the speaker reveals the parallel between the nipping wind that comes "whistling through [her] halls" and the people who knock on her door. The winds are symbolic of prying people, making the house and her clothing ("wraps and all") symbolic of her refuge and protection. Since the clothing is her protection from the weather/those who pry, then her nose, in line 19, is symbolic of her secret, which must not be shown (18) to the "Russian snows" (i.e., the intrusive meddlers).

46. (E) The speaker's playful tone (see questions 37 and 44) and figurative descriptions of her reasoning for not revealing her secret (see questions 41 and 45) do not attack or anger her speaker (A, C). She even acknowledges his kindness in asserting that he would not "peck" like the bothersome winds (other prying people) when she says, "I thank you for good will,/ Believe" (21–22). Once she has gone through the seasons, articulating why winter and spring preclude her from wanting to share her secret, she arrives at summer, with its calm and warm stillness, and the addressee (if he is indeed paying attention) would recognize that this season (or the time when the overzealous meddlers quiet down) may lead to her disclosure. Her words, "Perhaps my secret I may say,/ Or you may guess" would lead the speaker to feel hopeful. The words "Perhaps" and "may" make (D) not likely.

47. (D) The final stanza consists of one **periodic sentence**, a sentence in which the independent clause appears only after a series of dependent clauses. The speaker continues the sense of anticipation that has built up in the first two stanzas by further delaying the declaration ("my secret I may say") when she places it after a series of dependent clauses. There are **end rhymes**, but the beat is not exactly steady, and the poem does not end with an actual revelation, just a suggestion of one to come ("perhaps"), making (A) incorrect. The word "perhaps" is repeated, but the speaker does not communicate antipathy (dislike, aversion) (see questions 37 and 44), making (B) incorrect. The adjectives "warm," "still," "loud," and "drowsy" are hardly uncommon (C), and the independent clause ("I may say") is not in passive voice. The subject performs the verb, which makes it active voice, so (E) is incorrect.

Passage 5. William Wordsworth, "The world is too much with us"

48. (C) There are two visibly distinct stanzas. The first contains six lines (**sestet**) and the second contains eight lines (**octave**). While there are some instances of two lines ending in exact rhyme, the entire poem does not consist of **couplets** (B).

49. (B) The phrase "Getting and spending" is modifying the subject that appears immediately following the modifier, which is "we." The context of the poem helps clarify that the speaker would be referring to "we" as the subject of "getting and spending" because he goes on to assert that "we" also "give our hearts away" (4) and "are out of tune" (8) with the beauty and powerful sounds of nature.

50. (D) The phrase "sordid boon" is an **oxymoron** because two opposite words are placed together for effect. "Sordid" describes something that is disgusting and distasteful, and a "boon" is a benefit, a gift, an advantage. The surrounding context explains that the speaker deplores (disapproves of) people's negligence of the natural world and preference for modern technological and industrial advancement. He claims, "we lay waste our powers:/ Little we see in nature that is ours" (2–3). He is saying that people do not bother to appreciate what they can see in nature because they prefer to look at their own man-made structures. They ignore the "Sea that bares her bosom to the moon;/ The Winds that will be howling at all hours" (5–6). We have lost the "tune" (8), the ability to harmonize with nature and to hear the winds howling.

51. (C) Line 5 contains **personification** of the sea, who "bares her bosom to the moon," and line 6 uses a **simile** to describe the winds as "howling at all hours/ And are up-gathered now like sleeping flowers." Both devices reveal the majestic beauty and power of nature. The next line clarifies the speaker's intention with these descriptions. He bemoans, "For this, for everything, we are out of tune;/ It moves us not" (8–9). Clearly, the speaker laments that the sea and winds' actions and qualities are going unappreciated by "us." (E) may be a tempting choice considering the winds "will be howling at all hours," but the context reveals that this howling is currently "up-turned now like sleeping flowers," which is hardly intimidating.

52. (E) Lines 5–6 contain figurative language that emphasizes the majestic beauty and power of nature, specifically the sea and winds. Lines 13–14 return to this motif by using figurative language (in the form of **allusions** to Greek gods Proteus and Triton) to illustrate that same inspiring beauty that would make the speaker "less forlorn" (12).

53. (B) The word "this" refers to the "Sea that bares her bosom to the moon" and "The Winds that will be blowing at all hours" (5–6). The speaker does not intend to say we are "out of tune" for the "sleeping flowers." The sleeping flowers are part of a **simile** that helps further illustrate the winds. The "hours" are also part of the description of the winds, making only II correct.

54. (C) The title and first line of the poem contain its theme: "The world is too much with us." Here, "world" does not necessarily mean the environment of the earth and sky because we know that the speaker appreciates the "Sea" and the "Winds." He capitalizes them to emphasize their importance. So, if the "world" is "too much with us" in a negative way, then "world" must refer to the industrialized, modernized, technologically advanced world in which we are "Getting and spending ... lay[ing] waste our powers" (2). The speaker characterizes this advancement as negative and destructive; it is a "sordid boon!" (4), a benefit/advantage that is dirty, grubby, foul.

55. (A) The **metaphor** compares Paganism ("a creed outworn") to a mother's breast and a Pagan to a baby being "suckled" by that creed/breast. The comparison implies that the outworn creed of Paganism provides comfort and nourishment to a Pagan, the way a mother's breast offers the same to a baby. Essentially, the speaker compares himself to a baby who is in dire need of such consolation. He would even go so far as to be a Pagan to get it.

56. (C) When the speaker says he would "rather" be a Pagan so that he might glimpse Greek gods like Proteus and Triton, which would make him "less forlorn [sad]," he is expressing his desire. This is not an actual solution (E). He says only that he would rather be a Pagan, not that he will actually convert to this "creed outworn" (10). While his references to the Greek gods do demonstrate his knowledge (D), that is not the primary intention of the allusions. (B) is also a vague and incomplete answer. He does not express sanguinity (optimism) (A) through these **allusions** because he is not actually going to become a Pagan and escape his forlorn state.

57. (D) The theme of the poem as a whole is best described by (D) because the speaker first laments that people ("we") have allowed the "world" to be "too much with us," meaning we are consumed by "Getting and spending" and we "lay waste our powers ... ." The "world" that is "too much with us" is the material world that we have created with our technological and industrial "powers," which the speaker describes as a "waste" because these powers only encourage "Getting and spending" and distract us from noticing Nature's "Sea" and "Winds." This is tragic because "we have given our hearts away." The "boon" (benefit) of progress is "sordid" (dirty, grimy) because we have paid a big price for such advancement. (A), while expressed in the poem, is an incomplete description of the overall theme. (B) is a slightly crude and extreme way to describe the theme. (C) and (E) are expressed in the second stanza but do not describe the poem as a whole.

Passage 6. William Butler Yeats, "That the Night Come"

58. (A) The poem as a whole describes the woman as desiring death, not being able to endure the "common good of life," and behaving as if the events of life are to be tolerated and "bundled away" until her anticipated death arrives. (B), (C), (D), and (E) are supported by the poem, whereas (A) indicates that the woman, though she herself does not appreciate the "common good of life," thinks that this common good is in general unappreciated. There is no evidence to suggest she has this view.

59. (B) The subject of the poem is "She" who "lived in storm and strife." Lines 2–12 directly refer to "her soul," which is still considered to be part of "She"/her. While "a king" is mentioned in the poem, this reference is part of a **simile** comparing "her soul" to a king who bundles time away in anticipation of his wedding night. He is not a subject of the poem, making (E) incorrect.

60. (D) Line 1 contains **alliteration** with the words "storm" and "strife," and line 2 contains alliteration with the words "soul" and "such," making (A) incorrect. Line 1 introduces "She" as the subject of the poem and lines 2–12 continue describing the subject by focusing on "her soul," making (B) incorrect. The phrase "storm and strife" provides a figurative description of the woman's hardships, not objective, making (E) incorrect. The figurative language continues throughout the poem, with a **simile** in line 6, among other examples, making (C) incorrect. The one distinguishing feature of line 1 is that it contains a complete thought, an independent clause.

61. (C) The subject to which "it" refers is the word "soul." When written as prose, the sentence reads, "Her soul had such desire for what proud death may bring that it could not endure the common good of life." The subject of the sentence is "soul," not "death" (A). It is the soul that cannot endure the common good of life, not the desire (D). "Her" and "She"—B, E—are not even in the sentence.

62. (C) The king is mentioned in a **simile** that compares the woman's behavior to that of a king who cannot wait for his wedding night so he can consummate his marriage with his queen. The purpose of such a comparison is to further illustrate the emotional state of the woman, who is the main subject of the poem. The simile shows that the woman is anticipating her death as eagerly as the king anticipates his wedding night. While their emotion of eagerness is similar, the actual things they each desire are different: death and marriage. They are different in gender (A) and possibly class status since he is a king (E), but these differences are not emphasized in the poem. Their way of living (B) is the same (she lives like a king who …), as are their attitudes (D) toward life (they do not live for the moment but for the future).

63. (E) The speaker appears to be intimately familiar with the inner state of the poem's subject ("She"). The speaker is able to describe the manner in which the woman copes with life and what her soul desires. This knowledge indicates the speaker is **omniscient** in his point of view. Because the speaker conveys the woman's predicament, desire, and inner state with imagery and figurative language, it cannot be said that he is indifferent, making (B) incorrect. His description is more sympathetic and understanding than harsh, making (A) incorrect. There are no details to indicate the speaker is providing guidance like a mentor would (D) or indulging the woman (C).

64. (E) The **simile** compares the woman's anticipation for "what proud death may bring" (3) to a king who is so excited for his wedding night that he needs to fill his day with loud and exciting distractions to "bundle time away"(11). The comparison makes the woman's excitement for death more vivid by providing an image of an eager and impatient king.

65. (C) The speaker uses multiple conjunctions ("and") to string together a list of loud and exciting distractions, which continue the **simile** comparing the woman to a king who must "bundle time away." This device is called **polysyndeton**, and it emphasizes the anticipation felt by the woman (and the figurative king in the simile) by including a reminder ("and") that there are more and more distractions needed. The device almost mimics the tone of a young child who is so excited that she does not take a breath or pause between thoughts, but rather strings thoughts together with a rushed "and … and … and." There are no examples in lines 8–10 of **alliteration** (B), **enjambment** (D), or **internal rhyme** (E), and there are no verbs in these lines (A).

66. (A) Both the woman and the king are so impatient for something (death and the wedding night, respectively) to come that it seems remote and far away. The king longs for night because at night the king will be able to consummate his marriage, which is compared to the woman reaching "proud death" (3). Night, however, is not characterized as unavoidable— II—because that would imply that the woman and king want to avoid night. Night is also not interminable (never ending)—III; it is only the day that is presented as interminable because the king (and woman, through comparison) must "bundle time away" (11) to pass time until night comes.

67. (A) The poem is about a woman who "had such desire/ For what proud death may bring" (3–4) that she lived like a king who filled his day with fanfare and distractions to pass time until his wedding night came. The woman's anticipation for "proud death" is equated with the king's impatience for his wedding night. Wasting time (C) implies that they indifferently idle away the hours, which is not what the king is doing when he packs his day with "[t]rumpet and kettledrum" (9). They definitely do not ignore time (E) because they see it as something that needs to be "bundle[d]" and spent; they see it as an obstacle in the way of attaining their desired goals.

Chapter 2: American Poetry

Passage 1. Anne Bradstreet, "The Author to Her Book"

68. (C) Throughout the entire poem, the speaker addresses her own book as "Thou," "thee," and "thy" in the **extended metaphor** that compares her book to her child. Since the book is not actually a person who can respond to her, this address to her book is an example of a device called **apostrophe**.

69. (B) The "friends" are the ones who "snatched" the book and exposed [it] to public view. The next verb is "Made" in line 5, which refers to the same subject performing the previous actions of snatching and exposing: the friends.

70. (C) The speaker confesses, "I washed thy face, but more defects I saw,/And rubbing off a spot, still made a flaw./ I stretcht thy joints to make thee even feet,/ Yet still thou run'st more hobbling than is meet" (13–16). It is ironic that in her attempts to amend the book, she actually makes it worse. (A) is true but does not express the **irony** of her attempts to improve the book actually having the opposite effect.

71. (D) The speaker tells her book, "In better dress to trim thee was my mind,/ But nought save home-spun cloth, i' th' house I find" (17–18). She would have trimmed the book in better clothes (edited, improved it), but all she had in the house was mediocre home-made cloth, which would not be acceptable to her or worthy of her book. In this comparison, the speaker expresses her belief that she lacks the proper tools and skills to create the book she expects from herself.

72. (E) The speaker implies that her book is unfinished/unedited (A) when she describes it as "snatcht" from her side when it was only dressed in "rags" (5). The book was disseminated prematurely (B) because it was "snatcht … by friends, less wise than true,/Who [the book] abroad exposed to public view" (3–4). She goes on to describe the numerous "errors" (6) in the book that make it fallible (C) and how she tried and tried to "amend" its "blemishes" by rubbing, washing, and stretching it. Regardless of all these attempts, though, "more defects [she] saw" (13), making the book irreparable (D). There are no details that imply the content of the book is polemical (controversially argumentative) (E).

73. (C) The speaker's tone is self-deprecating (undervaluing oneself) because she has little confidence in her unedited and unrevised writing. She is mortified that her book would be "exposed to public view … in rags" (4–5). She is concerned that "all may judge" (6) her for a piece of writing she does not have confidence in. She admits that even with revision (rubbing, washing, and stretching), the "more defects [she] saw" (13) and the revision itself "still made a flaw" (14). Even though she does compare the book to her offspring, her tone is not nurturing (B) because she speaks about the book/child with harsh diction like "rambling brat" (8), "unfit for light" (9), and "irksome" (10). She is also more concerned about what others will think of her because of her sloppy book/child; she is not as concerned for the actual book/child. The subject of the poem is the author and her relationship with and attitude toward her book, and she is not vengeful (D), acerbic (bitter) (E), or mournful (A) toward it because she tries to improve it. Also, the poem is composed of **heroic couplets** (rhyming pairs of lines in iambic pentameter), making the tone less severe and harsh, so while the speaker is disappointed in her work, she can make fun of herself (self-deprecate) and not get angry.

74. (C) The speaker laments that the book was prematurely "snatcht" and "exposed to public view" and taken "to th' press to trudge" (3–5). She then tells her book, "In critics' hands, beware thou dost not come,/ And take thy way where yet thou are not known" (20–21). The speaker is deeply concerned about how critics view her work, and this worry is so intense as to make her actually unproductive, making (A) and (B) incorrect. Though perhaps unhealthy, this relationship may not be unconventional. Regardless, the poem does not suggest that it is normal or abnormal (D). (E) is too extremely negative.

75. (D) Only **heroic couplets** contribute to the musicality of the poem, not the parenthetical phrases or first person point of view. Heroic couplets are a series of two rhyming lines written in **iambic pentameter**—III. Each line in the poem contains nearly five (*penta*meter) iambs (a pair of unstressed and stressed syllables), such as "Thou *ill*-formed *off*spring *of* my *fee*ble *brain*/ Who *after birth* did *by* my *side* re*main*" (1–2). Heroic couplets can lighten the tone of a poem because they create a songlike sound.

76. (D) Like a fastidious (careful, picky) artist would view her painting with a critical eye (D), the speaker also views her book as not good enough to be published and read. She rubs, washes, and stretches (13–15) the book in an attempt to lessen the errors, but only creates more. She is embarrassed that her book has been "snatcht" from her prematurely and "exposed to public view … in rags" (3–5). Though she does use the **extended, implied metaphor** (see question 68) of a child to talk about her relationship with her book, the relationship cannot be described as nurturing (B) because she speaks about the book/child with harsh diction like "rambling brat" (8), "unfit for light" (9), and "irksome" (10). Teachers (A), bosses (C), and directors (E) serve in supervisory roles, but the speaker implies, through the metaphor, that she is not merely disappointed in her pupil or subordinate; rather, she sees the flaws in her book as flaws in herself. She takes the criticism more personally than a teacher, boss, or director would. The book, like a child, is a part of her.

77. (A) Though she is disappointed in her unrevised writing, the poem conveys a lot more emotion than mere dislike (B). Through the **metaphor**, the speaker shows how a writer views her work as part of herself, that she has "affection" (11) for it and an innate drive to improve and take care of it. Though the poem does suggest a work can always undergo more and more revision and still not be perfect, this is not the overall purpose of the poem (C). The harsh critics are referred to, but they are not the focus of the poem (D). The hardships of motherhood (E) are implied only tangentially through the discussion of the poem's main topic, the artist's relationship with her work.

78. (E) While the poem does contain **rhyme** (A), **iambic pentameter** (B), **simile** (C), and **metaphor** (D), it is developed mainly through the device known as the **conceit** (E). The entire poem hinges on the **extended metaphor (a conceit)** that compares the speaker's book to her child. The metaphor does not exist only in one line or one segment of the poem; rather, it continues throughout all 23 lines and drives the poem forward. All the other devices occur within the conceit.

Passage 2. Countee Cullen, "I Have a Rendezvous with Life"

79. (B) If a reader is not familiar with the word "Ere," the context establishes that it must mean "before." In lines 1–4, for example, it makes sense that the speaker hopes his rendezvous will come *before* his "youth has sped" and *before* "voices sweet grow dumb" due to the loss of hearing in old age.

80. (E) Lines 1–4 contain references to time and create anticipation ("In days I hope will come,/ Ere youth has sped…")—I, II. Lines 5–6 contain a reference to time with the word

"When" and a sense of anticipation for spring's arrival—I, II. Line 4 ends with "dumb," which forms a rhyme with "hum" in line 6—III.

81. (D) Lines 5–6 say, "I have a rendezvous with Life,/ When Spring's first herald hums." The word "herald" means the "first sign, signal, or indication." The signs of spring that would hum are insects and birds buzzing and singing, signaling spring's arrival. (C) is incorrect because vexing means annoying and bothersome. The speaker anticipates spring and its pleasures; he is not bothered by them.

82. (C) "Some would cry" that it is better to sleep through life in order to avoid its obstacles ("the road, the wind and rain") than to "heed the calling deep," the calling to seize the day and experience life. The speaker indicates that it is the challenges in life that inhibit "some," not their introversion (E) or their obliviousness to what life has to offer (A). They may be aware of life's positive experiences, but they are too fearful of its challenges to experience them.

83. (B) The "some" who "cry it's better" to avoid "the road, the wind and rain" (7–9) by sleeping are fearful of life's challenges. In line 12, the speaker admits, "Yet fear I deeply, too, … ", drawing a parallel between the fear of "some" and his own fear that he may miss out on life's pleasures. "Fearsome" means "causing fear," not feeling fear, so (A) is incorrect.

84. (D) See question 83. Note that the question asks what the speaker is *literally* doing. He draws a comparison between himself and "some." In doing so, it may be said that he is also humanizing himself by revealing that he, too, feels fear, but this would require some analysis and interpretation, and the question does not ask what the speaker is *figuratively* doing (B).

85. (E) In line 9, the speaker describes "some" as fearful of "the road, the wind and rain." In lines 11–14, the speaker compares and contrasts that fear to his own. He says, "Though wet nor blow nor space I fear," and the "wet," "blow," and "space" are parallel to the fears attributed to "some." The word "wet" corresponds to the "rain," the word "blow" corresponds to "wind," and "space" must correspond to "the road." The speaker says he does not fear the same things as "some," but he does share the emotion of fear because he fears that "Death should meet and claim me ere/ I keep Life's rendezvous" (13–14). The speaker does fear an untimely death, but the reference to "space" precedes mention of this fear so it cannot be *in response* to this fear (C). The "wet" and "blow" refer to potential stormy obstacles, but "space" does not (A).

86. (D) The speaker does say that he is motivated to seize life before his "youth has sped," before his mind and hearing weaken, but he does not intend to convey "Life" as consisting strictly of youthful pleasures (E). In lines 9–11, he recognizes the harsher aspects and experiences in life ("the road, wind and rain") but decides that they are not to be feared but to be braved in order to benefit from the more positive experiences. He keeps life's rendezvous, which means he fully engages with all that life has to offer so as not to miss out on the pleasures that can be fully enjoyed only in youth.

87. (E) The context of the poem as a whole indicates that the "rendezvous" the speaker keeps and has is a meeting. He encounters the experiences of life, whenever and however they come, which also implies that the "rendezvous" does not have to be planned ahead, making (A) correct. He engages (C) with life's positive and negative experiences. He does not interview (E) life, which would imply a sort of power structure with the speaker assessing life's merits.

88. (B) The speaker is greatly influenced by the concept of "Life" and all that it embodies, the good and bad. The possibility of an untimely death also greatly motivates the speaker to "keep Life's rendezvous." While the capitalization does indicate **personification**, the speaker does not *fear* life and he views Death as inevitable and unpredictable, *not* as calculating and threatening (C), (E). The word "intimidating" indicates that Life and Death make the speaker do something unpalatable, against his will, but enjoying the pleasures of spring is not intended to appear unpalatable (A). Life and Death are not Greek gods (D).

89. (E) The speaker's main concern is the need to make the most of life before his "youth has sped, and strength of mind,/ Ere voices sweet grow dumb" (3–4). The speaker does allude to youth's temporality, but he does not intend to say that dying young is guaranteed (A). He wants to seize the day ("keep Life's rendezvous") "Lest Death should meet and claim" him before he has had a chance to fully experience life. The drawbacks of aging are mentioned, as is the crippling fear of "some," but neither is the main concern (B), (D).

Passage 3. Emily Dickinson, "Success is counted sweetest"

90. (E) The speaker says lines 3–4 ("To comprehend a nectar/ Requires sorest need") to provide an image that supports the claim in the first sentence: "Success is counted sweetest/ By those who ne'er succeed" (1–2). In this context, "comprehend" means to truly know something. People who do not attain success *truly know* what success is, just as one must be in need of a nectar to truly know what it is. (B), (C), and (D) are all definitions of the word "comprehend," but in the context of the poem (E) makes the most sense.

91. (E) The **alliteration** of "*s*uccess … *s*weetest … *s*ucceed … *s*orest" and "*n*ever … *n*ectar … *n*eed" in the first stanza creates a soothing, pleasing, appealing sound, which complements the appealing and pleasing feeling of success. While the alliteration may soothe the reader (A), (E) is a more specific answer. There is no **assonance** in the first stanza (C) or **consonance** in the second stanza (D). The tone is not envious (B) (see question 98).

92. (C) The phrase "purple host" refers to those who are victorious, "Who took the flag today" (6). The speaker says "Not one" of the victorious "Can tell the definition,/ So clear, of victory,/ As he defeated, dying"—making I incorrect. The defeated hear "The distant strains of triumph/ Break agonized and clear" (11–12)—III. "The subject of the poem is that "Success is counted sweetest/ By those who ne'er succeed" (1–2)—II.

93. (B) The words "day" and "victory" are meant to rhyme to fit the **rhyme scheme** of *abcb defe ghih*, in which the second and fourth lines of each stanza rhyme. However, these two words do not make an exact rhyme; they almost rhyme, which makes them an example of **slant rhyme**. *The AP Exam rarely asks about rhyme scheme and types of rhyme, but this question is answerable by eliminating the other choices and looking at the pattern of rhyme in the poem as a whole.*

94. (D) Lines 5–6 say, "Not one of all the purple host/ Who took the flag today," indicating that the purple host are those who won, who were victorious, who "took the flag." In this context, purple is associated with victory.

95. (C) The sounds of victory are "distant strains" and "agonized" because the defeated are far (figuratively and literally) from the sounds of triumph that surround the victorious. When one is defeated and dying, the sounds of victory are agonizing because they are in such stark contrast to their own experience of defeat, and they are a painful reminder of the loss. The other answer choices make assumptions that are not directly supported by the text.

96. (A) The poem primarily contrasts the victorious ("purple host") to "those who ne'er succeed." The comparison is made clear with the word "As" (9). To paraphrase, the speaker says not one of the victorious can tell the definition of victory as clearly <u>as</u> those who are defeated and dying. There is no evidence to suggest that the victory was not earned (B). Collaboration is not mentioned in the poem (C). Soreness and sweetness (D) do appear to be contrasting concepts; however, in the poem, those who are sore due to their defeat are also those for whom "Success is counted sweetest" (1).

97. (C) The first sentence (1–2) of the poem is an example of a **maxim**, a self-evident truth, a proverb or wise saying. The other two sentences of the poem provide images (the nectar and the winning army) that illustrate the maxim. The opening statement is not stated as a hypothesis (A) or a theory (D) that the speaker is proposing (B) for consideration or research; on the contrary, she is posing the statement as a known truth, which she elucidates with images.

98. (D) The speaker opens the poem with a **maxim**, (a wise saying or proverb), which can also be described as an adage. The tone of the poem is similar to the tone of an adage—which offers a piece of thought-provoking wisdom. (B) and (C) assume that the speaker is lecturing to the reader when she is actually providing her own insightful observation about life. She is not envious of those who have achieved success (E). (A) is a tempting choice, as the defeated do experience sorrow; however, the poem as a whole includes this sorrow to share the larger maxim, making (D) the better answer.

99. (D) The poem's main point is communicated in the first two lines, "Success is counted sweetest/ By those who ne'er succeed." The other two sentences offer more images to elucidate the same idea—the nectar is understood only by those who are in *need* of it and the sounds of triumph are clearest to the defeated.

Passage 4. T. S. Eliot, "Morning at the Window"

100. (B) In an **implied metaphor**, the speaker says, "The brown waves of fog toss up to me ... " (5). The fog is presented as waves because it rises up from the street below to the speaker's window, from which he is observing the scene. The fog is also presented as a wave because it provides an illustration of how the fog carries the images of people's faces up to the speaker to see; it is as if the faces are riding the wave of fog. This metaphor does not exactly compare the scene below to an ocean. The souls are "damp" and the skirts are "muddy" more due to the fog and the literal environment than to a figurative ocean (C).

101. (C) The sentence that contains the word "tear" reads "The brown waves of fog toss up to me/ Twisted faces from the bottom of the street,/ And tear from a passer-by with muddy skirts/ An aimless smile … " (5–8). The subject of the sentence is the brown waves of fog, and they perform two actions: they toss and they tear. The waves tear an aimless smile from a passer-by and toss it up to where the speaker is.

102. (E) The words "*fog … faces from*" are an example of **alliteration** because the same letter and sound is repeated at the start of multiple words in close succession.

103. (C) Assonance occurs when the internal vowel sound of multiple words in close succession is the same, as in "f*o*g" and "t*o*ss." In this example, our mouths open vertically to pronounce the sound of the "o," which complements the tall rise upward of the waves and fog being described. None of the other answer choices includes examples of assonance.

104. (A) The speaker is physically removed from the scene he is describing; he is up at his window, and the people are at "the bottom of the street" (6). He observes the people below from afar and describes his subjective impressions of their souls (3), clothes (7), and faces (6, 8). The speaker sees the scene as grubby and sad ("despondent"), which could indicate that he himself is upset (B) and depressed, but it is too extreme to say that he is obsessed (B) with the scene below his window. While there is a moment of optimism in the descriptions ("an aimless smile"), the rest of the descriptions are more gloomy and sad. Since there is that one moment of observing a smile, the speaker is not entirely fatalistic (D) either. He is definitely not apathetic (lazy, indifferent) (E); he vigilantly watches the people below and carefully describes what he observes in vivid detail.

105. (A) To describe the scene below his window, the speaker uses ghostly **diction** like "rattling" (1), "damp souls" (3), "waves of fog" (5), "twisted faces" (6), "muddy" (7), "aimless" (8), "hovers in the air" (8), and "vanishes" (9). Even though the people do appear to be penurious (poor) (B), the specific word choice clearly creates a ghostly image that communicates the people's poverty and their haunting, deadly, empty auras. Also, even though the people are poor, dirty, and working class, there are no details to suggest the speaker sees them as pathetic (D). Only the "twisted faces" characterize the people as grotesque (E).

106. (D) The speaker is, unlike the people he describes, up at the window—II. Also unlike the people he describes, he is merely observing the people who are "rattling breakfast plates" (1) and "[s]prouting despondently" (4) —III. While we can infer that the speaker is perhaps from a higher class than the working class he watches, there are no actual details to suggest he is wealthier—I.

107. (A) The tone is developed through the speaker's eerie **diction** ("rattling," "damp souls," "[s]prouting despondently," "fog," "twisted faces," "aimless smile," "hovers in the air," "vanishes"). The speaker also uses **sensory images** that allow us to hear the "rattling" of breakfast plates and see the "brown … fog" (5). The **metaphor** of the "waves of fog" (5) also communicates the speaker's attitude toward what he is describing—he sees the people below him as ghostlike; their faces rise up to him on the waves of fog and then vanish "along the level of the roofs" (9). The poem does not contain rhyme (B), a **simile** (the comparisons are not set up with the words "like" or "as") (C), **allusions** (D), or **couplets** (E).

Passage 5. Phyllis Wheatley, "An Hymn to the Evening"

108. (E) The verbs in lines 1–6 are "forsook," "shook," "Exhales," "purl," "renew," and "floats." All these verbs evoke our senses. We hear the thunder shake the plains, we smell the incense that is exhaled, and we see and hear the music float and the notes renewed. These verbs are not literal (D) because the spring does not actually breathe. They are not repetitive (C); each one is unique. They are not mundane or ordinary (B); the thunder is not commonly referred to as *forsaking* the eastern main and birds are not ordinarily described as *renewing* their notes when spring arrives. The verbs are not passive (A), as "sun" precedes the verb "forsook," so the subject performs the action, making the construction active.

109. (B) If read as prose, the entire independent clause containing the word "their" says, "Soft purl the streams, the birds renew their notes, and through the air their mingled music floats." The mingled music is mingled because there are multiple birds renewing their notes. The music belongs to the birds.

110. (B) The speaker describes her environment with exclamations like "Majestic grandeur!" (3) and "what beauteous dies are spread!" (7). The exclamations reveal that her awe is not restrained (held back), making (A) incorrect. Her respect for the environment's grandeur is shown through her detailed descriptions and figurative language. She respects the power of the thunder, as it "shook the heav'nly plain" (2). She alludes to the wind as "zephyr's wing" and notes that the "blooming spring" carries not merely a scent but "incense" (3–4). The speaker's enthusiasm is not meant to reveal fear of her environment (C); rather, her amazement is generated from appreciating its power and grandeur. Her enthusiasm is not exactly whimsical (D) because her word choice clearly indicates reverence.

111. (B) Lines 1–8 focus on describing the environment with unrestrained awe and careful figurative language (see question 108), but line 9 introduces people ("our") into the poem. Lines 10–18 continue to focus on people ("our" and "my"), those who "wake more heav'nly," and whose "drowsy eyes" are sealed. Lines 9–18 do not contain consternation (worry, dismay), making (C) incorrect. The entire poem is subjective, not just lines 9–18, making (A) incorrect. The sun is setting in the west, creating a deep red in the sky, in line 8, so line 9 does not signal a change from daybreak to nightfall (D). Also, the entire poem conveys an appreciation of nature and God (E).

112. (A) If read as prose, the sentence in lines 8–10 says, "But the west glories in the deepest red: so may our breasts with ev'ry virtue glow, the living temples of our God below!" The speaker says that the glorious beauty and grandeur in "all the heav'ns" (7) that glows deep red may also live inside "our breasts," in our hearts and souls, when we are virtuous. The virtue is what would make our breasts glow because it would mean we are living temples of God here on earth; that is, we follow in his footsteps and develop his virtue within ourselves. The temples in this case are metaphorical, not actual churches erected in honor of God (B). "Secular" describes something having no religious or spiritual basis, and the "living temples" are certainly a religious reference (D).

113. (E) The slumbers will be placid (calm, peaceful, restorative) only if we are virtuous and live by God's example. (See question 112.) We are "living temples" when "our breasts" glow with virtue. Our "weary mind" will be soothed because we are living virtuously, which will allow us to "wake more heav'nly, more refin'd," and "guarded from the snares of sin."

The drawn curtains do not *cause* the slumbers to be placid; they signal that night has arrived (B). The scepter does seal the speaker's eyes, but the scepter does not *cause* the slumbers to be placid (D). The slumbers are likely quiet (A), but the question asks *why* the slumbers are placid/quiet.

114. (C) The placid slumbers "sooth each weary mind" (13), which means that sleep can mollify (B). Placid slumbers allow us to "wake more heav'nly, more refin'd ... More pure, more guarded," (14–16), making (A), (D), and (E) correct. Sleep will seal our eyes and our song will cease; we will be soothed and placid, not stimulated and awake, making (C) the only incorrect choice (and the correct answer).

115. (E) See question 114. She is grateful for the restorative powers of night and sleep and views the scepter with respect.

116. (B) The speaker portrays God as regulating day and night, since he "draws the sable curtains of the night" (12), which signals nightfall—I. God inspires his devotees to live virtuously, to glow with the deepest red of the heavenly skies (7–10)—II. The speaker's reverential tone and word choice indicate respect, appreciation, and awe for God; she does not feel intimidated, forced, or coerced. A reader may be tempted to choose III if misreading the reference to "Night's leaden sceptre" (see questions 114–115).

117. (C) A **couplet** is two lines of verse, usually in the same meter and joined by rhyme, that form a unit or complete thought. The final couplet is in lines 17–18. The **alliteration** is evident in the words "*s*cepter," "*s*eals," "*c*ease," and "*s*ong." The lines describe the soporific power of night, and the repeated "s" sound complements this description with its smooth and sleepy sound.

118. (E) "Night's leaden scepter seals [the speaker's] drowsy eyes," which makes her song cease until the morning. The context reveals that Aurora must be a reference (in this case, an **allusion** to a Roman Goddess) to the morning.

119. (E) The **alliteration** (see question 117) and **personification** of Night in the final two lines contribute to their soothing and sleepy tone. The speaker seeks to evoke a feeling of slumber here. Repose means lying down and resting. Readers focusing on the "leaden sceptre" may be tempted to pick (A), (B), or (D), but the scepter is not threatening or intimidating; rather, the speaker is grateful for the restorative and protective powers of night and sleep, which are symbolized by the scepter.

120. (A) Considering the reliance on exclamations and the reverential tone, the poem does not make repeated use of understatement to convey its message. There are three instances of exclamation, which show the speaker's unabashed reverence for her environment (see question 108). The poem consists of multiple **couplets** (see question 117) that contain essential ideas. There are numerous instances of **metaphor**: living temples, sable curtains, leaden scepter. Sensory **imagery** permeates the entire poem (see question 108).

Passage 6. Walt Whitman, "O Captain! My Captain!"

121. (A) Line 4 is part of the independent clause that begins in line 3: "The port is near, the bells I hear, the people all exulting,/ While follow eyes the steady keel, the vessel grim and daring." The clause "While follow eyes the steady keel" refers to the noun in the preceding clause, which is "the people" who are exulting. They are exulting (rejoicing, triumphant) because "the prize ... is won" (2), and they are not yet aware of the captain's demise. "Formidable" describes a noun that inspires awe or intimidation due to its grandeur, size, strength, power. The observers are exulting while in awe of the ship's formidable features that helped assure victory. It has been victorious, and the people are exulting, not lamenting the damage done to the vessel (E) or worrying about it pulling into the port (C). The boat is returning, not departing (B). The speaker is not looking at the vessel; he is looking at "the people all exulting" and describing their eyes (D).

122. **(A)** The speaker tells his heart to not leave "the little spot" where the Captain lies "cold and dead." In other words, he is telling himself (his heart) never to forget the moment and place of his captain's death. (E) is a close answer, but the command to his heart ("O heart! heart! heart!") indicates that he is telling himself not to forget, hoping and pleading with his heart to always remember, while (E) indicates that he is certain he will not forget.

123. **(C)** The "bells," "flag," "bugle," "wreaths," and crowds in the third stanza serve dual purposes in that they describe the celebration the crowd planned to have upon the captain and the ship's victorious return and also happen to describe a funeral, which is appropriate since the victory parade must turn into a funeral upon receipt of the news that the captain has died.

124. **(D)** The captain has not arrived home safely; he has died on the ship. Both the captain and the ship achieved their goals ("the victor ship") (B), ended their heroic journeys ("its voyage closed and done") (A), and are being celebrated (E). They are both **metaphorical**; the captain is actually Abraham Lincoln, and the ship is the United States of America, but without this background knowledge, a reader can interpret the metaphorical potential of the "captain" and his "ship" (see question 129) (C).

125. **(A)** In the fifth stanza, the speaker no longer refers to the captain in exclamatory sentences like "O Captain!" (1, 9, 13). Instead, his references are calm statements like "My Captain does not answer ... " (17). While these calm statements may be called internal thoughts (C), this would not be considered a change because the references to the captain in the previous stanzas can also be considered internal thoughts.

126. **(B)** The first segment (stanza 1) shows the speaker discovering his captain has died (... on the deck my Captain lies,/ Fallen cold and dead"). The second segment (stanza 3) shows the speaker is in a state of denial about the death ("It is some dream ... "). The third segment (stanza 5) shows the speaker accepting the reality of his captain's death (" ... he has no pulse nor will").

127. **(B)** The tone of the poem is not uplifting (A); rather, it is elegiac, which means it has the tone of an **elegy** (a funeral song, a mournful poem). The word "captain" is not part of a rhyme at any point in the poem (D), the message is not that mourning can be musical (C), and the speaker is not exulting (rejoicing) in their victory (E); rather, he is clearly mourning.

128. (C) In the final stanza, the speaker exhorts the shores to "Exult" and the bells to "ring." This noisy celebration is in contrast to the speaker's "silent tread" due to his mourning the loss of the captain.

129. (A) In the poem, the captain and the ship are **metaphors** for a political leader and his citizens who have just achieved an important victory. The actual leader is Abraham Lincoln, the victory is the Civil War, and the country is the United States of America. Though this would be diffficult to determine with just the poem at hand, the references to the captain and the ship are definitely metaphors for some kind of leader and group since the **diction** in the poem carries multiple levels of meaning. The speaker refers to the captain as his "father" in the final stanza, which also provides a clue to the metaphorical value ascribed to the captain. (B) is the literal interpretation of the captain, not symbolic. There is no evidence to suggest the captain was controversial (C); rather, the poem portrays him as victorious, loved by the speaker and the people, who are exulting in the victory he was instrumental in achieving. (D) is incorrect because the captain is a person and would symbolize another person as opposed to an entire industry. The references to the captain more logically apply to a person than the naval industry.

130. (E) See question 127.

131. (E) The speaker has moved from denial in the third stanza ("It is some dream") to acceptance of the captain's death in the final stanza. He acknowledges that the captain "does not answer" and "has no pulse or will" (17–18). Once he realizes this, he is in a mournful state as he decides to remain on "the spot [his] Captain dies" (23) while the shores and bells ring and "Exult" (21).

Chapter 3: World Poetry

Passage 1. Kahlil Gibran, "Defeat"

132. (E) The poem as a whole is written as an **apostrophe**; the speaker addresses defeat as if it were a person who can answer back ("Defeat" is also capitalized as if it were the name of a person), even though it cannot.

133. (D) In the second stanza, the speaker refers to "Defeat" as "my self-knowledge" (4) because it is through "Defeat" that the speaker *knows* he is "young and swift of foot" (5). He has found joy in "being shunned and scorned" (8). "Defeat" is valuable in that it makes the speaker more self-aware.

134. (C) In the third stanza, the speaker lists the messages he has "read" in Defeat's "eyes." The messages are listed using **parallel structures**: "to be … is to" is repeated in lines 11–13, emphasizing the cohesion of the messages. Ordinarily desired qualities, like being "enthroned," "understood," and "grasped," are viewed by Defeat as associated with negative qualities, like being "enslaved," "leveled down," and "consumed." The speaker does not appear overwhelmed (B) by these messages since he opens the stanza by addressing Defeat as "my shining sword and shield." He clearly uses Defeat's wisdom as guidance (A). The parallel structures create a predictable and steady sound, not a discordant one (D). The parallel structures do contribute to a steadier beat and rhythm (E), but the primary purpose is best described by (C).

135. (A) The **metaphor** of the "sword and shield" (9) is meant to emphasize "Defeat's" emboldening powers. The speaker calls defeat his sword and shield and then explains what he has learned from "Defeat"—namely, that success enslaves people and keeps them "leveled down" (12). The context does not indicate that "Defeat" is a sword and shield because it is brave or valiant (E), but rather that the knowledge "Defeat" has given the speaker has emboldened him the way a sword and shield would. It has made him feel strong, powerful, and protected.

136. (C) In the third stanza, the speaker describes different types of success ("enthroning," being "understood," and "grasped") and how they result not in happiness but in enslavement. In other words, success is overrated.

137. (D) Lines 13–14 say, "And to be grasped is but to reach one's fullness/ and <u>like</u> a ripe fruit to fall and be consumed." Here, the speaker compares "one," or a person who is "understood" and "grasped," to a ripe fruit that falls and gets consumed.

138. (A) The speaker characterizes "Defeat" as distinct (B) ("none but you"), useful (C) ("You are dearer to me than a thousand triumphs ... ," "In your eyes I have read ... "), brave (D) ("my deathless courage"), and bold (E) ("my bold companion"). He does not, however, think "Defeat" is second best to success; rather, success is described as overrated in the second stanza (see question 136).

139. (D) The poem's **refrain** is found in lines 1, 4, 9, 15, and 21 and enhances the poem's ode-like quality because, through the repetition of the same phrase, a lyrical, chorus-like sound is created, which coincides with the style of the **ode**. The poem is also ode-like because the speaker addresses and praises "Defeat."

140. (E) The speaker's address to "Defeat" as his "deathless courage" (21) shows that with "Defeat" comes temerity (fearlessness). Even though "Defeat's" courage is "deathless," meaning it is without death, the speaker does not use the phrase to mean that "Defeat" is immortal (D) but rather that "Defeat" provides him with an almost invincible courage, "with a will" that allows him to "be dangerous" (24–25).

141. (B) The speaker sees "Defeat" primarily as his mentor in that "Defeat" teaches him ("Through you I know that I am ... ") about himself and the world. Though "Defeat" is also his "companion" (15), their relationship is not primarily one of friendship (A), which implies an equal balance of give and take. The poem indicates that the speaker learns from and receives guidance from "Defeat" and does not necessarily offer the same in return.

142. (A) The mood that is established by the end of the poem is one of confidence: the speaker and "Defeat" will "laugh together" in a storm, "dig graves for all that die within" them, and "stand in the sun with a will" (22–24). These lines indicate that the speaker, with "Defeat" next to him, can face anything with confidence.

Passage 2. Jayadeva, Excerpt from *Gita Govinda*

143. (A) The first verse serves as the poem's **overture**, the introductory part or prologue. An introductory speaker (who is not the speaker for the remaining verses) sets up the scene by introducing Radha, her love-interest Krishna, and the maiden who will sing the remaining verses.

144. (A) The **appositives** in lines 1–5 provide epithets for Radha and Krishna. An appositive is a noun or noun phrase that further describes a noun nearby. For example, the appositive after "Beautiful Radha" is "jasmine-bosomed Radha" (1), which is also an **epithet**, any word or phrase applied to a person or thing to describe an actual or attributed quality.

145. (E) The **simile** in line 25 serves to highlight the commanding powers of spring when the speaker compares the dazzles from the blossoms to "Kama's sceptre, whom all the world obeys." Since everyone obeys Kama's sceptre, the simile makes us see how commanding spring's influence and bounty is, which almost justifies Krishna's infidelity—he has succumbed to spring's influence. The flowers are not compared to a person (D) but to a sceptre.

146. (B) The phrase "pink delicious bowls" (26) is primarily a **metaphor** for the nourishing flower petals that "fill drowsy bees." People eat from bowls, in the way that bees get their nourishment from the petals of a flower that look like and serve the purpose of bowls. While the bowls do evoke the bees' hunger, the phrase does not primarily symbolize their hunger (E); rather, it provides a new image of the flower petals. The flowers are not being **personified** in this description because "pink" and "delicious" are not human qualities (A).

147. (A) One can understand the meaning of the phrase based on both its vocabulary and the context. Throughout the poem, the maiden sings of the feelings of love that arise with the arrival of spring. A "goblet" is a drinking vessel; "nectar" means both the sweet secretions of flowers and, classically, the life-giving drink of the gods. This particular nectar "steeps" human souls in "languor", languor being a feeling of laziness or tenderness. Therefore, the best answer is (A), the drunken feeling of love.

148. (B) The **repetition** of "alone" as the closing word of many verses emphasizes the contrast between what Krishna is doing (cavorting and likely mating with other "damsels") and what he is avoiding (being alone during such an amorous season). The repetition of "alone" also explains and justifies Krishna's behavior by reminding Radha that "'tis sad to be alone" (11), "'tis hard to be alone" (17). In the third repetition of alone, the speaker asks, "who can live alone" (23), revealing her own understanding of Krishna's many romances. In the fourth and fifth mentions of "alone," the speaker insists, "none will live alone" (29) and "he will not live alone" (41), removing any judgment towards those who seek the romantic company of multiple damsels. This is a state Radha must accept. The poem does not specify that Radha is Krishna's wife or that the other damsels are additional wives (D). The speaker of most of the poem is Radha's maiden, and the word "alone" does not contrast the maiden to Radha (E).

149. (B) The poem's **refrain** serves to reinforce the speaker's empathy for Krishna by repeating the idea that "'tis sad to be alone" (11) at the end of each verse (11, 17, 23, 29, 35, and 41), which serves as a type of justification for Krishna's flirting and cavorting with many women. The maiden who sings the song seems to have understanding and empathy for Krishna, given the difficulty of being alone during sensual springtime. While this refrain may make Radha feel lonelier (C) since she is, in fact, alone while Krishna is enjoying himself with other women, the refrain first and foremost shows the maiden's understanding of Krishna's actions, which she is describing throughout the song.

150. (B) Although "fair," Krishna is "all-forgetful" and consumed with "earthly love's false fire" (3–4). This would suggest that Krishna's attitude toward Radha is best described as (B), indifferent (unconcerned, uninterested).

151. (A) In line 34, "thine other self, thine Own" refers to Krishna. The maiden sings this song to Radha. "Thine" is an archaic form of "your" and signifies familiarity. Therefore, the "you" here is Radha. Her "other self" then refers to her beloved Krishna, who dances with "those dancers" (34).

152. (E) While the maiden may be incriminating (D) Krishna by singing of his trysts with other women besides Radha, the best answer is (E), apologetic. In celebrating the fertility and bounty of springtime, she would seem to be justifying Krishna's behavior. He, too, is following the natural order of things. Furthermore, the repetition (**refrain**) at the end of each verse that such an environment makes it impossible to be alone would seem to further excuse Krishna's transgressions (see question 149).

153. (E) In context, the word "Love" (40) is a reference to Krishna. The maiden sings this song to Radha, whose love is Krishna, and in this line she says to her, "There dances and there laughs thy Love, with damsels many and one." We also know "Love" is Krishna because he has already been described as dancing with other women and the word has a capital letter that suggests it is personified as Krishna.

154. (D) We can infer that all these names are the names of types of foliage. "Kroona" is paired with the word "flowers," indicating that it is a type of flower (18). "Ketuk" is paired with the word "glades," indicating that it is perhaps a type of grass or plant (20). "Keshra" is described as yellow and with blossoms (24), "Pâtal" is paired with the word "buds" and feeds sleepy bees (26), and "Mogras" are "silken" and exude a "perfume fine and faint" (31–32).

155. (A) The song does not imply that Krishna is at all faithful. He is certainly promiscuous (B); he flirts, dances, and cavorts with many others besides Radha. He must be dexterous (agile, skillful) in that he dances, presumably well, with the dancers in the jungle (C). He also must have some charm (D) to captivate these other lovers. He indulges (E) in his desires by cavorting with other damsels.

156. (B) The overall mood is exultant. As the first verse reveals, Radha waits with her maidens while her lover Krishna is elsewhere, cavorting with other women. Radha may very well be jealous (A), but it is one of her maidens who sings the song that follows. Rather than being admonishing (scolding) (D), the maiden may be attempting to make excuses for Krishna's unfaithfulness through the song when she repeats at the end of each verse that it is "sad" or "hard" to be "alone" (11, 17). But this is hardly conciliatory (appeasing, soothing) for Radha (E). The maiden describes at great length the fertility and bounty of nature in springtime; the mood is celebratory, even ecstatic. Therefore, the best answer is (B), exultant.

Passage 3. Rabindranath Tagore, "The Home"

157. (B) The **simile** in line 2 compares the sun to a miser (scrupulous saver) to convey the disappearance of sunlight. The sun's light is compared to gold, and the sun holds on to its light (gold) as scrupulously as a miser (cheapskate) holds on to his money. (C) and (D) both say the simile contrasts two things when the purpose of a simile is to show similarities between two things, to compare them. While the simile does emphasize how dark it has become, similes do not symbolize things. (E) is not as specific as (B).

158. (E) Line 3 contains an abundance of **alliteration**. Four words in this line start with the same letter/sound: "*d*aylight ... *d*eeper ... *d*eeper ... *d*arkness."

159. (D) In context, the phrases "widowed land" (4) and "her arms" (13) are examples of **personification**. The land is given the human characteristic of being a widow, and the "darkened earth" is given human characteristics with the phrase "surrounding with her arms." In the first instance, the land is widowed because it has been harvested, presumably to nourish those who live there. In the second instance, the earth's "arms" surround the homes, which reinforces the idea of the land as nourishing and nurturing.

160. (A) The second sentence of the poem differs from the first in that it introduces "stillness" into the poem, whereas the first stanza describes the speaker as pacing alone on the road (1). The first stanza contains the **simile** ("like a miser"), not the second (B). Both stanzas allude to the setting sun and approaching darkness (C) (D). The first stanza, not the second, mentions the speaker's action of pacing (E).

161. (D) The third stanza contains a contrast between sound and silence, describing the boy's voice as "shrill" and the "track of his song" as noticeable against the "hush of the evening." There are no references to light (E) or day (A), only the "dark" and the "evening." The boy's boyhood is not compared to manhood (C), and even though the boy and the sky are mentioned (B), it is the boy's noise that contrasts with the sky's hush.

162. (E) The fourth stanza describes the location of the boy's village home; it is "at the *end* of the waste land," implying that it is somewhat isolated, being at the end of a long stretch of unused land. It is also "*beyond*/ the sugar-cane field" and "*hidden* among the shadows ..." (9). All these specifics mean that the home is somewhere, not nowhere, making (B) incorrect.

163. (D) The fourth stanza provides rich visual details of the boy's village home. We can imagine its geographical location ("beyond the sugar-cane field, hidden among the shadows of ... "), we can see the tall and slender trees loom over the home, we can feel the coolness of the shade created by the slender trees, and we even see the precise colors of those trees and smell their fruit. The preponderance of fruit trees and mentions of color provide a noticeable contrast to the "waste land" beyond, the "widowed land" nearby.

164. (A) The speaker notices that the families are happy ("glad") and their happiness does not know its own "value for the world;" in other words, happy families are unaware of how valuable their bliss is to the world (A). The earth is described as "darkened" (13), but there are no clear details that suggest the families light it up (B). The final sentence can be interpreted to mean that the speaker wishes he were a part of these families (C), but this is an inference and the question asks for a paraphrase. The earth opens "her arms" around the glad families, but there are no details that suggest the earth makes the families happy (E). In fact, it is implied that the comforts of home and "mothers' hearts" contribute to the happiness.

165. (E) The speaker feels reassured upon seeing that there is life, joy, love, and comfort for others, beyond the waste land, among the shadows and darkened earth. The gladness of those "young lives," blessed by "mothers' hearts," has value for the world, according to the speaker, who characterizes himself as "lonely." Ascribing value to the scene he observes means that he does not feel envious (B) or only mildly satisfied (C). The common comforts of the homes and love from mothers are not luxuries and do not create a sense of indulgence (D). The speaker is separate from those in the homes because he is a passerby, not because the homes are exclusive and excluding him (A).

166. (E) The poem's form and style are characteristic of a **free-verse poem** because the poem does not adhere to any regulated, standard patterns or styles of poems. There is no rhyme scheme or consistent beat, so it cannot be a **ballad** (A). It also does not have 14 lines, so it is not a **sonnet** (D). It does not overtly praise something, so it is not an **ode** (B), and it does not commemorate a death, so it is not an **elegy** (C).

Chapter 4: British Fiction

Passage 1. Frances Burney, *Evelina*

167. (A) The mercers "took care by bowing and smirking, to be noticed" because they are eager to be noticed by the patrons, perhaps so that they may receive more business, making them solicitous (anxiously concerned, eager to please). The speaker even notices, "they recommended them all [the silks] so strongly," indicating that their primary motivation is to persuade customers to "buy everything they showed" (10–11). While there are "six or seven men belonging to each shop," which may imply they are excessive and redundant (B), (C), the question asks for the *primary* characterization and this is secondary to their solicitous manner. The mercers are "bowing" and pleasing in order to make a sale, not because they are guided by principle and doing what is right (E).

168. (C) The speaker is most "diverted" by the fact that the women are served by men who "seemed to understand every part of a woman's dress better than" they do themselves. She is surprised and confused as to how and why this can be the case, indicated also by the exclamation point. There are no details to indicate she views these men negatively (D), (E), (A), (B). In fact, she is more impressed by their knowledge than bothered.

169. (A) In context, the word "affected" means assuming or pretending to possess that which is not natural. The speaker finds it abnormal that "such men!" exist, men who know women's clothes better than women. She finds this unusual, affected.

170. (C) The speaker remarks, "The dispatch with which they work in these great shops is amazing, for they have promised me a complete suit of linen against the evening." The word "dispatch" means haste, speed, efficiency. While the shops are accommodating her need to have her garments by "this evening," it is their efficiency that impressively allows them to accommodate her, making (C) more specific than (E).

171. (E) The speaker is disoriented; she finds her hair "odd," and does not recognize herself, which is an unsettling feeling. Even the terminology to describe her new hair style is unfamiliar. She sees it as "entangled" while "they" euphemistically call it "frizzled." She *fears* it will be difficult to comb it. (C), though true, does not encapsulate the unsettling feelings the speaker conveys. She is confused, perplexed, and a little bewildered by this strange new style.

172. (D) She is insecure about dancing well in front of different people, outside of her "school" (28). She is apprehensive (nervous, fearful) and wishes "it was over" despite reassurances from Miss Mirvan. (E) indicates that her dance skills are actually poor, and this may not be the case. When considering *the passage as a whole*, it is clear that the speaker suffers from a more general insecurity and apprehension. The speaker's aforementioned reference to her "fear" (26) about her frizzled hair, along with an earlier admittance that she "was almost afraid to go on" (8) while shopping reveal her apprehension towards the strangeness of these new experiences. (C), however, is not as good as (D) because she is not "half afraid" due to the newness of *everything she* has experienced; for example, she does describe the shops as "really very entertaining" (5).

173. (B) It is stated that the speaker is here to "improve by being in this town." She claims that once she has improved, her letters will not contain this "wretched stuff" and "will be less unworthy." The wretched stuff likely refers to the subject matter of the letter we have been reading, which reflects her confusion and naiveté about her upper-class environment. Since she is here to improve, and she describes her experiences only with shopping and balls, we can infer that she is here to become more refined, sophisticated, cosmopolitan. The reference to being "less unworthy" may lead to (C), but the purpose of her being here is not solely to please the reader of her letter.

174. (E) The closing of the passage is written as the closing of a letter. The passage is clearly an excerpt of a missive (a letter) from Evelina to her "dear Sir" (29). *Missive* is perhaps an unfamiliar term, but the other answer choices are recognizably incorrect.

175. (B) Evelina closes her letter, "Your dutiful and affectionate, though unpolished, Evelina," which emphasizes her balanced perception of herself. She acknowledges her strengths and what she perceives to be a temporary weakness, her unrefined nature, which she is currently devoting herself to improving (see question 173).

176. (D) In the passage, the speaker describes what she has seen and experienced and how she felt about it. She reveals emotions such as "half afraid," "almost afraid," and "almost ashamed" to express her reactions to what she has experienced. While she does appear to be tenacious (determined) because she is dedicated to "improving" herself, she is not characterized as wise (E) because she is naive and new to the environment. She is merely recording all that is new and weird to her, not insightful analyses or criticism of her society (A). Also, while she does appear guileless (open, honest), she does not appear uncouth (bad-mannered, rude). This adjective is too extreme (B).

Passage 2. Joseph Conrad, *Heart of Darkness*

177. (A) The word "it" in line 3 refers to the "*Nellie*," a cruising yawl, which is a boat or a vessel.

178. (E) The Director's work is not actually "out there in the luminous estuary," out on the sea, as one would expect, "but behind him, within the brooding gloom," the gloom that is earlier referred to as "brooding motionless over the biggest, and the greatest, town on earth." The Director's job is more municipal, focused on matters of the city/state (political, governmental, beauracratic).

179. (B) The mood of this sentence is lugubrious (gloomy, sorrowful), as indicated by the "mournful" gloom that "broods."

180. (E) The first and second paragraphs contain **simile** ("*like* the beginning of an interminable waterway"), **metaphor** ("red clusters of canvas"), **personification** (the air broods, "the haze rested"), and sensory **imagery** ("the air was dark," "flutter of the sails"), which together create a rich illustration of the setting that readers can see and feel. There are no examples of **oxymoron**, two words that have opposite meanings paired together.

181. (C) The Director of Companies is described as "nautical" (naval) and venerable (deserving of respect) when the speaker claims that he and the other crew members "affectionately watched his back" and saw him as the equivalent of a pilot, who is "trustworthiness personified." There are no details to suggest the Director is particularly sociable (gregarious) (E) or affectionate (demonstrative) (A) (B). The environment is brooding, not the Director (D).

182. (B) The narrator mentions four people who are on the boat with him: the accountant, the lawyer, Marlow, and the Director of Companies. (C) would be correct if the question asked about the total number of passengers aboard the yacht, including the narrator.

183. (A) After stating, "For some reason or other we did not begin that game of dominoes," the narrator elaborates with, "We felt meditative, and fit for nothing but placid staring." The context indicates that they are staring at their environment (the dynamic setting imbued with light and gloom).

184. (A) The "mist" on the marsh is compared to a "gauzy and radiant fabric" that "drapes" in "diaphanous folds." The folds are part of the **metaphor** that compares the mist to gauzelike fabric. "Diaphanous" describes thin, gauzelike transparent fabric.

185. (D) The context of the final paragraph reveals a setting sun that appears to be "without heat, as if about to go out suddenly, stricken to death" by the same gloom that is also "brooding over a crowd of men." Those poor hapless men appear to be trapped under this deathly gloom. The word "crowd" does not indicate reverence (A) or specifically indicate bureaucrats (B). The crowd is not restive (restless, refractory); on the contrary, the descriptions suggest it is more likely paralyzed or trapped under the brooding gloom (C).

186. (D) Lines 30–36 compare light and dark. The ending of the day creates "exquisite brilliance," shining water, "unstained light," and radiance. This light is contrasted with the "*gloom*" in the west, which can be interpreted as darkness because it is "angered by the approach of the sun [the light]," as if they are in battle.

187. (B) The final sentence creates an ominous (threatening) mood. The light, which is described as magnificent throughout the passage, is suddenly extinguished by the darkness—it has lost the battle and disappears as if "stricken to death by the touch of that gloom brooding over a crowd of men." This sentence has a threatening tone because something that was great and brilliant has suddenly been extinguished.

188. (C) The passage appears to use **symbolism** to **foreshadow** later events because the descriptions of the setting (the battles/conflicts between light and dark, the waterway/horizon and land, nature and man) are likely symbolic of future conflicts that are only hinted at by the descriptions of the setting. It is unclear who the main character—III—is from this passage. Several people are mentioned, but the narrator reveals more about the setting than himself and a main character of the novel (Marlow) is barely mentioned in this passage.

Passage 3. Joseph Conrad, *Heart of Darkness*

189. (E) The sea's glitter is "blurred by a creeping mist" (9), making it obfuscated (concealed)—III. It is also "always mute with an air of whispering" (5), making it laconic (not talkative)—II. The sea is also compared to an enigma and described as "smiling, frowning, inviting, grand, mean, insipid, or savage … " (4–5) and as whispering, "'Come and find out'" (6), making it cryptic (mysterious)—I.

190. (A) The speaker describes his job as perfunctory (done in a routine way without much care or passion) when he implies that the crew on the boat just "pounded along" (14), doing the same thing every day, in a monotonous routine. The settlements that are centuries old are "still no bigger than pinheads" (12–13) and regarding the workers, "nobody seemed particularly to care" that some drowned (18). The speaker explains that the soldiers were "just flung out there, and on we went" and he refers to himself as "idle," all indicative of a perfunctory and passionless approach to the work.

191. (B) The repetition of the word "landed" at the start of three clauses in the sentence is an example of **anaphora**, which, in this context, helps establish the speaker's attitude, or tone, of how repetitive and perfunctory he noticed the work to be (see question 190).

192. (E) The speaker remains "within the toil of a mournful and senseless delusion" (25) because of "idleness" (A), "isolation" (B), "the oily and languid sea" (C), and the "uniform sombreness of the coast" (24) (D). The "voice of the surf," however, "was a positive pleasure, like the speech of a brother" (25–26) (E).

193. (C) When the speaker describes his fascination with the "black fellows," he explains that they were "as natural and true as the surf … . They wanted no excuse for being there" (33–34). This is why "They were a comfort to look at" and why he felt "for a time" he "belonged still to a world of straightforward facts" (33–34). They provide him with a sense of verity (truth).

194. (B) In this line, the speaker **foreshadows** what will happen later in his story— that, for him, the world of truth would not last long.

195. (D) The sentence contains a **simile** ("Her ensign dropped limp *like* a rag"), and **alliteration** ("*s*limy *s*well *s*wung … *s*waying") in order to fully illustrate the lazy stillness and futility of the "man-of-war," which adds to the speaker's overall sense that there is "a touch of insanity" to the scene. One would ordinarily not expect a war ship to appear so disheveled and ineffectual. There are no examples of **onomatopoeia** (A) **hyperbole** (C), or **allusion** (E). The sentence contains multiple independent clauses, so it does not have a simple syntactical structure (B).

196. (D) The "she" in line 41 refers to the man-of-war ship that is described previously as "shelling the bush" (37). In lines 41–42, the description continues, describing her as "incomprehensible, firing into a continent."

197. (E) The word "Pop" is an example of **onomatopoeia**. The first sentence, containing independent and dependent clauses, is juxtaposed with the second sentence, consisting of only one independent clause, creating sentence variety—I, III. The series of descriptions ("a small flame *would* dart and vanish, a little white smoke *would* disappear, a tiny projectile *would* give a feeble screech") follows a **parallel structure**, and the phrase "nothing happened" is repeated, which contributes to the sense of purposelessness and futility—II.

198. (D) What the speaker has been describing is dark and absurd—a ship is "incomprehensible, firing into a continent" with no visible targets (41–42). He goes on to call this proceeding "insanity", making the "lugubrious drollery" (45) a clear reference to the dark absurdity of what he is observing.

199. (B) The speaker is incredulous (surprised disbelief) that "somebody on board" was so certain he was firing at enemies. While the speaker may feel distress (C) and perhaps remorse (D) since he is describing past events, the em dashes and the exclamation point in the quoted phrase show the speaker's shock, and the previous lines suggest his incredulity because he clearly does not see any enemies—the ship is *incomprehensibly* firing at nothing and the proceeding is insane.

200. (C) In the passage, the speaker describes countless scenes he witnesses while aboard a French steamer, such as the cold indifference with which his shipmates treat the possible drowning of the clerks they are dropping off, settlements that look "centuries old" but still "no bigger than a pinhead," trading places that appear more like "sordid farce[s]" than legitimate enterprises, and of course the "incomprehensible" man-of-war that fires into the jungle with no visible "enemies" in sight. The speaker's tone when describing these scenes is slightly tragic—he longs for truth and a world of "straightforward facts" because what he has seen is confusing. The settlements, the French outposts, are not functioning the way he may have expected or hoped.

Passage 4. Mary Shelley, *Frankenstein*

201. (E) The speaker observes, "There was a sense of justice in my father's upright mind which rendered it necessary that he should approve highly to love strongly" (3–4). The narrator goes on to reason that perhaps his father had suffered before due to loving someone who was not worthy of his devotion, "and was so disposed to set a greater value on tried worth" (6). His love is not unconditional; a person must have proven herself worthy in order to be loved by the father. The father felt "a desire to be the means of … recompensing her for the sorrows she had endured" (9–10) (A)(D), he is "inspired by reverence for her virtues"

(8) (B), and the "considerable difference between the ages … seemed to unite them only closer in the bonds of affection" (1–3) (C).

202. **(C)** The sentence begins with the subject to which "it" refers: "There was a show of gratitude and worship … for it was inspired … ."

203. **(C)** The speaker's mother is described as virtuous in line 8 (A), generous in lines 14, 37–40 (B), convalescent (recovering from illness) in line 14–19 (D), and enervated (weak) in line 19 (E). While the speaker's father is eager to attend to her needs, there are no details to suggest that the mother demands this attention and care; therefore, she is not presented as importunate (annoyingly demanding).

204. **(C)** While the comparison of the father to a gardener and the mother to a fair exotic might imply that the father is officious (overbearing and fussy) in his protection of the mother, the tone of the lines does not indicate that the speaker intends to portray the father in such a negative way. The speaker makes the comparison, more likely, to emphasize how his father nurtures his mother the way an attentive gardener would care for a rare flower.

205. **(D)** The first paragraph gives helpful background for comprehending the details in the second paragraph. The first paragraph explains the relationship between the speaker's parents and characterizes the mother. These details are useful in interpreting the second paragraph, in which we see the mother's specific actions and behavior (she helps the poor). The background from the first paragraph helps us understand the motives and reasons behind her actions.

206. **(A)** The **metaphor** compares the parents' love to a mine from which they extract unlimited amounts of affection for their son. The speaker implies that, even though they expended so much love and devotion on each other, their capacity to love was so inexhaustible that they still were able to love him without conservation.

207. **(E)** The speaker mentions that his parents saw him as "their plaything and their idol … ," implying that they adored him so much it was as if they worshiped him the way an acolyte (a religious follower, a worshipper at an altar) might worship a religious idol.

208. **(D)** The sentence contains a series of explanatory dependent clauses, one of which contains a list: "With this … added to the … it may be imagined that while … I received *a lesson of patience, of charity, and of self-control,* I was so guided by a silken cord that all seemed but one train of enjoyment to me." This string of clauses and phrases reinforces the *train* of enjoyment the speaker intends to convey.

209. **(A)** The children that "spoke of penury in its worst shape" are described as "poor," "half-clothed," "afflicted," and "hungry," all suggesting destitution (poverty).

210. **(E)** The girl is characterized as visually striking by the words "very fair" and by the contrast made between her and her "dark-eyed, hardy little vagrant" peers. Her gold hair "set a crown of distinction on her head"—I. She is otherworldly; she is described in line 53 as heavenly, celestial, and "of a distinct species." Her distinguishing qualities evoke strong emotions in the speaker and the mother: "none could behold her without looking on her as of a distinct species, a being heaven-sent … "—III.

211. (A) The description of the girl contains **alliteration** ("*s*o expressive of *s*ensibility and *s*weetness") (C), **polysyndeton** ("thin *and* very fair … clear *and* ample … her blue eyes cloudless, *and* her lips *and* the moulding of her face") (E), **simile** ("*as* of a distinct species") (B), and **hyperbole** ("heaven-sent, and bearing a celestial stamp") (D). There are no **allusions** in these lines.

212. (C) The tone is not factual; the speaker speculates and recalls his impressions of his parents (B)(E). It is not resentful but rather exceedingly praiseworthy of his parents (D). It is not grave (serious); he mostly recalls sweet, sentimental moments (A). Even his mother's physical weakness is described in the context of how much his father loved and cared for her. The tone is best stated as earnest because the speaker appears to genuinely feel the emotions his word choice suggests he feels. There is no hint of irony, sarcasm, humor, self-deprecation, hostility, regret, remorse, etc.

213. (E) While the passage does include more characterization of the mother than of the father, the speaker himself, and the sister (A), the main purpose of the passage as a whole is to characterize the family. The passage opens with the speaker speculating about the father's past, his reasons for loving the mother, and details about his devotion and sacrifice. In doing so, the narrator touches on the remarkable characteristics of his mother that have earned the devotion of the father. This background is necessary in order for readers to comprehend the parents' devotion to their son (the focus of the first half of the second paragraph) and to comprehend the descriptions of the sister and the mother's reaction to her (the focus of the end of the second paragraph). The passage intends to show the dynamics among the family members, and in order to do so, must spend time focusing on each character's features. One particular character is not the sole focus.

Passage 5. Jonathan Swift, *Gulliver's Travels*

214. (C) In the first paragraph, the speaker mentions that he "obtained [his] liberty" in the past "fortnight," indicating that he has been recently emancipated (B). He mentions that he was willing to give Reldresal his time "on account of his quality and personal merits, as well as of the many good offices he has done [him] …," making him grateful (A). He shows that he is gracious when he "offered to lie down, that he [Reldresal] might the more conveniently reach [the speaker's] ear" (D). Since the speaker has to either lie down so Reldresal can speak into his ear or hold Reldresal in his hand, it is clear that the speaker may be quite large (E).

215. (E) The word "it" in the phrase refers to the speaker's "liberty," suggesting that Reldresal will pretend that the speaker entirely earned his liberty but does not actually believe he did. He "added, that if it had not been for the present situation of things at court, perhaps [the speaker] might not have obtained it so soon" (11).

216. (A) Line 11 begins with "For, said he, as flourishing …" The "he" in this line refers to Reldresal, who is identified in the first paragraph as the principal secretary. After line 12, Reldresal continues as the speaker of the second paragraph.

217. (D) In lines 15–22, the speaker explains that the empire has "two struggling parties" that are distinguished by the high or low heels of their shoes. In the sentence "It is alleged, indeed, that the high heels are most agreeable to our ancient constitution; but, however this may be, his majesty hath determined to make use only of low heels in the administration of the government … ," the clause beginning with "but" suggests that there is some perceived problem with his majesty's partiality toward (preference for) the low heels. His majesty's shoes are indeed part of the problem (A), but the shoes are only problematic in that they indicate his majesty's partiality, making (D) the better answer to the question about the empire's problem.

218. (C) In lines 24–25, the speaker says, "We compute the *Tramecksan*, or high heels, to exceed us in number; but the power is wholly on *our side*," implying that he is a member of the opposing party, that of the low heels, also called "*Slamecksan*."

219. (B) The speaker explains, "We apprehend his imperial highness, the heir to the crown, to have some tendency towards the high heels … we can plainly discover that one of his heels is higher than the other, which gives him a hobble … ." Since it has already been determined that the speaker and his imperial majesty are low heels, it would make sense that they would be apprehensive (nervous, fearful) that the heir to the crown has displayed some preference to the high heels by wearing one high heel and one low heel, resulting in his hobble. The hobble then implies that the heir could be considering defecting (switching, betraying) from one party to the other.

220. (D) "These intestine disquiets" that the speaker has been describing have been the domestic (existing within their home country) problems and strifes (struggles) between opposing factions in the empire. (B) is not as specific as (D), which explains the "disquiets" as strife. No one has actually been found to have committed treason (C); there are merely speculations about potential defection.

221. (E) The speaker explains that the empire is skeptical about the truth of the addressee's claims "that there are other kingdoms and states in the world, inhabited by human creatures as large as [himself]" because their "philosophers … would rather conjecture that [he] dropped from the moon" (B). The word "rather" suggests that the philosophers find it more convenient to formulate a cursory dismissal of the addressee's claims than to have to contend with the frightening certainty "that an hundred mortals of [the addressee's] bulk would, in a short time, destroy all the fruits and cattle of his majesty's dominions." Their reasoning is not research-based (B) (D) or even that logical (A), as it stems from avoidance and fear. They are willing to believe something even more absurd—that he dropped from the moon or stars—than to engage with his assertions that "there are other kingdoms and states in the world" with creatures of his large size.

222. (A) The word "fomented" most closely means goaded (motivated, encouraged) in this context because the speaker goes on to explain that the monarchs of Blefuscu contributed to the war's continuance by providing "refuge" to Lilliput's "exiles." By doing so, they keep the enemy protected, which allows the rebellions to continue.

223. (E) When he describes Blefuscu's "*Blundecral*" as "our *Alcoran*," he suggests that the *Alcoran* is Lilliput's equivalent to Blefuscu's *Blundecral*. Both of these texts are implied to be each nation's sacred holy text because they contain chapters and "fundamental doctrine" of a prophet.

224. (D) The argument between Blefuscu and Lilliput is an argument about semantics, the study of language's meaning, of linguistic signs and their signifiers, because both nations interpret the words of the "great prophet Lustrog" differently. The words "the convenient end" are interpreted by one nation to be the "big end" and by the other nation to be the "small end." The speaker says, " ... which is the convenient end, seems, in my humble opinion, to be left to every man's conscience."

225. (E) The style of the passage is similar to a lampoon in that the author is clearly satirizing the silly nature of a country's wars and civic disputes, comparing them to quibbles over nonsensical things like arguing over which side of an egg the citizens should crack and what size heel a citizen wears on his shoe. A **lampoon** is a work of literature or art that sharply satirizes a person, issue, concept, etc.

226. (C) All of the words printed in italics (*"Slamecksan," "Tramecksan," "drurr," "Alcoran,"* and *"Blundecral"*) refer to objects or names in Lilliput and Blefuscu's language. (A) is incorrect because a "drurr" is not a person or a place. It is also not that important (B)—it is a unit of measure.

227. (E) Reldresal explains that "his imperial majesty, plac[es] great confidence in [the first paragraph's speaker's] valor and strength" (70), making him doughty (brave)—III. His strength is suggested to come from his large size—II—which is described in the first paragraph. The first paragraph also explains that the speaker of that paragraph has recently been given his freedom—I—for which he may be so grateful that he would return a favor to his majesty for his acquittal.

228. (A) While the passage as a whole carries an **ironic** and **satirical** tone, Reldresal's tone in lines 11–71 is quite serious. He describes Lilliput's problems in a grave tone to persuade his addressee to assist the nation in its war against Blefuscu.

Passage 6. Oscar Wilde, *The Picture of Dorian Gray*

229. (E) In lines 16–17, the author compares two things, London and the bourdon note, using the word "as," making the sentence an example of a **simile**—I. There is an example of passive voice—II—in the second paragraph: "Persian saddle-bags on which he was lying" (5). The subject of the sentence is placed after the action it performs, making the sentence passive instead of active. The entire first paragraph is a compound sentence—III—as is the sentence in lines 5–14 ("From the corner ... motion") because they consist of more than one independent clause with no dependent clauses necessary.

230. (B) The shadows of "birds in flight" (9–10) on the curtains make Lord Henry recall the Japanese painters who "seek to convey the sense of swiftness and motion" in the "immobile" medium of art (12–14). The narrator recalls this art form because the birds in motion are in contrast to the "oppressive" stillness of the room (16) the way that the immobile art form is at odds with the motion it attempts to convey.

231. (B) The tremulous (trembling) branches can hardly bear the burden of the beauty of "the honey-sweet and honey-coloured blossoms of a laburnum" (7–8), the subject to which "theirs" refers.

232. (A) While there are some details to suggest Lord Henry could be bored (A), he is actually described as having thoughts (11–12) and being relaxed (5–6), which do not imply boredom. The characters appear to be familiar with the art of foreign countries (B) because Basil Hallward's studio contains a "divan of Persian saddle-bags" (5) and Lord Henry describes Japanese painters with some familiarity. Both the characters are presented as upper class (C) through their familiarity with luxury items and foreign art. The first two paragraphs describe both the abundance in nature (the "odour of roses," the "heavy scent of lilac," the burdensome beauty of the blossoms and the "unmown grass") alongside the introduction of Lord Henry, who rests on a luxurious and imported divan, relaxing and smoking (5–6), implying the abundance of material wealth in the room (D). There is a lethargic (sluggish) mood (E) to the scene, indicated by the "monotonous insistence" of the circling bees (14–15), the oppressive stillness (16), and the image of Lord Henry "lying, smoking, as was his custom, innumerable cigarettes" (5–6).

233. (D) The emphasis in this paragraph has been on the silence and stillness, "the sullen murmur" (14) in the room. London's "roar" is "dim" (16–17) because of its distance to the stillness and calmness of the current environment. All of that urban activity and movement sounds as dim as "the bourdon note of a distant organ." There are no references to the cultural attractions of London (B), Lord Henry does not want to be somewhere else (see question 232), the narrator is not intending to critique London (A) or indicate the geographic location of the setting (E).

234. (D) Lord Henry speaks in **epigrams** (quips, witticisms, often ironic), such as in lines 39–40, which are *not* cliché (D) because they are original and witty. Much of what he says to Basil is advice (exhortation) on what he should do with his painting (27–33), that he should send it somewhere so as to be "talked about" and to make others "jealous" (42–44).

235. (C) Basil Hallward's assertion that he won't "'send it anywhere'" (34) is not indicative of insecurity (C). There are no details to suggest that Basil is insecure about his work; on the contrary, he has a "smile of pleasure" (24) when he looks at his painting, which indicates that he likes his painting (E). That he is well educated (B) is indicated by the mention of his having studied at Oxford (35); he has been the subject of idle talk (gossip, speculation) in the past (D), indicated by the many "conjectures" about his absence (22) and the friends who would laugh at him for the way he "tossed his head back" (34). He is a notable painter (A) since he is publicly known as an artist and, as Lord Henry suggests, he already has a reputation (40–41).

236. (C) The dialogue in the passage is predominantly comprised of Lord Henry's exhortations (urgings) to Basil Hallward to display his painting. In his speech, Lord Henry expresses his views on artists, the Academy, the Grosvenor, reputation, and old men.

237. (B) Lord Henry (and the reader) wonders why Basil Hallward will not send his painting anywhere: "Lord Henry elevated his eyebrows and looked at him in amazement … " What odd chaps you painters are!" (36–39), making (B) correct and (C) incorrect. Lord

Henry continues to express his views about the painters in the final lines of the passage (E). We know the stillness in the room is due to "the rich odour of roses ... the heavy scent of the lilacs ... the sullen murmur of the bees ... circling with monotonous insistence" (1–15) (A). Basil's painting is "a full-length portrait of a young man of extraordinary perfect beauty" (18–19) (D).

238. (D) While both Lord Henry and Basil share the scene and speak to each other, the focus of the passage is not on their friendship (B). The subject of their dialogue, however, is the painting, the galleries, and the artist's reputation. Lord Henry's views on the subject are evident in the counsel he offers Basil, and Basil's perspective is implied through his refusal to "send [his painting] anywhere" (34). The ornate descriptions of the setting help set a mood and tone, but are limited to the first two paragraphs only (E) and serve to communicate the purpose; they are not the purpose themselves.

Passage 7. Virginia Woolf, "An Unwritten Novel"

239. (C) Line 1 explicitly refers to the expression as one of unhappiness. It is "enough by itself" to pull one away from her newspaper, and the "poor woman's face" would be "insignificant without that look" and it is "almost a symbol of destiny with it." The reference to "a symbol of destiny" conveys the expression as overwhelming in its significant sadness. While (E) is true, the surrounding context suggests it is the actual expression itself, its weightiness and significance, that is hard to avoid. (B) is incorrect because the narrator does have a newspaper she attempts to use as a distraction, and the other passengers appear to be able to distract themselves (27–28).

240. (D) According to the passage, "Life's what you see in people's eyes; life's what they learn, and, having learnt it, never, though they seek to hide it, cease to be aware of" (lines 3–5). (B) is incorrect because "they" do not disregard what they learn in life; rather, they "never . . . cease to be aware of it" even though "they seek to hide it." (A) is a tempting choice, but the narrator does not ever indicate that life only consists of knowledge *reluctantly* gained. Even though there is an undertone of misery and avoidance of "life" due to its burdensome experiences and memories, the definition of life is more generally given as "life is what they learn." Also, the narrator refers to the *Times* as a "great reservoir of life" and she lists positive news (not solely reluctantly gained news) like births and marriages along with mundane news like court circulars among the events that make up "life."

241. (E) All five faces are "mature," so the fifth person is not older than the others (B). The narrator at first says, "Marks of reticence" are made by "each one of the five," each one "doing something to hide or stultify his knowledge" but soon reveals in line 10–11 that "the terrible thing about the fifth is that she does nothing at all." She does not have a mark of reticence, making (C), (D), and (A) incorrect. What distinguishes her from the others is that she does not play the game of concealing life with "marks of reticence": "Ah, but my poor, unfortunate woman, do play the game—do, for all our sakes, conceal it!" (11–12).

242. (E) The narrator only describes the other passengers as examples to support her assertion that "Life's what you see in people's eyes; life's what they learn, and, having learnt it, never, though they seek to hide it, cease to be aware of—what?" (3–5). The "faces opposite" have the "marks of reticence" that the narrator sees as customary attempts to "conceal" life. The four passengers also serve as a contrast to the fifth, who "does nothing at all," who does not "play the game" and "conceal it" (11–12). The narrator's intent is not to portray the other passengers as cold, indifferent, apathetic, or secretive (B–D) because of their "marks of reticence" and attempts to "conceal" life; rather, she mentions these behaviors as examples of what is expected and common and to highlight the strangeness of the woman's refusal to play along. The passengers are certainly not garrulous (talkative) (A).

243. (C) See question 242. The fifth person does not "play the game" of concealing life (what she has learned and experienced, particularly her sadness) with "marks of reticence" like the other passengers do.

244. (A) The author does not use actual dialogue in the passage. The only phrases/sentences in quotation marks are qualified with "she <u>seemed</u> to say to me" and "I answered <u>silently</u>." Though they are in quotation marks, these words are not actually part of a verbal conversation. There are several instances of auditory **imagery** and visual imagery in the second paragraph, along with a **simile**: "she looked up, shifted slightly in her seat and sighed . . . she shuddered, twitched her arm . . . and shook her head. . . . Again with infinite weariness she moved her head from side to side until, <u>like</u> a top exhausted with spinning, it settled on her neck." We can hear the woman sighing and see her moving. These observations are certainly subjective, as they are provided through first-person narration (E).

245. (A) The narrator observes the woman as possibly thinking, "'If only you knew!'" which is in context of the woman not concealing her sadness, her life experience, like everyone else does. The narrator insists, silently, "'I do know … I know the whole business … the *Times* knows. . . . We all know.'" She goes on to cite the news coverage in the paper, such as a peace deal, a train collision, births, deaths, marriages, court cases, and more. The variety of these examples suggests that what they "know" is the various events, details, and emotions that make up life, not the specific details of the woman's experiences (B), (C).

246. (D) The speaker attempts to use the *Times* as a shield (B) to protect her from the woman's unconcealed sadness, but "The *Times* was no protection against such sorrow as hers. . . . She pierced through my shield" (27–31), making the *Times* penetrable, not impenetrable. The *Times* is exhaustive in its full coverage of life events and news (see question 245); she even refers to it as a "reservoir of life" (A), (E). Because she relies on it "for manners' sake" and to help her "play the game" of not looking at life, the *Times* is also a kind of crutch (C).

247. (C) The passage is narrated in the **first-person point of view** ("me," "I"), not in **third person** (B). The passage consists of the narrator's thoughts as she rides the train and observes the behaviors of her fellow passengers, one in particular. She ponders, speculates, and makes assumptions about the significance of their actions while also revealing her own perspective on "life" and customary behaviors. There is no actual dialogue in the passage. The quoted speech is introduced as the narrator's silent expressions (E) or an assumption about what the woman might say (13–14).

248. (A) The narrator is most definitely *curious* about the fifth passenger, the woman, whose "expression of unhappiness was enough by itself to make one's eyes slide above the paper's edge" (1–2). She has *pity* for the fifth passenger, referring to her as "the poor woman" (2) and finding it difficult to resist "intercourse" with "such sorrow as hers" (27–28). In fact, she feels *compelled*, twice, to look over the paper's edge, the paper that is meant to be her protection from engaging with others' lives (2, 19–20). She experiences *hope* when she tries, yet again, to use her shield (the *Times*); she folds the paper "so that it made a perfect square, crisp, thick, impervious even to life" (27–29). Once armed, she "glanced up," hopeful that her protection would work. It does not work, however, as the woman "pierced through [the] shield" and dampens her courage to clay. The narrator is *resigned* as all hope is "denied" (30–33). The narrator does not experience extremely negative emotions like anger (B), disgust (C), audacity (D), or antipathy (E).

249. (B) The narrator uses a **simile** in the final lines to compare her own eyes to a body of water that the woman searches for any "sediments of courage . . . and damping it to clay" (31–32). The woman is characterized here as prowling and ultimately successful and powerful against the narrator, who is characterized as vulnerable, without any sediments of courage. (C) is a tempting choice, but the woman is portrayed more as a foe that the narrator must use a shield against, not specifically as a leader.

250. (E) The narrator opens the passage by contextualizing the woman's strangely captivating expression of sadness. She explains that we all play "a game" of concealing "life" with customary "marks of reticence." This woman, however, does not play along. The narrator silently pleads, "Ah, but my poor, unfortunate woman, do play the game—do, for all our sakes, conceal it!" (11–12). The second paragraph details the narrator's repeated attempts at staying focused on her own "mark of reticence"—the *Times*, and her compulsion to creep "over the paper's rim" (20) due to the woman's audible and obvious expressions of sadness. The final paragraph reveals that all hope is "denied"; the woman has "pierced through" the newspaper shield and dampened any "sediments of courage" that remained. (C) is true, but falls under the purview of (E), which is a summary of the entire passage.

251. (D) The narrator has made several attempts to arm herself against the woman's exposed unhappy expression. In the final lines, the narrator uses a **simile** (see question 249) to reveal what little courage she has left to fight the woman's attempts at intercourse. The woman gazes into her eyes as if "damping" any "sediments of courage" that remain. The woman appears to be successful: "Her twitch alone denied all hope, discounted all illusion" (32–33). The twitch, along with the other physical movements and sounds emanating from the woman (see question 244) and making it difficult for the narrator to avoid looking at her, denies all hope for the narrator. The passage ends on a note of surrender, capitulation.

Chapter 5: American Fiction

Passage 1. Louisa May Alcott, "An Old-fashioned Girl"

252. (D) Tom's indignant resolution is that he proclaims he will never "bother" about with Fanny's friends without her being there, but this decision is not the source of the humor (A). In this assertion, he does not directly attack Fanny (B) and his comment in reference to "bothering about [her] friends" is hardly biting (C). What is funny, however, is that Tom's decisive words and his "air of indignant resolution" are "somewhat damaged by a tousled head, and the hunched appearance of his garments generally." The tousled head alone (E) does not create the humor; rather, it is the juxtaposition of the disheveled appearance with the intended authoritative declaration that is comical (D).

253. (A) The narrator appears to know that Fanny is "hoping to soothe [Tom's] ruffled feelings" when she offers something to Tom in return for his picking up Polly—I. The narrator appears to know that Tom "regarded girls as a very unnecessary portion of creation"—III. These are both instances where the narrator reveals her access to characters' internal thoughts, as these details could not be gleaned from the characters' actions or speech alone. The description of Tom rising from the sofa (11–14) does not reveal the narrator's access to the characters' internal thoughts. There is no reference to Tom's internal state. Any objective viewer could observe his "air" and how it contrasts with his appearance—II. The narrator herself observes that "Boys are apt to think so …." These lines provide commentary from the narrator about boys in general, so they do not reveal the narrator's access to characters' thoughts—IV.

254. (A) The somersaults are used literally to indicate a movement/exercise boys of Tom's age enjoy and figuratively to indicate the complete reversal these boys will experience in a few years when they often become infatuated with the same girls they now loathe. The narrator does not intend to convey arrogance with this observation; it is meant to be an insightful observation about the nature of boys of Tom's age (B), (C). She does not regret this behavior or see it as negative (D). She is not intending to educate (E) the reader about boys, either; she is providing context for and insight on the events in the story.

255. (E) With the phrase "abject slaves," the narrator exaggerates the boys' eventual devotion and infatuation with "those bothering girls" they shun in younger years in order to emphasize the complete reversal, or "somersault" (see question 254), they experience as they age. This phrase is not literal; the boys do not actually become the girls' slaves (D). It is not meant earnestly or seriously, so it is not a somber description of actual male-female dynamics (A), (C). Though the commentary is humorous, the narrator does not mean to ridicule boys; rather, she is merely bringing our attention to a perceived pattern of behavior that she notices is funnily appropriate since boys of that age actually like "turning somersaults."

256. (E) The phrases are not part of a dialogue or conversation (B) and they are not specialized vocabulary terms that require background knowledge (D). The narrator does not use these phrases sarcastically to point fun at the boys who say these expressions (A), nor is she quoting an expert (C). The quotations indicate that these phrases are distinct from the narrator's voice. They likely belong to Tom himself or more generally to boys of Tom's age (E).

257. (E) After Fanny says that she described Tom's appearance to her friend Polly, Tom "gave a hasty smooth to his curly pate and a glance at the mirror, feeling sure that his sister hadn't done him justice. . . . " The context reveals that Tom is certain Fanny has underestimated his attractiveness, since sisters always do. His actions demonstrate this distrust—he does one quick touch-up and check in the mirror to make sure to contradict what Tom assumes Fanny has said to describe him, whatever it may have been. Tom is not looking in the mirror because he is overly concerned with his superficial appearance (C), nor is he overly-confident and arrogant about his good looks (D). Fanny's actual opinion of Tom's appearance is never provided in the passage, so it cannot be confirmed or belied (A), (B).

258. (D) While Fanny is working on her hair and refuses to accompany Tom because the rain will damage its "crimp" (3), she is not primarily concerned with her hair. She qualifies this behavior by explaining, "I want to look nice when Polly comes" (4) (E). Later, she adds that Polly is "ever so nice; and I shall keep her as long as she's happy" (20–21), which shows her intent to please Polly. When it appears that Tom will likely be late to meet Polly, Fanny cries, "'what *will* Polly think of me?'" (37). Tom jokes that Fanny appears to care more for her hair than for Polly (E), but Fanny consistently expresses a desire to please Polly. Fanny is annoyed that her brother is stubborn about going by himself and begs him to hurry (A), (B), but these concerns fall under the larger desire to make Polly's visit a happy one. Nowhere does the passage indicate that Fanny is in competition with Polly over their looks (C).

259. (C) The revelation that "he ran himself off his legs to make up for it afterward" is significant to the portrayal of Tom because, for the first time, it is suggested that Tom intends to do what is expected, despite all his ornery resistance. Before he runs, though, he is careful to affect a "leisurely" saunter because he "is bent on not being hurried while in sight" of Fanny. Perhaps he is posturing (adopting an affected or artificial manner) and does not want to give her the privilege of thinking she holds sway over his actions. Perhaps he wants to punish her in some small way for not accompanying him as she had said she would. Or, more likely, he knows that being late would only add to the awkwardness and discomfort of the whole experience, but he does not want Fanny to know he is that concerned. The posturing works, as Fanny observes his "slouchy" strolling and declares boys to be "'the most provoking toads in the world'" (46).

260. (C) See question 259. While in Fanny's sight, Tom intentionally acts as if he intends to be late ("sauntered") as a way of hiding his true intention of hurrying. When out of sight, "as soon as he turned the corner, his whole aspect altered." The description in lines 49–51 reveals the contrast between Tom's true intention and his feigned one. (A) provides a parallel action, not a contrasting one.

261. (A) It is stated throughout the passage that Tom's hesitation to meet Polly hinges around his fear of interacting with "strange girls" by himself, equating Fanny's delightful friend to "a wild woman of Australia" (7). It is meeting them alone that utterly frightens him, as he apparently agreed to go when Fanny was planning to accompany him (10). Once Tom arrives at the station, he feels "rather daunted at the array of young ladies who passed" (57). The narrator puts the word "chig-non" in quotation marks and makes sure to attribute this pronunciation to Tom alone (E). We can assume his pronunciation is incorrect since he seems overall very unfamiliar with and flustered by "such a flapping of sashes, scallops, ruffles, curls and feathers" (64). The added detail of his comical mispronunciation adds to the development of his intense anxiety and awkwardness around young girls. They wear hairstyles he does not even know how to pronounce. The narrator does not intend to portray Tom as laughably uncultured or ignorant (B), (C) because such a portrayal would not develop the wider characterization of him as "utterly" fearful of the opposite sex.

262. (D) There are two **similes** in these lines: "panting *like* a race horse, and as red *as* a lobster." Both comparisons add to the revelation that Tom truly intends to do what is expected of him, despite his posturing while in Fanny's view. The similes provide a strong image of Tom having run incredibly fast to make up for his earlier posturing ("sauntered leisurely . . . while in sight"). There is no **personification** or **metaphor** in these lines (A), (C). These similes do create dynamic visual imagery (B), but they are not indicative of his posturing since they reveal Tom's true intention to be on time.

263. (B) See question 261. Tom initially agreed to meet Polly when he thought his sister would accompany him (10). As soon as he discovers this is not the case, the fear and anxiety set in. He is "arrested at the awful idea that he might have to address several strange girls before he got the right one" (29–30), he runs "himself off his legs" (44) to avoid being late, which would only add to his anxiety, he repeats that it is "too bad of Fanny" to send him alone when he views the daunting "array of young ladies" at the station (57), and he has the "air of a martyr" while "nerving himself" to approach a damsel that appears, from Tom's perspective, as strange and foreign as an exotic bird ("flapping of . . . feathers"). Tom does appear to want to follow orders (A) and arrive on time since he runs "himself off his legs," but that intention is framed by his larger nervousness around interactions with girls. He does not want to be late and perhaps miss Polly because that would mean he would have to "nerve" himself to approach a "daunting array" of strange girls. He does antagonize Fanny (C) when he discovers she is not accompanying him to meet Polly, but this reaction also falls under the purview of (B). He does not hurry because he is concerned with appearing to be a gentleman (D) who pleases girls (E). The dominant portrayal of Tom is that he is almost crippled ("utterly quenched") by his fear of interacting with strange girls, and his speech and actions serve this portrayal.

264. (A) See question 263. Tom's nervousness about approaching "the damsel" is carefully articulated. We see him "nerving himself to the task" as he "slowly" approaches what appears to him as strange, unpredictable, and forbidding as a wild and delicate bird ("such a flapping of . . . feathers"). His discomfort is perhaps exacerbated by the stranger's "breezy" and "cool" demeanor, which stands in stark contrast to flustered and "meek" Tom, who was just now "panting" and "red as a lobster with the wind and the run." Tom is earlier described as "arrested by the awful idea that he might have to address several strange girls before he got the right one" (29–30) and here we see this feared exchange occur. Once Tom gathers up the nerve to approach her, the young lady responds, "'No,'" with a "cool stare" that "utterly quenched him." When used in context of thirst and drinking, quench carries a positive connotation of satisfying and appeasing. The context here, however, does not support this usage of the word as Tom is nowhere near satisfied that he now must repeat this dreaded interaction with yet more strange girls. In this context, "quenched" carries a connotation of extinguished, overcome, quelled. He gathered up all that nerve to no avail. (E) is not wrong, but "frustration" is not as apt a word as "anxiety" to describe Tom's emotional state.

265. (C) Fanny is primarily concerned with pleasing Polly (see question 258). She wants to look nice when Polly arrives, and she wants Polly to be picked up on time. Earlier in the passage, it is suggested that Fanny is not aware of the depth of anxiety Tom feels at approaching "strange girls" because she insists that he will not have trouble finding Polly because she (Fanny) has described Tom to her (32). Of course, this only creates additional anxiety as now Tom is "sure that his sister hadn't done him justice" so Polly is likely *not* to recognize him immediately. Perhaps Fanny is aware of Tom's anxiety, but she insists that he go anyway. Tom, similarly, is concerned with the potential embarrassment around meeting a strange girl at the station, and not with meeting his obligation to his sister. He does agree to go, but only once Fanny promises to "get mamma to let [him] have that horrid Ned Miller" pay him a visit.

Passage 2. Kate Chopin, "The Kiss"

266. (E) Even though the setting appears to be romantic (A, B) because of the fire, darkness, and the word "ardently" (5), a closer look at the imagery of the opening paragraph reveals a surreptitious (sneaky, underhanded) atmosphere, especially with the phrases "uncertain glow" and "deep shadows." The shadows alone evoke darkness and deception, but their depth evokes an even more extreme trickery. These deep shadows added to the "uncertain glow" further cement a surreptitious tone to the story. We cannot be certain that the glow is even a glow. These phrases conjure up doubt, skepticism, mystery, and perhaps even fraud.

267. (D) Brantain is meek compared to the more up-front and audacious Harvy, who "pressed an ardent, lingering kiss upon" Nathalie's lips (22–23), confidently responds to her angry questions (37–41), and "with an insolent smile" (75) rejects her kiss (81). Brantain, on the other hand, is less confident in expressing his desire for Nathalie. In the second paragraph, he is relieved by and thankful for the dark shadows because they allow him to develop the "courage to keep his eyes fastened as ardently as he liked upon the girl" (5–6). While the word "ardent" is used to describe Harvy's kiss, it merely describes Mr. Brantain's stare, further contrasting their personalities. Brantain is also hesitant in confessing his feelings for Nathalie, unlike the more up-front Harvy: "She was confidently waiting for him [Brantain] to declare himself … " (14). Brantain also unquestionably believes and accepts Nathalie's dubious explanation of her kiss with Harvy (55–56, 65).

268. (D) Up until these lines, we may have still assumed that Nathalie is genuinely attracted to and sexually interested in Brantain because of her occasional "slow glance into the shadow where [he] sat" (9–10) and the fact that "she was confidently waiting for him to declare himself and she meant to accept him" (14–15). However, the next sentence (15–17) reveals that she is primarily interested in Brantain for "the entourage which [his] wealth could give her" (16–17). Her flirtations reveal her to be opportunistic (one who seeks opportunities for advancement without regard for morals or principles).

269. (C) The phrase "'deuced awkward'" is an example of Harvy's own colloquial style of speaking, an example of his slang and vernacular (daily language, lingo).

270. (E) The adjective "delicious" is not usually paired with the noun "frankness," and this pairing makes the reader question the authenticity of Nathalie's frankness. The adjective "delicious" conjures up an image of Nathalie licking her lips, eagerly anticipating approaching Brantain with such a frank manner. It depicts Nathalie as more wily (cunning, strategic) than frank. She clearly has some ulterior motive in approaching Brantain; perhaps it has to do with her desire to marry him for his "wealth" (16). Also, the question asks about the phrase in context of the passage. Later it is confirmed that Nathalie is not being frank and candid with Brantain. She is like a chess player "who, by the clever handling of his pieces, sees the game taking the course intended" (76–77).

271. (C) In her explanation to Brantain, Nathalie contextualizes Harvy's bold kiss by explaining that he is her brother's friend and "often fancies that he is entitled to the same privileges *as the family*." She means to imply that he assumes he can be intimate with her the way a brother or cousin would. (B) is not as specific as (C) and does not consider the specific context of the phrase.

272. (B) A careful read of Nathalie's speech to Brantain reveals that she never actually admits to any wrongdoing herself. She cleverly assuages him with a logical explanation (A) (see question 267), a tactful evasion (55) so as not to remind Brantain of the details of the embarrassing scene (C), the trappings of genuine concern and remorse ("an engaging but perturbed smile," "almost weeping") (D), and appealing to his ego when she insists "it makes so much difference to me what you think of—of me" (E).

273. (B) While Brantain's face is "radiant," Nathalie's is "triumphant." The word "triumphant" implies that she has achieved something great, that she is happy because she has accomplished a task or goal and not because she is genuinely pleased to make Brantain happy. The word helps to characterize Nathalie as someone who is guileful (full of trickery and deceit) and has ulterior motives beyond love and affection when flirting with men.

274. (E) In contrast to her "delicious frankness" and "triumphant" face when speaking with Brantain, Nathalie's face is now "bright," "tender," and "hungry" in front of Harvy. With Brantain, she uses trickery and deception to convince him that she genuinely cares what he thinks and is honestly interested in him when she is, in fact, interested only in his "wealth" (16). However, with Harvy, she abandons such ruses, and her face is described with straightforwardly honest emotion. Also, it is never mentioned that Harvy has wealth, which would indicate that is not Nathalie's primary motivation (C).

275. (A) In the **simile** in lines 76–77, Nathalie feels as if she is a chess player who has cleverly handled her pieces and sees her triumph is imminent (definite). This same feeling is also revealed when she is described as having a triumphant face in line 67, after it is clear that she has assuaged (eased) Brantain's doubts and restored his interest in her, as she had cleverly planned to do.

276. (D) After Harvy rejects Nathalie's kiss, she recovers by reminding herself that "she had Brantain and his million left." She does not mind that she cannot have "everything," meaning both Brantain's money (financial needs) and Harvy's kiss (emotional needs), because she at least has secured her financial stability.

277. (E) In the final paragraph, the narrator adopts Nathalie's voice and thoughts. It is Nathalie who reacts to Harvy's news with the resignation to "Brantain and his millions." Because there are no indications that Nathalie is speaking these lines, there is no clear distinction between the narrator's voice and the character's, which makes these lines examples of **free indirect style**. The **third-person narration** is not merely omniscient (A) because the narration actually adopts Nathalie's own speech style.

Passage 3. Nathaniel Hawthorne, *The Scarlet Letter*

278. (A) The mood is somber (sad, dismal, depressing), as indicated by the "sad-coloured garments" (1) and "grey steeple-crowned hats" and oppressive, as indicated by the "heavily timbered" door that is "studded with iron spikes." The fact that the paragraph is describing a prison and a throng (crowd) of people may convey a claustrophobic (B) mood, but it is not religious as these two details also support the broader, more prevalent mood of somberness and oppression.

279. (C) A quick read through the sentence might lead to answer (E), Utopia, because it is mentioned in the clause preceding the word "it." However, "it" is "among [the founders'] earliest practical [first] necessities to allot a portion of the virgin soil as a cemetery" (6–7). Reading the entire sentence will make the subject clear.

280. (E) Isaac Johnson's burial-ground and "round about his grave" (11) became the "nucleus," or center, of all other graves to be gathered there.

281. (E) The passage details the physical appearance of the prison. It is "wooden," "marked with weather-stains," with a "beetle-browed and gloomy front." Its iron is rusted and it appears antique, "never to have known a youthful era." The location is mentioned (see question 280) (A), its origins are discussed (5–10) (B) (C), and Ann Hutchinson is alluded to as one of its denizens (D), but the bulk of the description is devoted to its appearance.

282. (A) Line 22 describes the prison as a "portal," which is repeated in line 34, "that inauspicious portal." The phrase's antecedent can also be found by looking in the previous sentence. The "inauspicious portal" refers to "the prison-door" in line 32. It makes sense that the prison door would be the "portal" because a portal is an entrance, a gateway to something. If the portal in reference is the opening to a prison, that would make the portal inauspicious (unfavorable).

283. (C) The narrator mentions Ann Hutchinson as background and as a theory for why the rose-bush "has been kept alive in history" (28). It either "merely survived" or "sprung up under the foot-steps of the sainted Ann Hutchinson" (28–32). Even though "there is fair authority for believing" this, the narrator insists, "we shall not take upon us to determine" (32–33) because he does not mean to be definitive on the matter. While it may appear that the narrator's positive description of Ann Hutchinson as "sainted" suggests he is criticizing the colonies' disenfranchisement of citizens, such criticism is certainly not explicit (A). The protagonist of the larger text from which this passage is adapted finds herself in similar circumstances to Ann Hutchinson. She is mentioned here for her symbolic significance, but that would not be gleaned from the excerpt alone.

284. (C) The rose-bush, "by a strange chance" has survived, and conveniently (I) "finding it on the threshold of our narrative," the narrator offers it to readers for its potential to "relieve the darkening close of a tale of human frailty and sorrow" (III). He hopes it will "symbolize some sweet moral blossom" (II), but he does not refer to its use or connection to the character of the tale (IV).

285. (E) While the passage as a whole is dark and depressing, the tone of the final paragraph is one of optimism and sanguinity because the rose-bush is presented to serve as a mollifying (healing, soothing) agent to alleviate (lessen) the pain of the tragic tale we are about to read. The speaker says that perhaps one of the flowers that strangely grows by the prison door may serve as a symbol of a "sweet moral blossom that may ... relieve the darkening close of a tale of human frailty and sorrow" (36–37). The last paragraph also speculates and anticipates (B)(C) by wondering and conjecturing about the flower's role in soothing the reader by the end of the tale, and it introduces a **metaphor** (A) by assigning a bigger symbolic meaning to the flower, comparing it to a panacea (cure) of sorts. Any cynicism from earlier in the passage is eased by the offer of the comforting rose and its symbolic potential. Though some cynicism arguably remains, the final paragraph cannot be said to be *establishing* that tone.

286. (B) As explained in the final paragraph, the reader is about to hear a "tale of human frailty and sorrow" (37). The passage prefaces that tale.

287. (B) The narrator's critical attitude toward the setting is evident in his characterization of the new colony as depressing—the clothes are "sad," the prison is "ugly," the vegetation is "unsightly," and the wilderness is "stern" and "old." The narrator is critical of the setting and the new colony for its emphasis on condemning criminals who deserve the "deep heart of Nature" and its "pity" (26). The narrator's diction belies (contradicts) objectivity (A) and reverence (D). There is no evidence to suggest the narrator is bewildered (C) by the subject.

288. (E) As the final paragraph indicates, the passage precedes a "tale of human frailty and sorrow" (37), so its primary function is to establish a setting (the prison, the throng, a brief history of the community) and introduce meaningful symbols, like the rose-bush that will "symbolize some sweet moral blossom" (36). It also establishes the mood as lugubrious (mournful, grave, serious, gloomy) through severe descriptions of the people, their clothes, and the structure of the prison.

Passage 4. Nathaniel Hawthorne, *The Scarlet Letter*

289. (E) The narrator repeats the phrase "It may seem marvellous that ... " several times in the opening paragraph to denote the strange, impressive (E), intriguing, unexpected nature of Hester Prynne's choice to remain in the town where "she must needs be the type of shame" (9–10). The amazement at her choice is communicated through the narrator's list of alternative settings that Hester could have chosen as her home.

290. (D) The afterthoughts set off by em dashes suggest other paths Hester Prynne could have taken instead of staying "within the limits of the Puritan settlement" (2). She could have returned to "her birth-place, or to any other European land" (3) or "the passes of the dark, inscrutable forest" (5–6).

291. (C) After the series of clauses beginning with "It may seem marvellous that ... " Hester Prynne would stay at the location of her crime and punishment, the narrator responds to the assumption of it being "marvellous" with a generality of human nature. It is not so marvelous because, he explains, "there is a fatality, a feeling so irresistible and inevitable that it has the force of doom, which almost invariably compels human beings to linger around and haunt, ghost like, the spot where some great and marked event has given colour to their lifetime" (10–13). He goes on to qualify the apparently marvelous decision by saying that "the darker the tinge that saddens" one's life, the more irresistible the urge to remain at that spot.

292. (B) The "fatality" is explained in the following sentence to be "[h]er sin, her ignominy" (14), her transgression.

293. (E) In lines 14–21, the narrator compares Hester's sin to roots that strike the soil, birthing a "converted forest-land" that anchors her to the setting of her crime, which provides a unique perspective on sin's powers—II and an illustrated explanation of why Hester has stayed—I. These lines also include description of Hester's childhood home, including a **simile** ("*like* garments put off long ago") that evokes memories of purity and innocence and starkly contrasts the home to which her sin has rooted her—III.

294. (E) As opposed to the previous paragraph that articulates the narrator's generality about sin anchoring human beings, the second paragraph explores Hester's most probable justifications for why she specifically continues "a resident of New England" (31–33). According to the narrator, she reasoned it is for "retribution" (28), for "her earthly punishment" (35), for purging her soul (36), and for becoming more "saint-like" (37). The paragraph does refer to her sin (B), and her fatal choice to remain at the location of her crime (A) but these references are not unique to the second paragraph. Her predicament (staying at the scene of her crime) and chosen setting (the setting of her crime) are also thoroughly discussed in the first paragraph (C) (D).

295. (E) Since this person is described as one who will join Hester Prynne "before the bar of final judgment … for a futurity of endless retribution" (27–28), we can assume he has been her partner (accomplice) in sin.

296. (D) The second paragraph explains that Hester stays in New England, in the town where she committed her crime, to endure punishment, cleanse her soul, and achieve a "saint-like" "purity," and "martyrdom" (36–37). (A) and (C) are false and not mentioned in the passage. (E) is mentioned in the first paragraph, so it is not suggested by the second paragraph as the reason Hester remains in New England. Hester may have felt ambivalent (torn) about remaining, but the question asks why she decides to stay. Ambivalence would not be a reason to stay (B).

297. (B) The second paragraph introduces Hester's secret: another reason she may have decided to stay in New England is in order to be near her accomplice, "one with whom she deemed herself connected in a union that … would bring them together before the final bar of judgment, and make that their marriage-altar, for a joint futurity of endless retribution." Hester cannot marry her accomplice "on earth," so she secretly longs to be joined with him in eternity by their shared retribution for their crime. The "tempter of souls had thrust this idea upon Hester's contemplation, and laughed at the passionate and desperate joy with which she seized, and then strove to cast it from her."

298. (D) The passage is written in third person and contains insights into Hester's psyche but is not limited by her viewpoint (A), making him omniscient. The narrator is not objective, impartial (B), or detached (E) because he reasons as to why Hester has chosen to remain in New England and provides possible justifications. Though he is invested in exploring Hester's predicament, he does not judge, criticize, or condemn her (C) (see question 299).

299. (D) The narrator actively theorizes about Hester's motives, fears, thoughts, emotions, etc., showing curiosity about the character. He never treats her as a saint (C) because he does not automatically assume her to be moral and great. He acknowledges and is intrigued by her sins and quest for redemption. He is not aloof (distant) (E); on the contrary, he appears almost to be sitting on her shoulder as he observes her battle with a secret and attempts to "cast it from" herself. There are no details that depict the narrator as condescending or pejorative (insulting) (A, B) toward Hester.

Passage 5. Henry James, *The Turn of the Screw*

300. (E) The speaker conveys her anxiety by explaining that she was caught between a "succession of flights and drops," "right and wrong" (1–2). She is full of doubts, yet also "certain" she "had made a mistake" (4). This "seesaw" (2) of emotion suggests she is full of anxiety over a decision she has made.

301. (A) The convenience refers to the "vehicle from the house" that would meet her (6). It is described as a "commodious fly," or a spacious carriage. *Conveyance* means a mode of transportation.

302. (C) The speaker describes how the "summer sweetness" of the June air was a "friendly welcome," which dispelled her former feelings of anxiety and restored her mental and emotional strength.

303. (E) The speaker recalls the "greatness" (17) of the scene (B), the "curtsy" that would ordinarily be meant for "a distinguished visitor" (19–20) (A), "the summer sweetness" that "seemed to offer … a friendly welcome" (9) (D), and her expectation of "something so melancholy that what greeted [her] was a good surprise" (12–13) (C). The speaker recalls noticing that Mrs. Grose was "on her guard not to show [her gratitude and happiness] too much," (40–41) and the speaker admits to this making her "shrink again" (38), which is a reference to the "drops" in emotion she experiences (see question 300). Mrs. Grose is not forthright, and this is noticeably strange to the speaker (E).

304. (A) The speaker strings together her memories of the impressive features of the house with conjunctions, a device known as **polysyndeton**: "its open windows *and* fresh curtains *and* the pair of maids looking out … the lawn *and* the bright flowers *and* the crunch of the wheels on the gravel … ." The repeated conjunction conveys an almost childish sense of excitement. The "crunch" of the wheels on the gravel and the "cawing" of the rooks are **onomatopoeic**. The "circling rooks in the golden sky" is just one example of the rich imagery in these lines. There are no examples of **allusions, irony, understatement,** or **simile**.

305. (B) The first paragraph implies that the speaker is not upper class herself because she explains that the descriptions of this grand home "had a greatness that made it a different affair from [her] own scant home" (17–18) and she says that the curtsy given her by the civil person at the door was as decent "as if [she] had been a mistress or a distinguished visitor" (19–20), suggesting that she is neither of those (C). There are no details to suggest that the speaker is precocious (knowledgeable beyond her years) (A), the overseer (D), or the proprietor (E).

306. (C) The "drop" echoes the drops mentioned in line 1 of the passage—the flights and drops that characterized the speaker's emotional state as she set out on her journey. The drops referred to her hesitation, so in the second paragraph she explains that she did not have any more drops, or doubts, until the next day.

307. (C) What "remained" with the speaker in line 30 is the same thing that she says "astonished [her] too." The subject, "this," which refers to her excitement, both astonished and remained with her, which adds to her sense of the "liberality" with which she was treated.

308. (B) While the first paragraph focuses on the speaker's arrival and first impressions of the house itself (the setting—D), the second paragraph adds description and impressions of other characters, namely "the most beautiful child" (28) she has ever seen and Mrs. Grose. Both paragraphs include a reflective tone (C) and share the same point of view (E). The speaker describes her emotions throughout the passage (A).

309. (D) The speaker explains that it is the "sense of liberality [generosity, munificence] with which [she] was treated" (30–31) that makes her so excited she cannot sleep. She goes on to list the things that she has been given: "The large, impressive room, one of the best in the house, the great state bed, as I almost felt it, the full, figured draperies, the long glasses … " (31–33). Mrs. Grose surprises the speaker with her friendliness (gregarious), but this is tempered by her suspicious "guard against showing it too much" (A).

310. (C) Regarding Mrs. Grose, the speaker recalls feeling "fear" and brooding over the idea of Mrs. Grose, but she is relieved that "from the first moment [she] should get on with Mrs. Grose" (35–36). However, this relief is tempered by hesitancy when she notices "the clear circumstance of [Mrs. Grose] being so glad to see [her] … . " She is also confused by Mrs. Grose's "guard not to show [her gladness] too much." This observation makes the speaker "shrink again" (38) and feel "uneasy" (42). (E) is incorrect because it does not mention the relief the speaker feels upon first discovering that the relationship with Mrs. Grose is not one to brood over, as she had expected.

Passage 6. Sinclair Lewis, *Babbitt*

311. (B) Babbitt "kept himself from the bewilderment of thinking" (1–2), suggesting that he performs his job without thought or effort, in a routine, perfunctory manner. He does the same thing "[e]very evening" (2), and since "the days were blank of face and silent" (3), we can assume that he goes through his routine without much enthusiasm.

312. (C) The "days" (3) are described as having a blank face, a human attribute, making the phrase an example of **personification**.

313. (A) This sentence is set off in its own paragraph because it contains the essential point that will be reinforced in the next few paragraphs—Babbitt's apathy toward creating his own experience outside of his monotonous routine. He is excited to be free for the evening, but "not quite sure what" (5) to do, which is reinforced later in the passage by his boredom over "having to take so much trouble to be riotous" (11), his vague (20) desire to look for entertainment that would "enable a fellow to forget his troubles" (28–29).

314. (B) The word "emancipated" suggests that the house has been set free. From the previous sentences, we can assume that the house is set free from the routine of work, wife and neighbors, bridge, the movies, and blank and silent days (1–3). In the previous sentence, Babbitt is described as "free to do … " (5), indicating that the "emancipation" is from prescribed routines.

315. (C) The narrator adopts Babbitt's point of view when describing Verona's opinion. By repeating the word "opinion," he is clearly mocking Verona's fourth-hand knowledge of the topic she is discussing. (A), (B), and (C) are too extreme and do not recognize the humor in the repetition of the word "opinion."

316. (E) Babbitt only "vaguely" wants something more diverting than comic strips to read (20), which suggests he is not tenacious (B), determined, or passionately eager about making the most of his evening. He appears to be more apathetic (lazy) about finding something to do.

317. (E) Babbitt and Verona clearly do not share the same interests. It is stated that Babbitt "liked none of the books" (26) that he finds in Verona's room.

318. (E) Babbitt was "unusually kindly to Ted and Verona, hesitating but not disapproving when Verona stated her opinion … " (12–13). This line indicates that Babbitt would normally disapprove and potentially tease Verona about her opinions. (C) is too extreme and not supported by the text.

319. (D) This line is not written in quotation marks, nor is it prefaced with an indicator that it is one of Babbitt's thoughts, yet the statement is written from Babbitt's perspective, in Babbitt's voice. The narrator's voice and Babbitt's voice have commingled, making the sentence an example of the technique of **free indirect style**, where the narrator adopts the voice and point of view of character(s) in his/her own narration.

320. (E) The final paragraph follows a "restless" Babbitt upstairs to Verona's room, where he browses for something "diverting" to read. Settling on an "adventure story," he "clumped down-stairs and solemnly began to read, under the piano lamp." Babbitt is not desperate to seek escape (A) since he is described as "restless" and only "vaguely" wanting something diverting to read (20), which also indicates he is hardly reveling in solitude (B). His reactions to Verona's "highly improper essays" are not intended to portray him in an admiring light. The tone is still humorous and we get a sense that we are laughing at Babbitt and not at Verona (C). Babbitt settles on a book, so he is not perpetually unsatisfied (D).

Passage 7. Upton Sinclair, *The Jungle*

321. (C) In lines 4–5, the speaker explains that the word "this" in line 2 refers to "such cases of petty graft," or incidents involving unethical behavior.

322. (C) The speaker says, "After Jurgis had been there awhile he would know that the plants were simply honeycombed with rottenness of that sort—the bosses grafted off the men, and they grafted off each other … " (6–8). Graft is definitely abundant, and the word "simply" implies that this is simply what happens on a routine basis; it is so abundant that it is common.

323. (D) Tamoszius describes the plants where he and Jurgis work as "honeycombed with rottenness of that sort" (7), referring to the commonplace incidents of graft. To elaborate, he describes the ubiquitous (widespread) nature of the graft, how it is hierarchical and interconnected (III), with the superintendent grafting off the boss, the boss grafting off the men (as a queen bee is served by all her worker bees—I, II), and the men grafting off each other. The passage does not indicate or suggest anything positive or sweet about the graft.

324. (D) The comparison to men arranged in ranks and grades in the army is useful in its similarity to the hierarchical structure of Durham's that Tamoszius wants to explain to Jurgis. Durham is at the top, then the "managers, superintendents, and foremen … "

(10–13). Discipline (A) and patriotism (B) are not mentioned in the passage. The workers are not said to be conscripted (drafted) into the plants (E), and the context of the army **simile** does not imply that these workers and bosses have fortitude (mental and emotional strength) (C).

325. (E) Nowhere in Packingtown (in the plants or in Durham's), is there an appreciation of a scrupulous (conscientious, ethical) work ethic. It is noted that "old Durham in the beginning" must have handed down unethical business practices to his son (A), that "the men eventually "caught the spirit of the place" because "every man lived in terror of losing his job, if another made a better record than he" (16–17) (B, C). The widespread graft among the "managers, superintendents, and foremen … " (10–13) indicates the ubiquitous venality (openness to bribery) that is also evident at Durham's (D). (See question 321.)

326. (E) In line 30, Tamoszius explains that the type of man who rises in Packingtown is a "knave," which he later explains is "the man who told tales and spied upon his fellows" (31–32). A charlatan is a fraud, a swindler, a pretender, a knave.

327. (D) Before the phrase "'speed him up'" (33), Tamoszius is explaining what the bosses would do to a "man who minded his own business and did his work." They would "'speed him up' till they had worn him out, and then they would throw him into the gutter" (33–34). The description of speeding up a man to the point of exhaustion implies that the command is a **euphemism** (a substitution of a mild expression for one thought to be harsh) for overworking a man—I. The quotes also indicate that this phrase is distinct from the words of the current narrative voice (Tamoszius's)—III, not that the phrase is part of an actual dialogue/conversation occurring at this point in the text—II.

328. (B) Tamoszius uses **metaphors** when he describes the plants as "honeycombed with rottenness" (7) and as a "seething cauldron of jealousies and hatreds" (18). He uses a **simile** when he describes the superintendents and foremen as "ranged in ranks and grades *like* an army" (12–13) (A). **Rhetorical questions** (C) are found in line 21. Tamoszius also cites examples (D) to support his argument that the plants are corrupt places. He cites the examples of the bosses and the superintendents grafting off subordinates (7–9) and he gives a more concrete example when he says, "Here was Durham's, for instance … " (10). He speculates (E) when he wonders, "The reason for that? Who could say? It must have been … " (21). There are no examples of **anaphora** in these lines; though he does repeat the word "simply" twice, the repetition does not occur at the start of sentences or clauses.

329. (A) The **third-person narrative voice** is apparent in the first sentence of the third paragraph: "Jurgis went home with his head buzzing" (35). However, in the following sentence, the narrative voice moves into **free indirect style** again, and this time the narrator adopts the voice of Jurgis: "no, it could not be so" (36). This line is clearly the voice of Jurgis, not the third-person narrator. The free indirect narration from Jurgis's point of view continues for the remainder of the paragraph; the narration refers to Tamoszius from Jurgis's point of view ("a grumbler," "a puny little chap … that was why he was so sore"). The third-person narrator would not describe Tamoszius in these terms as he has no need to justify his own skepticism about the corruption of the plants, but Jurgis does.

330. (C) In lines 36–40, Jurgis doubts the validity of Tamoszius' claims about the company's graft and corruption. He reasons that Tamoszius is merely "sore" or making excuses because he "did not feel like work" (38–40). This response is typical of someone who is skeptical about believing new information. Jurgis cannot be said to be in complete denial (E) because he begins to notice multiple examples to support the opposing view: "And yet so many strange things kept coming to Jurgis's notice every day!" (40–41). The **free indirect style** of narration (see question 329) is evident with the exclamation point, indicating that the narrator writes this statement from Jurgis's own perspective.

331. (B) In the final sentence of the passage, Jurgis realizes, "And yet so many things kept coming to [his] notice every day!" (40–41), suggesting that even though he had his doubts about Tamoszius's claims, much of what Tamoszius described is becoming more and more visible at the company. The exclamation indicates his surprise at the legitimacy of what he was told. The passage ending in this sentence suggests that the following paragraph might explain exactly what Jurgis had been observing that corroborated Tamoszius's claims.

332. (E) Tamoszius explains that deception, graft, knavery, telling "tales," and spying are what help a man rise in Packingtown. In other words, men who are opportunistic and seek advancement through no concern for principles or ethics are the ones who will succeed here.

Chapter 6: World Fiction

Passage 1. Miguel de Cervantes, *Don Quixote*

333. (D) Nowhere in this passage is it indicated that Don Quixote feared his chivalric ambitions were too great (E). Quixote does leave his home "without giving notice of his intention to anyone" (4–5) (A); and he indeed doesn't know exactly where he is going since "he pursued his way, taking that which his horse chose" (21–22) (B). Also, later in the passage, we learn that an integral part of his heroic fantasy is the "grievous wrong" (42) that Princess Dulcinea has done him (C). Nevertheless, the best answer is (D), since the elucidation of the "terrible thought" (11) arrives immediately in the next sentence: that it "occurred to him that he had not been dubbed a knight" (12–13). The legitimacy of his entire adventure depends on his being a knight.

334. (B) All of the following are true: one, Quixote was unable to reason coherently (A), "his craze being stronger than any reasoning" (17); accordingly, two, he had a tenuous grasp on reality (C); three, he had faith in his good fortune (D), since he was willing to take a path "which his horse chose" (22); and four, he was unwilling to go home (E), given the fact that "he made up his mind to have himself dubbed a knight by the first one he came across" (18–19). Yet it is this last detail that confirms that the best answer is (B), his fantasizing was resourceful. In this instance where he encounters an obstacle to the carrying out of his "grand purpose" (10), it is the resourcefulness of his imagination that provides a way of overcoming that obstacle. His fantasy, in effect, offers both problem and solution.

335. (E) Quixote, as the speaker, believes that his adventures are and will be entirely veracious, or truthful. He is emphatic about this, making multiple references to the "sage magician" who will be "the chronicler of this wondrous history."

336. (D) In keeping with the playful layering of voices typical of *Don Quixote* as a whole, this sentence is a quotation within a quotation, where Don Quixote speaks in the antici- pated voice of his future "sage" chronicler. Quixote is imitating the lofty, pretentious style of medieval **heroic epic**. Some might describe this rhetorical style as sophisticated (C), but the best answer is (D), grandiloquent, because the language is courtly and lofty to the point of being bombastic and arrogant, which is not exactly sarcastic (B) or provincial (simple, unrefined) (E).

337. (D) In the sentence, Quixote addresses his anticipated chronicler, which is, slyly, a ref- erence to the writer himself (A), Cervantes, since he is, in fact, Quixote's chronicler, making (D), the narrator, the best answer. Quixote addresses the "sage chronicler" with, "whoever thou art, to whom it shall fall to be the chronicler," indicating it could not be Dulcinea (B) or himself (A), whom he obviously knows. The title "sage magician" means the chronicler is not suggested to be mediocre (E).

338. (D) Quixote laments to Dulcinea, the "lady of this captive heart" (42), that she has banished him from the "presence" of her beauty with "inexorable obduracy" (43). While her behavior very well might be construed as cruel (A), the best answer is (D), stubbornness, the definition of obduracy.

339. (E) *Don Quixote* as a whole satirizes heroic romance (A) or **epic** (B), narratives that center on the exploits of a hero. There is not enough information in the passage to claim it is part of a **tragedy** (C), which concerns itself with a flawed hero and usually ends in his death, or a **comedy** (D), which, while also satiric, usually ends in a marriage or union. As a **farce** (E), *Don Quixote* relies on stereotypical characters and outrageous situations and consists of a series of episodes that never culminate in a **denouement**, or conclusive unraveling of the plot. The given passage reveals the protagonist to be a parody of the stereotypical knight who is obsessed with his own heroism and image. In the passage, we see him embark on a journey, an episode, that is not given much serious weight.

340. (C) For Quixote, a knight must not travel directly and purposefully (A), but rather he should pursue "his way, taking that which his horse chose, for in this he believed lay the essence of adventure" (22–23). Quixote obviously does not value plain, succinct speech (B), preferring instead the grandiloquent (pretentious, wordy, long-winded) rhetoric of heroic romance. A knight must not avoid romantic entanglement (D), but rather embrace it, as Quixote does in swearing his undying fealty to the Princess Dulcinea. Although Quixote finds creative ways of circumventing the rules he imposes on himself ("he made his mind to have himself dubbed a knight by the first one he came across"), he certainly claims to make every effort to observe his own chivalric code, however seemingly unreasonable its precepts (E). From the passage, it is clear that Quixote sees self-flattery and extreme confidence (superciliousness) (C) as an acceptable and perhaps necessary quality for a knight to possess.

341. (A) Don Quixote thinks of himself in the most grandiose and epic terms. He fancies himself a heroic knight whose adventures, though they have not yet begun, will undoubt- edly be chronicled by a "sage magician." He almost calls off the adventure due to the color of his armor being inappropriate, but "being crazed" he is able to reason that scrubbing his armor shall do. Humorous details like this, along with the stark absence of any other characters who can legitimize Quixote's vision of himself, alert a careful reader to the farcical tone of the passage. There is no indication that Quixote is deserving of such exalted speech.

342. (A) The narrator's attitude toward his protagonist is neither sardonic (scornful) (B) nor acrimonious (bitter) (C), since he describes Quixote in sympathetic terms. He refers to him as a "novice knight" (15) and "our new-fledged adventurer" (24), both being expressions that Quixote thought of himself. Because the narrator does show some sympathy for Don Quixote's idealistic spirit, neither can he be said to be entirely dispassionate (unemotional, detached) (E). Although Quixote fails to give "notice of his intention to anyone" (4–5), he has a "grand purpose" (10) that includes "wrongs he intended to right, grievances to address, injustices to repair, abuses to remove, and duties to discharge" (3–4). By implication, the narrator endorses his ambitions but questions his methods and their likelihood of success. The best answer is (A), magnanimous (fair, generous). Even though the narrator pokes fun at his hero's folly, he demonstrates a subtly generous attitude toward his noble enterprise.

Passage 2. Fyodor Dostoyevsky, *Crime and Punishment*

343. (D) The paragraph opens with the declaration that the protagonist "had successfully avoided meeting his landlady on the staircase." In this paragraph, the narrator proceeds to describe the protagonist's living situation and how he always felt "a sick, frightened feeling" when passing his landlady. This feeling is clarified by the last sentence of the paragraph: "He was hopelessly in debt to his landlady, and was afraid of meeting her." This sentence could have been placed at the start of the paragraph, but delaying this clarification creates some suspense and curiosity for the reader.

344. (C) The third paragraph elaborates on the precise reason why the protagonist avoids his landlady. It does not refute (A) the analysis provided previously because the previous paragraph only hints that his fear may be due to his owing rent. There is no question explicitly raised in the second paragraph that the third can respond to (B). Both paragraphs mention the same characters (the protagonist and the landlady) (D), and the tone is constant throughout the passage (see question 353) (E). The second paragraph is more focused on establishing setting and context for the protagonist's feelings; it describes his room, introduces the landlady, and briefly mentions his fear. The third paragraph, however, expands on the reasons behind the protagonist's emotional state. It explains his "overstrained irritable condition" (13) by describing how he has isolated himself from others and "has lost all desire to" attend to "matters of practical importance" (17–18) (C).

345. (D) The second paragraph may lead a reader to believe that the protagonist avoids his landlady because he has a "sick, frightened feeling" due to his "debt" to her. However, the third paragraph elaborates on this fear. His fear is not due to his being "cowardly or abject" but more a result of being "so completely absorbed in himself, and isolated from his fellows that he dreaded meeting, not only his landlady, but anyone at all." The debt he owes her is not troubling to him, as he "had given up attending to matters of practical importance; he had lost all desire to do so." He is not actually fearful of her because "nothing that any landlady could do had a real terror for him." Instead, it is the torture of "trivial, irrelevant" pestering, "threats and complaints" that he wants to avoid. The subsequent paragraph will elaborate on what is preoccupying the protagonist to the point of complete self-absorption that makes simple interaction with his landlady so odious.

346. (A) The protagonist clearly lacks temerity (courage, boldness). He admits, "'I want to attempt a thing like that and am frightened by these trifles,'" He goes on to cite an axiom that states man's cowardice prevents action (B). He also recognizes his "chatter," "talking too much," "thinking" (C) and deliberating (D) over questions like "Am I capable of that? Is that serious?" contributes to him doing "nothing." He also vacillates (E), briefly considering his plans and ideas may be "a plaything!"

347. (B) The axiom is: "'all is in a man's hands and he lets it all slip from cowardice,'" which paraphrases as a man's cowardice causes a man to squander opportunities (let it all slip).

348. (A) The two sentences are **chiastic** because the order of words in one of two parallel clauses is inverted in the other. In the first clause "chatter" is the *cause,* and in the second clause "chatter" is the *result,* but the grammar and phrasing are parallel in both clauses. The sentences are not axiomatic (B) or veracious (truthful) (C) because they do not contain self-evident truths. The protagonist is not necessarily exaggerating, so the sentences are not **hyperbolic** (D). Perhaps he is in denial or deluding himself, but there is no evidence to suggest this, and the statements themselves are not delusional statements (E).

349. (C) In these lines, the protagonist thinks to himself about "his fears" (24). He says he wants "to attempt a thing like that" but is frightened by "these trifles" (25). We are not told what "that" and "these" are, and he goes on to refer to this deed as "there" (32), "that" (32), and "it" (32), keeping us in suspense and confusion over what he is actually contemplating that is so fear-inducing. In addition to creating a sense of mystery (A, D, E) the vague language characterizes the protagonist's own fear (B) because he clearly cannot even *say* what it is he is contemplating; he is afraid even of the words. The vague language definitely does not elucidate (clarify) the protagonist's actual desire (C)—we are purposely made unaware of what he actually wants to do.

350. (B) The detailed descriptions of Petersburg's "airlessness," "bustle," "stench," and "drunken men" show how the environment "worked painfully upon the young man's already overwrought nerves" (35–38). The setting, though not directly, does provide some justification—I—for the protagonist's isolation from others (14–15) and his overall state of petulance (irritability). The **imagery** used to communicate the odor, heat, and noise of the city "complete the revolting misery of the picture," undoubtedly adding to the overall tone of misery—II. There are no details to make III a viable answer.

351. (A) The final paragraph focuses on describing the putrid, squalid conditions of the protagonist's environment. The "heat in the street was terrible," and "that special Petersburg stench … worked painfully upon the young man's already overwrought nerves." The "drunken men" in the streets only "completed the revolting misery of the picture." The contrast between beauty and ugliness is apparent in the next sentence: "An expression of the profoundest disgust gleamed for a moment in the young man's refined face." The narrator goes on to describe the man as "exceptionally handsome, above the average in height, slim, well-built, with beautiful dark eyes … ." The contrast between the ugly city and the beautiful man makes it more understandable why the protagonist "walked along not observing what was about him … not caring to observe it." The contrast provides some understanding of his chosen isolation and indifference to people and "matters of practical importance" (17).

352. (E) The protagonist is emotionally detached (A) from his environment: "He had become so completely absorbed in himself, and isolated from his fellows that he dreaded meeting ... anyone at all" (15). He also "had given up attending to matters of practical importance; he had lost all desire to do so" (17–18). The protagonist has given up on life; he even ceased to care about the fact that he was "crushed by poverty" (16) (D). He is described as "irritable" (13) and disgusted (42), making him petulant (irritable, ill-tempered) (C). He is described as physically distinctive, due to his "exceptionally handsome" (43) features (B). He is not, however, intrepid (fearless) (E); he "was afraid of meeting [his landlady]" (10) and "on coming out into the street, he became acutely aware of his fears" (23–24). When he thinks to himself, he admits that he is "frightened" by his thoughts (25).

353. (A) The narrator observes the protagonist throughout the passage. He is not predominantly curious, intrusive, or pitiful (B, C, D) because he seems to know everything the protagonist knows and more (he describes him as beautiful, and perhaps the protagonist would not describe himself that way). While the narrator does agree that the city is putrid when he describes it as such in the final paragraph, these descriptions are more indicative of his being observant (A) than empathetic (E) because he is merely noticing the "heat ... airlessness ... and dust" (35–36), where the stench has come from ("pothouses") and why the city appears "revolting" (41) and not necessarily indicating that he feels the protagonist's pain.

354. (C) The protagonist admits, "'I want to attempt a thing like that and am frightened by these trifles'" (24). The "thing" is also referred to as "that" and "a plaything ... a fantasy." He does make a reference to "Jack the Giant-killer," but the reader never fully discovers exactly what he is "thinking" of while "lying for days in [his] den." He avoids his landlady because "he had given up attending to matters of practical importance" and "had become so completely absorbed in himself...that he dreaded meeting, not only his landlady, but anyone at all" (14–18) (A). He is physically weak because "for two days he had scarcely tasted food" (50) (B). The final paragraph provides the protagonist's impression of his environment (see question 352) (D) and a description of his "handsome" appearance (E).

Passage 3. Gustave Flaubert, *Madame Bovary*

355. (E) The speaker and his peers "rose as if just surprised at [their] work" (3), which indicates that they were *not* actually engaged with their work. In fact, some "had been asleep." As opposed to the "new fellow," who is "so attentive as if at a sermon" (17–18), the other boys have no difficulty tearing themselves away from the lesson to "fall into line." They also carelessly throw their "caps on the floor," in a manner that would purposely make "a lot of dust: it was the thing" (23–24). The boys are habituated to the routines and customs of their school, as opposed to the "new fellow," who appears in stark contrast to the others in his rapt attention and upright behavior.

356. (B) The speaker perhaps describes the boy's clothing to emphasize how awkward he appeared among the other boys in the school, how he does not fit in. We have already been told that he was "not wearing the school uniform" (2) and that "his short school jacket of green cloth with black buttons must have been tight about the armholes, and showed at the opening of the cuffs red wrists accustomed to being bare" (12–14). The jacket appears not to fit properly, and the red wrists imply that the boy is not used to wearing any kind of school uniform, unlike the other boys in the school. The speaker also notices his boots were "ill-cleaned," suggesting further that the boy does not fit in. The school servant does mention that he "recommends" the new student to the headmaster's "care" (6), but the speaker's description of the boy's clothing does not suggest his academic potential (E). (D) is incorrect because even though the boy may feel apprehensive and uncomfortable in his clothes, the speaker's intention is to convey his own (and the students') impressions of the boy based on his clothing, and what he seems to point out repeatedly is how he does not match everyone else and looks out of place.

357. (C) The new boy is described as "attentive as if at a sermon" during the lesson, making him rapt (deeply engrossed). The teacher "was obliged to tell him to fall into line with the rest" because he is so immersed in learning that he does not even realize the bell has rung. Though the teacher has to tell him to follow what the others are doing, (A) and (B) misunderstand the teacher's intention; the boy is not being reprimanded for not following the others. The speaker is carefully describing the observations he had of this boy. There is a greater purpose to all these observant details; they are meant to characterize the boy, not to belittle him (E) (see question 362).

358. (B) The phrase "'the thing'" is in quotation marks because it is what the students call the action to which "the thing" refers (throwing their hats). It is their own vernacular, a colloquial phrase, an **idiomatic expression** to describe an action they take regularly.

359. (B) The speaker notices the cap is ugly, "one of those poor things" but still "full of expression." The fact that it is full of expression shows that the cap carries meaningful significance as a **symbol**. It is poor but full of expression, just as the boy appears to be poor because of his "ill-cleaned" boots and "short school jacket" that does not quite fit. However, like the cap, the boy is also "full of expression"; he is "attentive as if at a sermon" and he "looked reliable, but very ill at ease." The speaker goes on to describe the cap's "composite order," every type of material, color, and texture that made up the cap. Since this detailed description of the cap follows other speculations and conjectures about the boy, we can logically assume that the cap is potentially symbolic of the boy. After all, the paragraph ends with a statement that easily suggests the cap's symbolism for the boy: like the boy, "the cap was new; its peak shone." The previous paragraphs have detailed exactly how the boy himself sticks out from the other boys, how his "peak shone." Though he notes how the boy is markedly different from others, and though he refers to his hat as having "dumb ugliness," the speaker is not harshly judgmental of the boy in all his descriptions of his cap, nor does he intend to describe it purely to ridicule him (D).

360. (A) The penultimate sentence contains three independent clauses, multiple dependent clauses, and it runs for nearly six lines. The last sentence, however, is short, direct, lacking any dependent clauses or appositives. The two sentences juxtaposed create **sentence variety**.

361. (A) The tone of the passage is attentive. The speaker is vigilant in his observations and descriptions of the new boy. He notices minute details of his clothes, body ("red wrists"), demeanor, behavior, and emotional state. The speaker is also not detached (D); rather he is quite involved in his impressions of the boy; he declares, somewhat passionately, that the boy's cap has "dumb ugliness" with "depths of expression, like an imbecile's face." Someone who is detached from a subject would not describe it with such specific and subjective detail.

362. **(C)** The passage as a whole is devoted entirely to characterizing the "new fellow." Each paragraph contributes to this characterization primarily through the speaker's (who speaks for his classmates) observations. We do learn a little about the culture of this school, but those details are in service to the characterization of the "new fellow"—I. While the passage does suggest class differences between the "new fellow" and the schoolmates, this is certainly not the primary purpose of the passage—II.

363. **(E)** The speaker observes and comments on the boy for the entire passage, beginning with the moment he first sees him. He describes his attire in great detail, along with the behaviors that appeared most distinctive to him. His impressions are purely subjective, from his own point of view. Since he was a classmate, he cannot be said to be unreliable (A). The style and content of the passage do not resemble that of a biography; even so, biographers may take liberties in their descriptions of their subjects, and the speaker's descriptions are not definitively unfair (D).

364. **(D)** The new boy differs from the speaker in his attire/clothing (2, 12–16, 24–33), his height (10), his deportment/manner/behavior (17–25), and his interests (17–20). Their environment is the same: the classroom and school.

Passage 4. Hermann Hesse, *Siddhartha*

365. **(C)** The first sentence contains repetition, specifically **anaphora**, because the phrase "In the shade" is repeated three times at the start of different clauses—II. The repetition is purposeful, so it is not redundant—I. The sentence also contains a **metaphor** when Siddhartha is compared indirectly to a "falcon"—III.

366. **(D)** An ablution is a cleansing with water or other liquid as a religious ritual. While (C) is correct, (D) is a better answer because it more specifically describes ablutions. We can understand the meaning of the word by looking at the context; Siddhartha performs the *sacred* ablutions when he is "by the banks of the river … bathing."

367. **(A)** The question asks for the dominant technique, and there are more examples of **anaphora** than any other technique listed in the answer choices. The phrase "in the shade" is repeated at the start of three clauses, the phrase "the sacred" is repeated twice, and the phrase "to speak" is repeated at the start of two clauses. There is only one sentence containing **personification** ("shade poured") (B). While the references to "Om" and "Atman" could be classified as **allusions**, there are still only two of them (D). While the tone of the passage is laudatory and the descriptions of Siddhartha appear exultant, they are meant earnestly, not **hyperbolically** (as exaggerations) (C). The only **metaphor** is the reference to Siddhartha as "a young falcon" (E).

368. **(D)** The word "Om" is mentioned to be something that one would "speak … silently" into oneself "while inhaling" and "out of" oneself "while exhaling." It requires "all the concentration" of the soul and "clear-thinking," indicating that it is a recitation that requires thought, effort, concentration—it is meditative (10–14).

369. **(A)** Siddhartha's parents are impressed that Siddhartha is "quick to learn, thirsty for knowledge" and likely to "become a great wise man" (B) (C); his ecclesiastical (religious) potential, as he is likely to become "a priest" (D); and his litheness, "slender legs" (E).

Siddhartha is not said to be impudent (arrogantly bold) (A); in fact, he is loved by his mother because of his "perfect respect" (21) (B).

370. (D) The only one of the options that indicates people covet (desire) Siddhartha is the quotation from lines 22–24, in which it is said that the young daughters think of love when they observe Siddhartha's attractive features, such as his "luminous forehead," "eye of a king," and, of course, his "slim hips."

371. (A) Govinda is described as loving Siddhartha "more than all the others" (25), and it appears he genuinely does. It is also indicated that, due to Siddhartha's inspiring qualities, Govinda knows he will not "become one of those ... tens of thousands of Brahmans," which Govinda "as well did not want to become." Consequently, he wants to "follow Siddhartha," potentially to learn from him in addition to serving and loving him, making his admiration partly self-serving.

372. (E) According to Govinda, many Brahmans are supercilious (proud, arrogant) and "vain" (31)—I. They are also venal (open to bribes), being "greedy" and "deceitful" (30, 31)—II—and banal (common, unoriginal) in that they are "stupid sheep in the herd of many" (32)—III.

373. (E) The entire passage is devoted to praising Siddhartha's many venerable qualities. Every person mentioned in the passage is mentioned only through their admiration for Siddhartha. The tone is thus lofty and exalted. Though the descriptions of the shade and the calming, meditative rituals may make the passage seem idyllic (A), the tone refers to the author's attitude toward the subject; the subject is Siddhartha, not the peaceful setting, and the attitude toward him is exalted (high-minded).

374. (B) Siddhartha is described to us through what others say and think about him. We learn what his father, his mother, Govinda, and "the Brahmans' young daughters" (22) all think of him. We do not actually meet Siddhartha in this passage, so he is not introduced as much as he is *characterized*. The descriptions are hardly objective since they are from specific characters' points of view (C). Figurative language is used in the descriptions of the characters' perceptions of Siddhartha, so (E) falls under the purview of (B). This community cannot be said to represent an entire culture, making (A) emphatically wrong.

Passage 5. James Joyce, "The Dead"

375. (C) The second sentence of the passage contains multiple clauses and conjunctions without any commas or semicolons. When it is read, we feel the frenzied and hurried state Lily must be in as she is "run off her feet" preparing for the party.

376. (A) The opening paragraph alludes to the spatial layout of the house, with a "little pantry behind the office on the ground floor," "the bare hallway," "the bathroom upstairs," and the stairs with a banister and a head that can be peered over to see downstairs. We also hear the "wheezy hall-door bell," and the "gossiping and laughing" upstairs. Several characters are mentioned, and we do feel sympathetic for Lily, who is in such a hurried state, but the imagery cannot be said to be partial toward her (E). There is no irony or regret in the tone (B), (D).

377. (A) The simple, concise statement that "Never once had it fallen flat" is emphasized by its placement between two rambling statements overflowing with detail about how splendid and well-attended the affair is. It does appear to be an essential point that the dance has never "fallen flat" because it helps explain the anticipation, nervousness, and frenzy permeating the scene.

378. (D) The mood in the house is anxious (jumpy, nervous, tense), as indicated by Lily feeling "run off her feet" (1), the two aunts feeling "dreadfully afraid that Freddy Malins might turn up screwed" (34) and "fussy" (32), and their peering over the banister "every two minutes" (38).

379. (D) Mary Jane is referred to as the "main prop of the household" right before it is mentioned that she was qualified to teach music and that her students were wealthy (19–23). The next sentence explains that the two aunts also contribute to the household as much as they can, making (A) and (B) incorrect. (C) and (E) are too rash and assuming. There are no other details to suggest that the aunts are merely using Mary Jane or that they actually see her as a prop, an object. Since they themselves contribute to the household in their own ways, it would not make sense for them to view Mary Jane as beneath them for doing the same.

380. (B) All the phrases are examples of the characters' vernacular and **free indirect style**. They are examples of free indirect style in that the characters' colloquial phrases are not flagged by the author (with phrases like "he said" and "she thought"); rather, they are written into the narration. The phrases are not **malapropisms** because they are not misusing words or confusing the meaning of words.

381. (D) The aunts may be demanding because Lily mainly gets on well with them due to her ability to carry out their orders without making mistakes, but since she does in fact get on well, it cannot be said that they are *overly* demanding. Lily does add that they are "fussy, that was all" (E). The aunts are discerning in that "they believed in eating well; the best of everything: diamond-bone sirloins, three-shilling tea and the best bottled stout" (28–29) (A). They both work in jobs related to music (B), indicating that they do have to earn their living (C).

382. (C) The first paragraph does set the scene; it introduces the event that is taking place by describing what the housemaid and hosts are doing. The second paragraph, however, provides background information on who these characters are, how they know each other, and what the event is. (D) is incorrect because the second paragraph does contain simple sentences ("They were fussy, that was all"). (E) is incorrect because the first paragraph mentions Lily and the two aunts, all of whom are also mentioned in the second paragraph. (A) is incorrect because the first paragraph does contain Lily's perspective. She (and the speaker) tells us that she is "run off her feet" because she is scampering around greeting guests. No problem is set up and solved in the two paragraphs (B).

383. (D) The closing sentence clarifies the reason Kate and Julia incessantly peer over the banister. They are anticipating the arrival of Gabriel and Freddy. The sentence does justify their behavior, but it is in no way a weak justification (C). They are eager about the arrival of these guests, but they clearly do not prefer Freddy over other guests since it is mentioned that they are concerned if he will arrive "under the influence" (35–36) (A). The anxiety has not been eased by this final sentence, as Gabriel and Freddy have not yet arrived (B).

384. (B) We are only told that the aunts' eagerness for Gabriel and his wife's arrival is "what brought them every two minutes to the banisters to ask Lily had Gabriel or Freddy come" (38–39). We learn that Freddy has a history of showing up intoxicated, but Gabriel's background is not shared. The aunts are interested in parties, of course, and "the best of everything … " (28) (A). The aunts are Mary Jane's aunts, who they have "taken" in after her father's death (15–16), and they are Lily's "mistresses" (30) (C). Their jobs and the history of the house is mentioned in the second paragraph (D), (E).

Passage 6. Franz Kafka, "Metamorphosis"

385. (C) While the descriptions of Gregor's insectlike appearance would potentially upset a reader (B), the main purpose of these descriptions is to pique the reader's interest by setting up a problem (C). The problem is Gregor's transformation into an insect, which will be described in more detail in subsequent paragraphs. By emphasizing the specific details of Gregor's bewildering transformation, the opening paragraph motivates readers to read on and learn more about his condition and how he might deal with this perplexing problem.

386. (B) Through descriptions of the objects in his room ("a collection of textile samples" and "a picture … in a nice gilded frame"), we understand a little more about Gregor as a person. The textile samples reveal his line of work, and the framed picture of a woman dressed in fur evokes masochism (for readers familiar with Leopold von Sacher-Masoch's story "Venus in Furs"), or less specifically, it reveals Gregor's desires. While the picture of the woman can be interpreted as a **metaphor**, (A) is incorrect because the first paragraph contains a metaphor as well (Gregor's insect body), which is a similarity between both paragraphs and not a difference.

387. (A) This question asks readers to consider the symbolic significance of Gregor's metamorphosis into an insect specifically. Gregor's repeated and failed attempts to turn onto his right side evoke the sense of futility he feels at his job. The following sentence, the start of the next paragraph, supports this interpretation, as Gregor exclaims, "'what a strenuous career it is that I have chosen!'" (23). The strenuous act of turning over is parallel to the strenuous task of having to go to his demeaning job every day.

388. (C) It is surprising to us that even though Gregor has awoken to find himself transformed into an insect, his thoughts are focused on his hatred of his job. We can assume that Gregor would be having the same thoughts on any morning since he does not reference his metamorphosis at all. This makes us see that Gregor's unhappiness with his daily routine and responsibilities is so great that even an insurmountable and grotesque problem like being turned into an insect does not outweigh his problem of just having to go to work for another day. It also makes us consider the symbolic significance of his turning into an insect. It does not weigh heavily on him because his daily experiences in the workplace are not that different from what an insect may experience. The difference is so slight that he barely notices it. (B) is incorrect because even though these thoughts can also be described as symbolic, they do not *introduce* a new symbol; rather, they further develop a symbol already introduced in previous paragraphs: his metamorphosis into an insect is likely symbolic of his experiences in the workplace.

389. (D) After Gregor says that getting up early "'makes you stupid,'" he goes on to explain that "'You've got to get enough sleep,'" implying that "stupid" in this context means foggy, in a daze from lack of sleep.

390. (E) Gregor's thoughts in lines 34–48 reveal how he is treated like an insect in his regular human life. He describes his boss as unrelenting and demanding, demeaning "his subordinates from up there." Unlike the "other traveling salesmen [who] live a life of luxury," Gregor has to scurry around like a weak and powerless insect. The **metaphor** of his physical transformation into an insect (introduced in the first paragraph) is further developed here by explaining how Gregor's emotional and working life is similar to that of an insect. While the lines may elicit some empathy from readers (B), their symbolic resonance is their primary purpose.

391. (A) The narrator's tone is clear and straightforward. It does not express dismay at Gregor's shocking transformation; on the contrary, the tone is more objective and matter-of-fact, as if Gregor has awoken this way every morning. The passage begins with a calm, objective description of Gregor's morning. The following sentence does not ask questions or reveal Gregor's own bewilderment; it merely goes on to offer a factual rendering of what Gregor does and how he looks.

392. (A) In the last sentence, Gregor declares that he has "got to get up [because his] train leaves at five." It is astounding to us that, despite his physical transformation into an insect, Gregor is still determined to go to his horrible job. His decision suggests that being an insect physically is not so shocking or noticeably terrible to Gregor because he is already like an insect emotionally because of his work situation. Gregor's indifference to his physical transformation emphasizes how habituated he has become to being treated like an insect in his life. We are not angry (D) at, impressed by (B), or distanced from (E) Gregor because of his decision. Also, we are not dumbfounded (C) by his denial because Gregor appears to be aware of his transformation—he does not insist that it has not happened. In fact, he confirms, "It wasn't a dream" (7)(C).

393. (A) In contrast to the narrator's objective and straightforward tone (see question 391), the tone of Gregor's thoughts is marked by frustration and annoyance toward his job. Exclamation points indicate his anger at choosing such "'a strenuous career'" (23). He thinks, "'It can all go to Hell!'" (28).

394. (E) Gregor's decision to go to work despite his condition is indicative of his dependence and desperate need to stay in his odious job to help his parents, who are in debt to his boss (C), (D). "Buoyed" indicates he is energized and motivated, but he is doing what he is compelled to do for his family. He is resentful of his predicament, counting the years until he can "give … notice" and tell his boss just what he "thinks of him" (40–41) (B), (A).

395. (A) Gregor's metamorphosis into a "horrible vermin" or insect is clearly the focus of the text, and a careful read of the passage reveals the metaphorical value of this transformation. The symbolic significance of the insect **metaphor** is developed in each subsequent paragraph, making the metaphor extended and central to the passage. (See question 390.) There are no other characters that Gregor interacts with in the passage (B). Though significant, the **allusion** to the lady in fur in the painting is not central to the passage (E).

Chapter 7: Drama

Passage 1. Hannah Cowley, "The Belle's Strategem"

396. (B) Once he is informed that his cousins are coming to town, Courtall "paints them" in his mind (since he has not seen them yet) as "Hebes . . . made up of rusticity, innocence, and beauty." Knowing that they are "from the farthest part of Northumberland" and have never "been in town," he imagines they fit his stereotyped image of country dwellers as innocent, simple, and beautiful, an image that will be challenged once he meets them in person. He is not disparaging (belittling) them (A) because "innocence, and beauty" have a flattering tone.

397. (A) While the word "Hebes" has been used as a contemptuous term for Jewish people, a careful look at the context reveals that Courtall uses the word in a flattering way to describe how he (mistakenly) imagined his country-dwelling cousins to be "made up of rusticity, innocence, and beauty." The use of the word as a slur did not actually appear until the 1900s, after the publication of this eighteenth-century play. The slur is an intentional shortening of the word "Hebrew," so the actual definition of "Hebe" is unrelated to the meaning of the slur. In the eighteenth century, the word would have referred to the Greek goddess of youth and spring. While knowledge of the word's etymology is certainly useful, a careful reader's attention to context would eliminate (B), (C), and (E) as options because Courtall does not intend the word negatively. Lovingly (D) is too extremely positive.

398. (E) Courtall first imagines his cousins fit his stereotyped image of country dwellers as innocent, simple, and beautiful (see question 397), an image that will be challenged once he meets them in person. Instead of being beautiful, he describes them as "maypoles," which conjures an image of awkward, towering height and rail-like thinness, not graceful stature and slenderness—III. Instead of "being made up of rusticity [and] innocence" (16), they want to escape their rustic culture and embrace the "fine" city in hopes of "leaving it—Wives" (28). Their bold demands to have access to "the first circles," by way of their cousin Courtall, contradict the expectation that they are innocently content rustics—I. Courtall's breakfast with his cousins does not serve to contrast his initial expectations of them—II.

399. (D) The word "fallow" is defined as "not in use, unseeded." Courtall's first mention of his "cousins Fallow" is in line with his initial image of them as rustic and innocent, meaning unmarried and virginal. (E) is too negative and not supported by the context of Courtall's positive tone. The word does allude to the cousins' being "virginal" (unseeded) but "fallow" does not imply they are particularly moral (A). It is also entirely possible that their last names happen to be Fallow, which is why he refers to them as "my cousins Fallow" with a capital "F." However, a close reader cannot overlook how apt the name is for the virginal rustic cousins.

400. (C) The cousins "bounced" in with a "violent bustle" and "opened at once, like hounds on a fresh scent" with a series of exclamations, greetings, and entreaties, making them audacious (E), eager, and talkative (not reticent, shy, reserved—C). They are referred to as "from the farthest part of Northumberland" and never having "been in town," making them country dwellers (B). Courtall discovers that they have "come to town with the hopes of leaving it—Wives," and they ask to be escorted to "all the fine places" in order to meet "Kinght-Baronights," making them opportunistic and aspirational (A), (D).

401. **(E)** Courtall contrasts his cousins to "the rustics of the last age" to highlight their "bold" demands as unappealing (40–42) (A). He quotes their repetitive (B) greetings ("'Oh, cousin Courtall!—How do you do, cousin Courtall! Lord Cousin. . . .'") and entreaties to emphasize their bouncing in and "violent bustle." The particular emphasis the cousins place on his name and title serve to highlight the affected manner they adopt, which is redolent of their aspirations to receive "entrée in the first circles" in order to become "Wives" of "Knight-Baronights." Their list of "fine places" is strung together with conjunctions (**polysyndeton**—C), which also serves to communicate their over-excited "hounding." He uses a **simile** to illustrate how they pursue him "*like* hounds on a fresh scent" (D). There are no examples of a **periodic sentence**.

402. **(C)** Courtall is immediately put off by his cousins' entreaties to be escorted to "'all the fine places'" (24–25), which is in contrast to the "the rustics of the last age" who are content with visiting less "fine" and exclusive places, such as ordinary tourist attractions like "Paul's, the Lions, and the Wax-work" (A) (40). At this point in the passage, Courtall has not learned of his cousins' true intention: to leave the city as "Wives," so he is merely suspicious of their requests that he take them to the "fine places" and not yet condemning them for their matrimonial ambitions (D). While (E) is certainly true, (C) provides a more specific interpretation of the quoted line, with particular attention to its context.

403. **(D)** Almack's is mentioned in context of Courtall listing "all the fine places" his cousins want him to take them in order to leave the city as "Wives" (28). Saville laughs at the mere idea of gallant Courtall damaging his reputation by being seen "at Almack's, with five aukward country cousins!" (37–38). Almack's is clearly an exclusive place for those who are deemed appropriately "fine."

404. **(E)** Saville's reference to Courtall as a "Man of Gallantry" cannot be seen as entirely sincere since the instances Courtall is regaling him with only seem to show him as the opposite of gallant. "Gallant" means "chivalric, gentlemanly, gracious, munificent," but Courtall is possessive of his corner of society from which he excludes his cousins, he lies to avoid interacting with them and is embarrassed to be seen with them. Saville does not necessarily intend to use the phrase ironically, but a careful reader (or viewer) would notice the nuanced insincerity suggested by the term's application to Courtall—I. Courtall tells Saville that he avoided his cousins by "complaining of [his] hard, hard fortune that obliged [him] to set off immediately for Dorcetshire" (35). He follows this with a hearty "ha! ha! ha!" indicating that there is no hard fortune or that the claim was merely an excuse—II. Courtall views the "cousins of our days" with distaste because they are not content to innocently sightsee but "boldly demand their entrees in the first circles" (45). His cousins "come up Ladies—and, with the knowledge they glean from magazines and pocket-books, Fine Ladies." Here, the aside reveals Courtall's insincerity in calling them "Fine" because a true sophisticated "first circle" lady would not "glean" the proper demeanor, pedigree, and education from a magazine. He is poking fun at the rustics who assume they can put on "fine" airs by gathering tips from magazines—III.

405. (C) See question 403. The cousins want to be escorted to "all the fine places" in order to leave the city as "Wives" (28). These are places they are likely to meet "Knight-Baronights." Courtall makes up excuses to avoid being seen at these places with his "five aukward country cousins" because it would damage his reputation. He says if they were "like the rustics of the last age" who were content with visiting "Paul's, the Lions, and the Wax-work" he would be "at their service." He goes on to explain that the cousins "boldly demand their entrées into the first circles," which indicates that it is the exclusivity that makes the "fine places" something to avoid when with his cousins. Paul's, the Lions, and the Wax-work, then, must be places that do not belong to the "first circles," since he would be content to take them there, and so are better suited to country folk (C).

406. (E) Early in the passage, Courtall does not genuinely mean that it would have been a "treat" for Saville to have his cousins as he may have been courted by them or trapped into accompanying them on their hunt for husbands (see question 402) (A). Courtall also knows that it is not genuinely "heroic" of him to stay for merely an hour with his cousins, but it feels heroic to him due to his intense dislike of their intentions and attitudes (B). Courtall tells Saville that he "gets off" the hook to accompany his cousins to "all the fine places" by pleading "a million engagements" (D). He follows this by admitting, "However, conscience twitched me," and Courtall reveals his brief moment of sincerity when he decides to actually arrange a meeting with his cousins, but at a location he deems more appropriate (and less damaging to his reputation): "the most private place in town" (33). After this engagement, however, his insincerity returns as he takes "a sorrowful leave, complaining of [his] hard, hard fortune," the mention of which induces him to laugh ("ha! ha! ha!") (C).

407. (D) Courtall is concerned for his reputation as a "Man of Gallantry" and would prefer to not be seen "with five aukward country cousins" who "boldly demand their entrées into the first circles." He is likely concerned they might embarrass him with their general "bouncing" and "violent bustle," along with their hound-like scents (21) and bold attempts to court a "fine" husband (C). (A) implies that Courtall prefers privacy in general, but he only prefers privacy when associating with his embarrassing (to him) cousins. Courtall does not specifically want to prevent his cousins from meeting men (C); rather, he does not want to help them do it or serve as their ticket into the "first circles."

408. (E) If his cousins had "come to town, like the rustics of the last age" to see the sights, and not assume the airs of "Fine Ladies," Courtall would be "at their service." Instead, they "laugh at the bashfulness of their grandmothers, and boldly demand their entrées into the first circles" (44–45). We already know that Courtall is vexed by his cousins' boldness and does not want to assist them in their attempts to become "Wives" of "Knight-Baronights." He longs for the bashful cousins of the last age (the current grandmothers), who were content as rustics.

409. (C) The comic tone of the passage is created by Courtall's detailed depictions of his rustically awkward and out-of-place cousins. Courtall first laughs at the idea of Saville arriving "half an hour sooner" because he would "have given [Saville] such a treat, ha! ha! ha!" (8–9). The laughter here is at the expense of the cousins because Courtall uses the word "treat" sarcastically. It is implied that Saville would have been equally vexed by the cousins' behavior had he met them. Later, Saville laughs at Courtall's narrow "escape" from having to accompany his rustic cousins to Almack's. The laughter here is not directed at Courtall, but to the "five aukward country cousins! ha! ha! ha!" (38) (E). This humor would fall flat were it not for Courtall's illustrative portrayals of his gauche cousins, including their actual speech, specifics about where they would like to be taken, descriptions of their unattractive appearance, and a contrast to what he had initially imagined them to be. Courtall does not have distaste for all country girls, since he contrasts his cousins to the more appealing "rustics of the last age" who are more "bashful" (40–45) (A), (D). These "rustics" are lauded as opposed to belittled so they cannot be the primary source of humor in the passage (B).

410. (B) Saville appears to share the sensibilities of Courtall. They both find the "five auk-ward cousins" humorous, they both agree that it would be embarrassing and tragic to be seen with them, and they both laugh at the casual lying and deception used to escape them. Choosing (A) would indicate a misread of the passage's humorous tone (see question 409). (D) implies that Saville servilely laughs along with Courtall in an attempt to please him, but this is not supported by the text.

Passage 2. Euripides, *Medea*

411. (D) In the first paragraph, Medea explains that she has come forth "from the house" out of "fear lest [the ladies will] be blaming her" (1–2), meaning if she were to stay in her house, "showing pride," she would gain an "ill name and a reputation for indifference"(3–4). She leaves and speaks to the "Corinthian ladies" so that they will not "blame" or judge her. She is trying to mitigate (lessen) their judgment of her. Though she does say that "there is no just discernment in the eyes of men" (6), labeling the people as unjust is not her purpose in leaving her house (B).

412. (C) Medea says that there is "no just discernment in the eyes of men" because they "loathe [a person] at first sight, though never wronged by him" (8), making I incorrect. People will form unrelenting judgments of others even if they are "stranger[s]" (8). Regard-ing II, Medea says that she does not wish to commend (praise) a citizen who "resents the city's will" (11) and out of "stubbornness of heart" refuses to hate those whom the city hates.

413. (B) In the first paragraph, Medea introduces the topic of her speech. She is here to persuade the Corinthian women not to blame her. She explains why she needs to leave her house to lessen their hatred for her. In the second paragraph, she develops this topic by explaining how she was wronged, perhaps to help them understand her situation and the reasons for her crime or sin. She says, "on me hath fallen this unforeseen disaster, and sapped my life; ruined I am … " (12–13). Both paragraphs are addressed to the "Corinthian ladies" (A). No questions are posed in the first paragraph (C). Both paragraphs contain specifics (D); the first gives examples of the men's unjust discernment, and the second gives examples of why "women are the most hapless creatures" (16). While the first paragraph does contain some mild excoriation (criticism) of the unjust discernment of men, it also contains understanding of such judgment (9–10) as well as explanations of why she has come forth from her house. It is not primarily an excoriation. Medea explains the hardships women have to endure, which indirectly allows her to present her desire for vengeance as warranted, but the justification here does not address any excoriation in the first paragraph, making (E) not as good as (B).

414. (C) Medea's commentary on women's lives opens with an arguable claim (thesis): "Of all things that have life and sense, we women are the most hapless creatures" (15–16). She uses transitions like "first" and "Next" to lay out her reasons and examples, which constitute lines 17–29. The transition "And yet" leads to a counter-argument ("they say we live secure at home, while they are at the wars"), which she claims is "sorry reasoning" and swiftly offers a rebuttal: "I would gladly take my stand in battle array three times o'er, than once give birth." There is no optimism in her commentary (D) and the examples do not appear to be ranked according to severity (E). She alludes to the privileges men have, but the commentary is not equally focused on men and women's experiences (B). There is certainly logic to her list of complaints (A).

415. (D) Medea's opening argument introduces the idea of misfortune and fate. She says "we women are the most *hapless* creatures." They are unlucky, first, in that they were even born female, and this misfortune continues when they marry because their future depends on this choice being "good or bad." Furthermore, a woman would have to have a "diviner's eye to see how best to treat the partner of her life" because she "hath not learnt the lesson in her home." She would only, by remote chance, be able to discover the ways to satisfy her husband. While (A, B, C, and E) would certainly help to alter a woman's fate, they all hinge on good fortune, according to Medea.

416. (E) According to Medea, when a man "is vexed with what he finds indoors, he goeth forth and rids his soul of its disgust, by taking him to some friend or comrade of like age," whereas women "must needs regard his single self," which means they are expected to stay at home and only have their husband as a companion—I. Medea points out that the pain of childbirth far outweighs the pain incurred in battle (30–32)—II. Women's happiness in a marriage is, in part, dependent on their ability to "best treat the partner of her life," making her submissive to the man. Also, she states that women cannot "disown [their] lords," which indicates that only a man has the power to divorce a woman—III.

417. (E) The word "yoke" means burden, oppression. In this paragraph, Medea complains about the sad plight of women. She says that if women do not resent the yoke/impositions/burdens of marriage to a man, they will be happy.

418. (C) In the second paragraph, Medea cites examples of women's unfortunate lot in life. She says they have to "buy a husband at a great price" (17) (B), and if they make a bad choice in spouse, they cannot be unfettered (E) from a bad marriage because "divorce is not honourable to women" (20), and while the husbands have the option to leave the house and seek the company of friends, women "must needs regard his single self" (28–29), which means they do not have that same option (A). A woman, according to Medea, also must "have a diviner's eye" (22–23) to be able to determine how best to please her husband, though she has not been taught how to do this. All these examples imply that women's submission to men causes their haplessness (D), but nowhere does she mention their obligation to *raise* children (she does indicate that she would rather fight in war than bear the pain of childbirth)(C).

419. (A) See question 414. As part of Medea's argument that "women are the most hapless creatures," she uses the phrase "And yet" to transition into an anticipated counter-argument: "they say we live secure at home, while they are at the wars." Men view themselves as more hapless because of the danger they incur on the battlefield. Medea calls this "sorry reasoning" and provides a rebuttal by citing child birth as a more painful experience. (C) does not mention the counter-argument and (B) and (E) suggest this is a digression; however, addressing a likely counter-argument actually strengthens one's claim.

420. (C) Medea says, "But enough!" after she has gone on complaining about the plight of women for nearly the whole passage. She is about to change the focus from general women to herself by admitting, "this language suits not thee as it does me." She acknowledges that she is the one in a compromised position, not them. This acknowledgment serves as a transition to her current quest for revenge and appeal for their tacit acceptance. Her detailed argument in support of her claim that "women are the most hapless creatures" was not a digression (D); rather, it was essential in order for her to garner sympathy from the Corinthian ladies in order to persuade them to grant her her wish: their "silence" (39). Also, perhaps by addressing concerns that can apply generally to all women, she hopes her audience may feel that her quest for vengeance is partly theirs, increasing the chances that they will grant her their "silence."

421. (D) In lines 33–38, Medea says that she should stop griping about the lot of women because it applies only to her situation and not to the women she is addressing. She goes on, "thou hast a city here, a father's house ... but I am destitute, without a city ... a captive ... ." Medea distinguishes between herself and them by assuming they all have what she does not. Though she does mention she is without a family or husband (A, B) she is assuming they still have these things, making (D) the better answer choice.

422. (C) Medea wants to devise a plan of revenge on her "husband for this cruel treatment, and on the man who gave to him his daughter, and on her who is his wife."

423. (E) Medea acknowledges that though women are "timorous" and "coward[s] at the mere sight of steel," she abandons this timorous nature and fills her heart with deadly thoughts.

424. (C) Of the options, the best choice is (C) because Medea is filled with deadly thoughts she intends to pursue, since she has just attempted to convince the Corinthian ladies to grant her their vows of silence. Her deadly plan means she is not undecided about her next steps (E) or entirely hopeless (A), despite her earlier focus on her hapless lot in life. She is not lecturing or moralizing here (D).

425. (B) Medea says women are "timorous in all else ... a coward at the sight of steel." She has already equated herself with all women in the first 29 lines, so Medea certainly does not view herself as innately courageous. She does not take responsibility for her situation, attributing it to the "hapless" state of womanhood (A). She is inciting sympathy and coop- eration from the Corinthian ladies by detailing the sad misfortunes they all share as women (C, D), and she makes several references to being alone ("without a city ... a captive ... with no mother, brother, or kinsman") (E).

Passage 3. Euripides, *Medea*

426. (D) After Medea says, "For dost thou think I ever would have fawned upon *this man* ... ," and every "he" and "him" until line 9 refers to the same man.

427. (B) Medea opens these lines with a question ("Whether shall I … "), followed by logical reasoning in which she considers the consequences and then decides to stick to using a method she is best skilled in ("to take them off by poison"). She then comes to a conclusion ("Let it be so"), but then considers more alternatives ("Waiting then yet a little time … But if … "). Though (E) is a reasonable answer because Medea does use rhetorical questioning, weighs consequences, and then becomes temporarily undecided, this answer is not as complete as (B) because Medea does eventually come to a firm decision. She even swears on Hecate that she will not allow her victims to live on and torture her with "impunity" (28–29).

428. (C) According to lines 11–26, Medea's primary obstacle is that she does not have a city to receive her, "a hospitable stranger affording a land of safety and a faithful home … . There is none." Without this protection, she must deliberate over alternate plans, like "waiting then yet a little time" for a "tower of safety." If this obstacle is still in place, she will resort to the "extreme act of daring," which entails sacrificing her own life in order to kill her victims.

429. (C) Medea does make a reference to wanting to avoid affording "laughter for my foes" and "ridicule from the race of Sisyphus" (D), but this is secondary to her swearing to never allow "any one of them wring [her] heart with grief with impunity" (29). Jason has abandoned her and remarried. Medea is clearly in pain and grieving over this shame and loss. She wants to kill him and his wife to prevent them from being able to torture her emotionally with grief, which they do just by being alive and reminding her of what she has experienced.

430. (A) From the context, we know Hecate is a mistress whom Medea "reveres most of all," making her a type of mentor. Hecate "dwells in the inmost recesses of my house," which indicates that Medea may not be referring to someone mortal (C, E). Hecate will serve as "assistant" in this vengeful act, making (D) incorrect and (A) the best answer.

431. (B) Medea speaks in first person during the entire first paragraph ("I"), but in line 31, she addresses herself as "thee" and "thou" (second person). We can imagine that Medea, on stage, looks at her reflection and speaks directly to herself, looking in her own eyes, to rally herself to action. It is fitting she use the **second-person address** because she is reminding herself of her own skills and talent, of her suffering and the potential humiliation she would incur from men. She needs to become two people in order to grant herself permission to "Proceed" with such a deadly act.

432. (E) Throughout the passage, Medea has a proud—I—tone. She belittles the man who "at such a height of folly" (7) allows her to stay in the city of her future victims instead of banishing her. She also tells herself twice, "thou art skilled" (32, 37). She has a tenacious (determined)—II—tone in that she is passionate about executing this plan—she carefully thinks it through in its entirety, using rational—III—reasoning, meaning she considers the consequences ("If I should be caught") and alternatives ("which shall I"), and comes to (what appears to her as) a logical solution to her problem ("Best then is to"). Her tenacity is clear when she swears by Hecate that she will go through with this, even risking her life to do so (25–28).

Passage 4. Zora Neale Hurston and Langston Hughes, "Mule Bone: A Comedy of Negro Life"

433. (B) When others wonder what bone he is carrying, Joe asks, "Don't y'all know dat hock-bone" (11), implying that it is from such a well-known mule that they should immediately recognize it. He goes on to explain it belongs to Brazzle's "ole yaller mule," who it is revealed is infamous for his evil, stubborn, and generally recalcitrant behavior. (C) and (E) are close answers but not as specific as (B) because they do not incorporate the wider characterization of the mule as infamous.

434. (B) Brazzle exclaims, "Well, sir!. . . It 'tain't my ole mule!" (17–18) upon seeing the hock-bone—I. He reflects on his time with the mule when he shares stories of its antics throughout the passage—III. He uses physical gestures to describe a particularly contrary action of the mule (39–40)—IV. He never avoids stating a truth about the mule or intentionally provides vague and unclear details to avoid revealing information about the mule—II.

435. (C) Brazzle shares a memory of the mule's aversion to carrying a rider: "you better not look like you wanter ride 'im!" (21). Corroborating that detail, Lindsay recalls a time when he saw Brazzle limping "down de road" (22). While the limping is surely humorous, its purpose is not to provide comic relief because the scene does not have a tragic or melancholy tone to break up with comedy (E).

436. (B) Throughout the scene, Brazzle recalls his mule's antics with a reminiscing and memorializing tone. He says, "This sho was one hell of a mule, too" (19) before he details evidence of the mule's less than favorable qualities, including his "evil" way of trying to "bite and kick when" Brazzle would "go into de stable to feed 'im" (25). The biting and kicking is not literally evil (C). In fact, it is humorously ironic that the mule would bite and kick the hand that feeds him. While frustrating for Brazzle at the time, the behavior is not brought up in this context as regrettable (A). There is not enough context in the excerpted passage to suggest the word "evil" is metaphorical or symbolic (D), (E).

437. (E) Lige's memory of the mule is not at all revealed to be fallible (false). It is full of visual **imagery** (A) as we can see the mule doing an about-face to avoid "dat crooked place in de road" and hilariously going "through de handle of dat basket . . . wid de boy still up on his back" (32–34). The extent the mule would go to avoid a little challenge in his path is surprising, and the absurdity of the resulting picture does have some shock value (C). The story incites laughter, as noted in the stage direction (B), (D).

438. (C) Brazzle's mule has been characterized throughout the passage as stubborn, contrary, and recalcitrant. It makes sense that Joe would be saying here that even in death (the after-life), the mule is likely causing trouble.

439. (D) All the anecdotes shared by the characters regarding Brazzle's mule share one feature: they highlight the mule's stubborn and contrary nature that they can all laugh and reminisce about years later. Brazzle tells how the mule would not carry riders, and would not cooperate in the fields (19–21) and reminds everyone of his stubbornness even in his dying moments (40–41). He also says the mule would bite and kick even when he would try to feed him (25). Lige's story shows the lengths the mule would go to in order to avoid a "crooked place in de road" (31–34).

440. (B) The characters' anecdotes about Brazzle's stubborn mule and the physicality indicated by the stage directions reveal a comic tone to the passage. The mule, though difficult and "evil," is viewed now in death as absurdly funny in his extreme recalcitrance. Though the characters appear to be memorializing a deceased animal that was an essential part of their community, the tone is not dirgelike (C) because of the multiple instances of laughter and the joy they take in sharing their memories with each other.

441. (D) As Joe says, "More folks went to yo' mule's draggin' out than went to last school closing . . .", which indicates that the mule's death was a significant moment for the community. The multiple anecdotes and responses to the memories of Brazzle's mule reveal that knowing that infamous mule was a shared experience in the community.

442. (C) The passage is written in the vernacular of the characters being portrayed. Their colloquial expressions, such as "die decent" (37) and "I God" (42), pepper the passage and give the dramatic scene a lively and realistic edge. The characters use figurative language in their observations, like Joe's claim that he "made de feathers fly" (5) when hunting and Walter's comparison of the mule's ribs to a washboard (27). The distinctive qualities of the grammar, idiomatic expressions, syntax, and style of the characters' speech, and the fact that all the characters follow those same distinctive patterns, indicate that the speech patterns are culturally specific to this community (E). The characters' speech does not appear to exaggerate the qualities of the mule. The mule's behavior and characteristics were genuinely extreme (C).

Passage 5. Sophocles, *Oedipus the King*

443. (D) The passage begins with Oedipus asking three questions. He asks why his "children," the citizens of his land, carry "suppliant branches" in prayer and entreaty (1– 4). He also inquires whether the priest stands there in "dread or sure hope" (12). He then asks if the priest knows that he is there for them "'gainst all" (13). As these are all actual questions directed to another person who is about to answer in the following lines, they are not **rhetorical questions** (B).

444. (A) The word "us" refers to the King, Oedipus. It is common for monarchs to refer to themselves as "we" and "us," the "royal we" form. Shakespeare's plays provide abundant examples of this.

445. (C) The **personification** in these lines characterizes the city and its people as desperately in need of assistance. The city "breathes/ Heavy with incense, heavy with dim prayer/And shrieks to affright the Slayer." A city cannot actually breathe, pray, and shriek; these actions all personify the city as pleading for help. While the technique of personification does imply that the object is alive (D), that is not the sole purpose of the device. It presents things as alive for a reason, and in these lines the city is given human qualities to emphasize its desperation. The incense and prayer may lead to choosing (E), but the personified "shrieks" and the heaviness of the breathing make (C) the best choice.

446. (C) Oedipus makes sure to mention that he is so moved by the citizens' plight that he has "scorned withal/ Message or writing" once he knew that he was called by his people—II. He calls himself "world-honoured Oedipus," clearly characterizing himself as venerable, deserving of great honor and respect—I. In lines 12–14, he emphasizes that he is there for the citizens above all else; his "will is [theirs]." He reiterates how moved he is by their hardships by saying only "stern" hearts would not feel for "so dire a need," indicating that he is not preoccupied but is here to assist the people—III.

447. (D) Oedipus was summoned (C) by the people, but he makes a point of saying that he has "scorned withal/ Message or writing" because "this [their plight] so moves [him]" (7–10). Instead of merely responding in writing, he has come in person to demonstrate his deep concern for their well-being.

448. (A) Oedipus first says that he notices how the city "breathes," is heavy with "dim prayer," and "shrieks"; then he says "this moves me." The word "this" refers to the city's heavy breathing, dim prayers, and shrieks; in other words, what concerns him is the city's plight.

449. (B) The people appeal to Oedipus because he "came to Thebes so swift, and swept away/ The Sphinx's song, the tribute of dismay/ ... That made [them] free" (39–41). They do not see him as a peer to God (34) (C), and do not believe he knows more than they know (42) (D). It is true that "the world saith" (44) Oedipus saved their lives, but the people are not relying on rumors, as they "say" and can confirm this themselves (E). Oedipus is described as filled "by God's breath" (43)(A), but his record of success is their primary motivation for appealing to him now.

450. (E) The priest explains that "A burning and a loathly god hath lit/ Sudden, and sweeps our land, this Plague of power" (30–31). Another word for a plague is a scourge. It is ruthless in having sent the land's people to "Hell's house" (33).

451. (A) The **metaphor** compares the ship to the city and its woes. Like the city, the ship is "weak and sore" (24). The ship is "shaken with storms" (25), and the city is shaken by the "Plague of power" (31). The ship cannot keep "her head above the waves whose trough is death" (26), like the citizens of the city who are dying in droves.

452. (D) Oedipus has previously addressed the people as the "fruit of Cadmus' ancient tree," which indicates that Cadmus is the founder of Thebes. The priest describes Thebes metaphorically as Cadmus' house to dramatize the extent of their suffering. In the **metaphor**, the people of Thebes would be the residents in the house, a house that grows empty "hour by hour" as a result of the "Plague of power." A house evokes ideas of unity, wholeness, and comfort. The swiftly emptying house illustrates how the plague is depleting an entire culture of people. The second reference to "house" develops the image further by illustrating where these residents have gone. They are now in "Hell's house," which is almost **oxymoronic** as Hell is so foreboding and nightmarish that the concept of it serving as a home or shelter is jarring. The vivid **imagery** contained in these metaphors also helps us imagine the depths of the people's despair. We can see and smell the "steam of tears and blood."

453. (D) The priest says to Oedipus that "we kneel before thine hearth,/ Children and old men, praying." The "we" refers to children and old men. Earlier, the priest directs Oedipus' attention to the crowd, which consists of "Some whose little wing/ Scarce flieth yet, and some with long living/ O'erburdened." He goes on to clarify that they are "priests ... And chosen youths" specifically. *Senescent* means old and aging, making (D) the best answer. *Senescent* is an obscure vocabulary word, but (D) is the only option that includes "the young."

454. (C) In closing, the priest again refers to Oedipus as their Lord and Chief before declaring, "we lay our grief/ On thy head, if thou find us not some aid." Oedipus is their lord and chief, and so he is responsible for helping them with their turmoil. If he cannot offer aid, their grief is on his "head," meaning he will carry the burden of their grief because he has not fulfilled his duty as their lord and chief to assuage it. The fault will lie with him. While the other choices do indicate feelings the people may have toward Oedipus, they are not correct summaries of the indicated lines.

455. (A) The priest's tone is grave as he explains to Oedipus the severity of the situation the citizens are in—they are suffering from a "Plague of power" (31). Oedipus's tone, on the other hand, is mostly compassionate. He urges the priest to tell him what causes them to approach him with "suppliant branches" (4), and he insists that their hardship "moves [him]" (7), that his "will/ Is [theirs] for aid 'gainst all" (12–13). (E) is an understandable answer choice, but the priest's tone is not entirely laudatory (full of praise). While the priest does praise Oedipus for freeing the people in the past, and for being full of "God's breath" (43), the main purpose of his speech is to convey the seriousness of the city's turmoil, which his tone reflects.

456. (A) Cadmus is the name of the founder of the city of Thebes, the setting of the passage. In the opening line of the passage, Oedipus addresses his city's citizens as his "children, fruit of Cadmus' ancient tree." Here, he uses a **metaphor** to compare the people of the land to fruit that has been born from a tree, implying that the citizens have been born from Cadmus; Cadmus is the father of the people the way a tree fathers its fruit. The second reference to Cadmus is also a metaphor. The priest now compares the city and the citizens to "Cadmus' house" and family. As the plague festers, "Cadmus' house grows empty, hour by hour/ And Hell's house rich with steam of tears and blood" (32–33). The dead citizens leave their land ("Cadmus' house") and enter Hell. In line 39, the city's name is revealed to be Thebes, making (A) correct.

Chapter 8: Expository Prose

Passage 1. Charles Darwin, *On the Origin of Species*

457. (A) In the first sentence of this passage (excerpted from a longer work), the writer summarizes the points he has made previously ("I have now recapitulated [summarized] the main facts … ") so that he may now address some of the anticipated objections to those points and provide **counter-arguments**.

458. (A) In the second paragraph of the passage, the writer states that "most eminent living naturalists and geologists" have rejected the notion of the "mutability of species." Throughout the passage, he offers **counter-arguments** to the position of these naturalists and geologists, namely, that species are immutable (unchanging). The question is asking about a theory that *would not* explain "the several large classes of facts above specified" (5–6). In a parenthetical aside, the writer refers to natural selection as a theory that *would* explain the aforementioned facts (D).

459. (D) The writer does not agree with (B) or defer to (E) the opinions of "eminent living" geologists, but he certainly understands them. By taking the time to address their opinions, he demonstrates that he neither discounts (disregards) (A) nor disrespects (C) those opinions.

460. (A) "Mutability" means changeability, variability. The writer asks why many have rejected the idea of the "mutability of species" and then responds by saying that "It cannot be asserted that organic beings in a state of nature are subject to no variation" (13–14).

461. (E) The first sentence begins with "It cannot" and repeats "it cannot" after the semi-colon. The sentence that follows also begins with "It cannot." The repetition of the same word or phrase at the beginning of clauses or sentences is called **anaphora**. In this instance, the strategic repetition allows the writer to emphasize all the reasons his detractors' assertions "cannot be" valid.

462. (E) The tone of the passage is expository. It sets out to explain in a calm, straight-forward manner the theory of natural selection and to provide **counter-arguments** to objections. The writer addresses his skeptical audience with respect; he reasons with their doubts and hesitations in an even-tempered tone, not in a pedantic (A), bitterly sarcastic (D), darkly humorous (B) or frustrated fashion (C).

463. (C) In response to the skeptics' view that the mutability of the species is not a viable theory, the writer explains, "we are too apt to assume, without proof, that the geological record is so perfect that it would have afforded us plain evidence of the mutation of the species, if they had undergone mutation." The writer addresses the skeptics' reasoning by pointing out that it rests on a mere assumption that there is a perfect geological record.

464. (C) Natural selection is certainly a theory (A). According to most philosophers of science, all theories must be both coherent and falsifiable; that is, evidence that contradicts a given theory can prove the theory wrong (B). The writer sees no contradiction between his theory and his religion ("I see no reason why the views given in this volume should shock the religious feelings of any one.") (D). The writer believes his theory to be coherent as it "does explain, the several large classes of facts" he has specified in the larger volume from which this passage is excerpted (E). The one thing natural selection is not is directly observable as it has occurred "in the course of long ages" and we cannot "assume [that] the geological record is so perfect that it would have afforded plain evidence of the mutation of the species" (C).

465. (E) According to the theory of natural selection, changes in species accumulate over many generations—II. And because humans live for only a relatively short period of time, it is difficult for us to perceive change over long periods of time—III. The writer insists that with respect to evolution most, if not all (not a few), variations are slight—I.

466. (D) The writer assumes that his audience is receptive but skeptical. As a consequence, he takes pains to address what he anticipates will be the key objections to his theory.

467. (D) The writer cites "a celebrated author and divine" to support his own claim that there is "no good reason why the views given in this volume should shock the religious feelings of any one." The divine has written that it is "a noble conception" that the "Deity … created a few original forms capable of self-development into other and needful forms" (9–10). In the same fashion, the writer cites Lyell to support his observation that "The mind cannot possibly grasp the full meaning of the term of a hundred million years; it cannot add up and perceive the full effects of many slight variations, accumulated during an almost infinite number of generations" (29–31).

Passage 2. Thomas Hobbes, *Leviathan*

468. (C) The condition refers to the descriptions provided in lines 1–3, in which "men live without other security, than what their own strength, and their own invention shall furnish them withall." Living without security makes them independent—II. Because of this state, "there is no place for Industry … Culture … Navigation, or use of commodities … no Instruments of moving or removing … And the life of man, solitary, poore, nasty, brutish, and short" (4–10)—II. According to the writer, when men are independent, they are not protected by "other security" like what the state could supply—III.

469. (D) It is a common rhetorical strategy in expository prose for the writer to address potential objections to his or her argument. In effect, the passage is imagined as part of a larger conversation or debate. While the writer (Charles Darwin) certainly had contemporaneous rivals, that he addresses "some man" suggests an imagined adversary rather than a known one (A). Furthermore, although the entire passage is addressed to an implied audience (C), this particular sentence singles out a participant in the larger debate who is less sympathetic to the writer's claims than an implied audience generally would be.

470. (A) The writer believes "some man" may find strange his views that nature renders men "apt to invade, and destroy one another," and perhaps "some man" "may desire to have the [views] confirmed by Experience." To make the views appear comprehensible to "some man," the author asks him to "consider with himselfe" his own experiences in which he has demonstrated a distrust of his fellow subjects, like when he "rides armed … locks his dores … when he locks his chests" (15–20). The writer does not mean to expose "some man" as hypocritical and ignorant (D), but hopes to point out the illogical nature of his hesitation toward the ideas expressed in the passage.

471. (B) To address the **counter-argument** that a hypothetical "some man" (11) may make, the writer provides examples that are "confirmed by Experience" (14) to defend his point that the natural state of man is to "dissociate" (12) into a state of war. An empirical method aims to give evidence based on experience in support of an argument. Apodictic (A), a priori (C), and deductive arguments (D), generally speaking, work by proving propositions through reasoning, irrespective of experiential evidence. An ad absurdum (E) approach attempts to refute an argument by reducing it to an absurdity.

472. (C) The writer asserts that desires, even, by implication, harmful ones, and actions motivated by those desires, are not sins if the perpetrator does not "know a Law that forbids them" (24). No laws can be made, he claims, except by someone with the authority to make those laws. Accordingly, the best answer here is (C), installment of a legitimate sovereign, since it is the legitimate sovereign who has the authority to make and enforce laws that check man's naturally selfish desires. A state of anarchy (B) is a situation of law-lessness, as is civil war (D); therefore, they are both akin to a state of nature, where conflict presides. The writer is not concerned with the church (E) directly in this passage but with secular political authority.

473. (A) Both first sentences begin with "It may," which expresses possibility and thus anticipation. In the second paragraph, the writer anticipates the objection to his assertion that in a state of nature "every man is Enemy to every man" (1–2). Given the boldness of this assertion, his hypothetical reader may require more tangible evidence than simply the inference he provides through his notion that human passion, such as it is, necessarily leads to conflict. In the third paragraph, the writer anticipates the **counter-argument** that such a state of nature akin to a state of war has never existed. He then provides two examples—natives in America and civil war—to back his original argument. The sentences do not have an ironic (E) or skeptical (B) tone. His attention to counter-arguments does not cast doubt on his own argument (D) but rather strengthens it. Nowhere does he suggest that these counter-arguments are in any way authoritative (C).

474. (D) While the writer does contend that Native Americans have a relatively small government that is essentially that of "small Families" (29), he says that government is not particularly effective, since life under it is "brutish" (31) (A), an allusion to the wholly natural state (B) of man where life is "solitary, poore, nasty, brutish, and short" (10). Accordingly, for the writer, there is nothing noble (C) about such a "savage people" (28). The problem for the writer is that the Native Americans, among others, do not enjoy the authority of an absolute sovereign (D), and thus they miss out on all the benefits of law-abiding subjectivity.

475. (A) One of the writer's most counterintuitive points in this passage is that independence (A) is generally undesirable as it results in reversion to a state of war, man's natural state. Kings watch over their subjects, protect (C) them from invaders and, significantly, from each other, through the enforcement of laws (B). This dependence allows the subjects of a kingdom, in turn, to be both neighborly (D) and productive (E), since they all enjoy the protection of the king.

476. (A) The main purpose of the book *Leviathan* as a whole is to argue for the legitimacy and value of absolute monarchy (B). An important preparatory element of this argument is to elaborate the natural state of man, which the writer describes in this passage as a state of perpetual and debilitating war. That the writer does disparage Native Americans as "savage"(28) (C) and does equate total "Liberty"(43) with this state of war (E) is secondary to his main point in this passage, that the natural state of man is war.

477. (E) The writer does not seem particularly idealistic (D) about humanity, since he suggests that, left to its own devices, a state of war inevitably results. For the writer, people are not naturally good, but must be induced by sovereignty to be so. On the other hand, it would be unfair to say that he is cynical (B) about or contemptuous (C) of humanity, since he does offer a way out of the naturally miserable state of man. While he writes with some aplomb (assurance, confidence) (A) about humanity, "aplomb" is self-referential—it describes his attitude about his own thinking and writing and the question asks about his attitude toward humanity. The best answer here is (E), realism. The writer seems to make a concerted effort to consider the best and worst of humanity and to provide a realistic political solution to the problems of the world, as he understands them.

478. (B) In the last paragraph of the passage, the writer points out that kings, "because of their Independency" (37), are in perpetual conflict with each other. On the other hand, since kings impose laws on their subjects, these subjects' relative lack of liberty allows them to be industrious and thus free from the misery of the natural state of man. Individual liberty, in effect, is akin to a state of war, which the writer elaborates in the first paragraph as a state of fear (A), ignorance (C), immobility (D), and misery (E). In such a state, no one is motivated to be industrious (hardworking, productive) "because the fruit thereof is uncertain" (4–5).

Passage 3. Friedrich Nietzsche, *Beyond Good and Evil*

479. (B) The writer asserts that because "obedience has been most practiced and fostered among mankind" (4–5), "Thou shalt ... do" and "refrain" reduce simply to "Thou shalt" (8), which he describes as a "need" that, with an "omnivorous appetite," fills "its form with a content" (9). Although many commandments are indeed unconditional (E), the point he is making is that specific rules of conduct are inconsequential (B). Rather, it is the compulsion to obey that is all important. This is a dynamic more in keeping with the notion that means are everything.

480. (C) The writer does not specify the command but merely writes "something" as a placeholder because the command is irrelevant in this context. He even reduces it to its most simple and essential form: "'Thou shalt'" to emphasize that any command is obeyed because "the need" for obedience "is now innate in every one" and it serves "as a kind of FORMAL CONSCIENCE" that governs individuals.

481. (B) The **simile** uses the word "as" to compare a desire to satisfy to a desire to devour. The writer writes, "This need tries to satisfy itself and to fill its form with a content ... it at once seizes as an omnivorous appetite with little selection ... " (9–11).

482. (A) The "herd-instinct" does indeed often manifest as "representative constitutions" (33) (B). And since it values obedience above all else, it does tend to encourage a cohesive public opinion in groups (E). Yet the writer clearly is more concerned that the "herd-instinct" (15) may result, eventually, in a dearth (total absence) of strong leadership (A) when he writes that if "one imagines this instinct increasing to its greatest extent, commanders and independent individuals will finally be lacking altogether" (16–17). He does not see Napoleon as a tyrant (C) at all, more as a worthy individual (37–39). In the passage, he has nothing explicit to say about class conflict (D).

483. (E) The writer certainly finds herds reprehensible (worthy of blame) (A) inasmuch as he takes pains to criticize them and the "herd-instinct" (15) in this passage. By implication he finds human herds obdurate (stubborn) (B), self-perpetuating (D), and autocratic (despotic) (C). What they are not is transitory, or short-lived. He asserts that "as long as mankind has existed, there have also been human herds" (1–2).

484. (A) (B) through (E) are certainly all conventional criticisms of leaders' hypocrisy. But the writer's point is an unconventional one: that rulers are hypocritical when they call themselves "'servants of their people'" or "'instruments of the public weal'" (25). According to him, leaders ought to command confidently without such backhanded justifications.

485. (C) The writer makes it clear that contemporaneous European leaders do all of the following: they celebrate self-effacing values (A) such as "kindness" and "deference" (28); they embrace public opinion (B) inasmuch as they claim to be "'servants of their people'" (25); they encourage collegiality (D) with values such as "public spirit," "modesty," and "sympathy" (28–29); and they would seem to respect consensus (E) in that they are members of "representative" governments (33). Counterintuitively, the writer suggests that what they do not do is vilify (or denounce) absolute rulers (C) such as Napoleon. Rather, they embrace them as a relief from the burden of having to rule.

486. (E) The writer seems to have nothing but contempt for democratic institutions ("representative constitutions"), which he describes as collections of "clever gregarious men" (33), where leaders, by justifying their rule as "executors of older and higher orders" (23), exercise a form of "moral hypocrisy" (21) and yet are quick to relinquish command as soon as an "absolute ruler" such as Napoleon appears on the scene (35). Given the writer's polemical tone (see question 488), one that relentlessly and ironically attacks conventional wisdom, his attitude toward democracy here can best be described as sarcastic.

487. (B) In this passage, the writer offers up Napoleon as a perfect example of a commander who rules resolutely without hypocritical justification, the kind of leader that represents for "clever gregarious men" (32) a "deliverance from a weight becoming unendurable" (34–35), that is, the burden of leadership. According to the writer, rulers like Napoleon, as "its worthiest individuals," can give an "entire century" a "higher happiness" (37–39).

488. (D) The writer at times does write with irony (A), such as when he calls democratic representatives "clever gregarious men" (33). But the best answer is (D), polemical (argumentative, controversial), because the writer unapologetically offers up counterintuitive arguments against conventional liberal notions of leadership, partially in an effort to be controversial. Providing evidence and addressing objections are only secondary concerns; therefore, the tone is not expository (E). Nor is it apodictic (C), a form of reasoning that works methodically to clearly and incontrovertibly demonstrate absolute truths.

489. (D) While the writer does take pains to describe the "moral hypocrisy of the commanding class" (21) (B) and implicitly makes a case against democracy (the rule of the people) (E) when he writes that "nowadays" in Europe there is "attempt after attempt" to "replace commanders by the summing together of clever gregarious [outgoing, sociable] men" (32–33), the best answer here is (D), criticize group behavior. The entire passage is dedicated to criticizing the "herd-instinct" (15), and the previous two points fall under its purview.

Passage 4. Zhuangzi

490. (C) The cook does not react to Wen Hui's visit in a way that would suggest that the ruler is being intrusive (A) or sarcastic (D). Wen Hui's responses, likewise, are more than merely tolerant (B), but rather enthusiastic toward what the cook is doing. Permissive (E) generally implies someone in authority allowing a subordinate to get away with bad behavior. The best answer here is (C), enlightened, in that the writer's portrayal of Wen Hui goes against the stereotype of a ruler being arrogant and aloof toward his subjects. The ruler is bright and secure enough to be willing and able to learn life lessons from the cook in the humble act of butchering an ox.

491. (B) While the cook's method of butchering the ox does make his work easier (E), appear somewhat mechanical or automatic in its execution (A), and require only the use of a good knife (D), in his speech he clearly emphasizes that "the method of the Dao" (10) is a form of meditative action where his "senses [are] discarded" and his "spirit acts as it wills" (13–14). There is something beyond conscious decision making (B) in this description of his mental state. That the ruler approves of his method is an important yet secondary concern for the cook (C).

492. (C) There would appear to be nothing hypnotic (A) or unconscious (B) about the cook's method in that he is fully aware while he works; for example, at times, he proceeds "attentively and with caution" (25). This approach would seem to be something more than instinct (E), in that instinct is generally understood to be basic innate behavior that is crude and reactive. As his "servant" (10), the cook does indeed defer to the ruler's wishes (D) but, in describing "the method of the Dao" (10), the cook is not talking about the spirit of service, but more likely a spirit of communion with right action in the context of his mind, body, and the situation at hand. As such, that he says that his "senses are discarded" is paradoxical. They are discarded so that he may achieve a certain heightened sensitivity (C) to the knife's movements within the ox carcass.

493. (D) There is no hint in the passage that the knife has magical properties of any kind (A), in spite of the seemingly miraculous results. The cook implies that he has not sharpened the knife for nineteen years when he says that it "is as sharp as if it had newly come from the whetstone" (19–20) (B). Clearly, by butchering the ox into pieces, he does not leave the carcass intact (C). Sometimes in his work he moves slowly, in particular when he comes "to a complicated joint" (24), but not always (E), as sometimes the knife moves "easily" along (23). The important point that the cook makes is that through his meditative approach, he is able to feel his way through the butchering in a way that avoids the kinds of abrupt collisions between knife and bone, ligament, and tendon that would quickly blunt the knife (D).

494. (B) The cook views himself as unparalleled, incomparable to good and ordinary cooks who unnecessarily dull their knives every month or "every year" (17)—I. He is clearly dexterous, in comparison to those whose methods blunt their knives, because he has used his knife "for nineteen years." His knife is "as sharp as if it had newly come form the whetstone" because he intentionally enters the "interstices" of the carcass where the thin knife "easily ... moves along." He uses "a very slight movement of the knife" when dealing with more difficult parts—II. The chef, though he has perfected his method over many years, is not plodding (proceed in a tediously slow manner) because his practice is full of care, intention, and thought—III.

495. (C) The final step in the process the chef describes does appear simple as he uses one "slight movement of the knife" and the difficult part of the carcass "is quickly separated." However, this success is not effortless (A) or simple (B) as the chef has made clear that this practice has been refined over many years and his success is attributed to his proceeding "attentively and with caution" when approaching the "complicated" joints. He also takes care to slide the knife mainly through the carcass's "interstices" so as not to unnecessarily blunt his knife or damage any of the carcass. In this context, the chef's "air of satisfaction," then, is attributed to the pride he takes in his carefully practiced endeavor. The chef mentions he looks "all around" upon completing the act of butchering the carcass, but there is no indication that he ever has an audience while performing the task (D). He is not portrayed as arrogant because the details of the passage suggest his pride is genuinely warranted (E).

496. (B) While the cook treats the ox carcass with respect, and therefore is not irreverent (disrespectful) (A), he is not necessarily courteous toward it either (E), since courtesy is usually behavior shared between people, not between people and things. Nowhere does the passage indicate that the cook is being religious (C) in the conventional sense of performing a ritual for the benefit of a deity. Nor does the passage suggest that the cook is animistic (D) by attributing a living soul to the inanimate ox carcass. The best answer then is (B), venerating, which suggests that he regards the ox carcass with respect and reverence in that its dismemberment is an occasion to practice a kind of communion with it through meditative action.

497. (C) The cook's account of how he butchers an ox is loosely **allegorical** (A) in that it suggests a mode of being—"the method of the Dao" (10)—that can be extended beyond that specific act. The ruler Wen Hui confirms this when he says that he has learned from the cook's words "the nourishment of [our] life" (32). The cook says that with a slight movement of his knife a part of the ox carcass "drops *like* [a clod of] earth to the ground" (27–28), which is a **simile** (B). To claim that he has butchered "several thousand oxen" over the course of "nineteen years" (19–20) certainly would seem to be an exaggeration—or **hyperbole**—for dramatic effect (D). In his responses, Wen Hui makes several exclamations (E), for example, "Admirable!" and "Excellent!" What is missing from the passage is **sarcasm** (C), as the tone of the passage is sincere (see question 499) and the chef's attitude toward his craft is respectful.

498. (E) Nowhere does the passage indicate which particular hand the cook uses to wield the knife; therefore, we cannot ascertain whether he is ambidextrous (A), or able to use both his right and left hand. The cook is certainly dexterous with the knife, though, so clearly not maladroit (awkward) (C). His "method of the Dao" (10) would seem to be anything but fractious (irritable) (D) or overwrought (B), or highly agitated. The one quality here that the cook's method does exhibit is meticulousness (E) in that he is both careful and precise.

499. (B) The tone of the passage is utterly sincere (B) and lacking in irony (C). While the ruler Wen Hui's responses may be described as ecstatic (E), the cook's tone, which dominates the passage, is decidedly more level-headed. There is careful attention to describing the details of the process and unique method of butchering, but such detail is not intended to provide step-by-step instructions that one can follow to imitate the process (D). The writer shows a clear sympathy for the cook's efforts and, through the dialogue between servant and master, implies a feeling of mutual accord or congeniality (B).

500. (D) Through the proxy of the cook, the writer clearly expresses a certain respect and enthusiasm for the task of butchering the ox. This is reinforced by the ruler Wen Hui's enthusiastic reaction to the cook's speech. *Avidity* means enthusiasm or dedication.

ALL PASSAGES USED IN QUESTIONS CHAPTERS HAVE BEEN SELECTED AND COPIED FROM PROJECT GUTENBERG (www.gutenberg.org).